Engaging Resistance

Engaging Resistance

How Ordinary People Successfully Champion Change

Aaron D. Anderson

STANFORD BUSINESS BOOKS
An Imprint of Stanford University Press
Stanford, California

Stanford University Press
Stanford, California

Special discounts for bulk quantities of Stanford Business Books are available to corporations, professional associations, and other organizations. For details and discount information, contact the special sales department of Stanford University Press. Tel: (650) 736-1782, Fax: (650) 736-1784

Printed in the United States of America on acid-free, archival-quality paper

Library of Congress Cataloging-in-Publication Data

Anderson, Aaron D.
 Engaging resistance : how ordinary people successfully champion change / Aaron D. Anderson.
     p. cm.
 Includes bibliographical references and index.
 ISBN 978-0-8047-6243-4 (cloth : alk. paper) — ISBN 978-0-8047-6244-1 (pbk. : alk. paper)
 1. Organizational change—United States—Case studies. 2. Portland State University—Administration. 3. Olivet College—Administration. I. Title.
 HD58.8.A385 2011
 658.4'06—dc22
                              2010020238

Typeset by Bruce Lundquist in 10/14 Minion

Contents

Exhibits

Preface

The work for this book began a little over a decade ago, in the late 1990s, when, as members of a W. K. Kellogg Foundation–funded research consortium, my colleagues and I grappled with the particulars of making change—and more broadly, transformation—happen in organizations. Our discussions and research efforts ranged from the mundane to the deeply philosophical (read: What exactly is the difference between change and transformation, and do we really care?). Our group, a blended mix of practitioners and scholars, examined and wrestled with real unfolding change initiatives as a means to generate meaning and understand how ordinary people, in practice, make organizational change happen. Through this work, I became fascinated with the phenomenon of resistance to change efforts. Subsequently, two questions emerged as the key focus areas for my independent research efforts. (1) How do organizational leaders plan for and execute change initiatives? And more specifically: (2) How do change champions experience and successfully work through resistance as they make organizational change happen?

As our conversations progressed, we took a long walk through the literature to discover what others had said about organizational change and transformation. There is a great deal of writing around planning and implementation; and universities even offer certificate programs in project management and degrees in organizational development. Many authors espouse ideas about the different steps and stages that change entails or requires. There is no shortage of books proclaiming that one recipe or another is the "right" way for executives or champions to plan for change. Yet many warn that the incremental, stepwise strategies that have been accepted for decades are long past their prime (Alfred and Carter, 1993; Burke, 2008; Cawsey and Deszca, 2007; Collins and Hill, 1998; Hamel and Prahalad, 1994; Presley and Leslie, 1999; Quinn, 1996). Still, to the date of this writing in 2010, the various models used in practice have been inadequate for empirically validating the emerging frameworks, particularly those that attempt to fully explain resistance (Furst and Cable, 2008; Goltz and Hietapelto, 2002).

The convergence of market forces is increasing the speed with which change must take place (Calabrese, 2003; Champy and Nohria, 1996; Duderstadt, 2000; Gumport and Pusser, 1997). Even though several helpful books have addressed the subject of organizational change since the turn of this century (e.g., Burke, 2008; Burke, Lake, and Paine, 2009; de Caluwé and Vermaak, 2003; and Demers, 2007), the existing empirical research on change, transformation—and resistance in particular—poses numerous problems. The literature is thick with practitioner-centric cookbooks and articles offering recipes for fostering change within single organizations. But the number of empirical pieces related to change, transformation strategy, and resistance in general is razor thin (Dunphy and Griffiths, 1994; Hearn, 1988; Klimecki and Lassleben, 1998; Piterit, 2000; Presley and Leslie, 1999; Sporn, 1999; Young 2000). There are three further weaknesses in the literature.

First, an encompassing and empirically based theory explaining transformation is missing from all fields reviewed (e.g., higher education; organizational behavior, change, and transformation; and business) (Dunphy and Griffiths, 1994; Eckel, 2000). Despite the importance of understanding the theoretical and practical implications of organizational transformation processes, macro-institutional change has not been fully explored, theories not fully specified, and frameworks not integrated (Demers, 2007; Sastry, 1997). While numerous models accounting for incremental and radical organizational change are offered, little theory explains why one theory or model applies rather than another or how the process of transformation proceeds within organizations (Newman and Nollen, 1998).

Second, much of the literature is anecdotal, based on first-person accounts or single-organization case studies (Galpin, 1996; Guskin and Bassis, 1985). Wading into the large collection of consultant-authored books and articles, one notices that the literature has a practitioner focus (e.g., Ashkenas, Ulrich, Jick, and Kerr, 1995; Brill and Worth, 1997; Cawsey and Deszca, 2007). Wary change agents are deeply familiar with trendy change techniques such as Hammer and Champy's (1993) "reengineering," and recognize the danger of applying

[handwritten margin notes: based on concerned with, or verifiable by observation or experience rather than theory or pure logic]

superficial management fads (Axelrod, 2002; Day, 1998; Nadler, 1998). Hamel (2000, 20) warns that "consultants, self-proclaimed gurus, and left-brain planners" have no real answers and no idea where new strategies and approaches to change should come from. In addition, it is difficult to obtain widely applicable results from single-organization case studies and first-person accounts (Merriam, 2002; Yin, 1993 and 1994). Burke (2008) goes further, identifying a paradox in the change literature: although change processes are rarely linear, the models used to describe them are typically presented in a linear fashion. Many describe the eight steps or six stages of change, but neglect to tell you what to do when things explode at step four (Burke, 2008; Cawsey and Deszca, 2007).

Last, there are very few articles or books that empirically explore the phenomenon of resistance to organizational transformation. Much of what we know about resistance to change efforts is anecdotal or theoretical, and is relegated to a chapter or less in related books. Although numerous authors address resistance to change in small sections of articles or books, two foundational works address resistance directly: specifically, Hultman (1998) and Judson (1966). However insightful, both are practitioner-authored books written from the authors' personal experiences in lengthy consulting careers. Since then, there has been almost no empirical support for strategy and approaches to surmounting resistance (some exceptions include: Fletcher, 1990; Furst and Cable, 2008; Macri, Tagliaventi, and Bertolotti, 2002; Rowley, Lujan, and Dolence, 1997).

In conducting the study that serves as the foundation for this book, I set out to add some empirical understanding to the mix of existing literature on the subject. Certainly not all change efforts are resisted, but many practitioners understand intuitively that change agents (or champions) almost universally experience resistance to organizational change and transformation (Backer and Porterfield, 1998; Burke, 2008; Cameron and Ulrich, 1986; de Caluwé and Vermaak, 2003; Hermon-Taylor, 1985; Likert, 1961). While the roots of resistance—power, emotion, control, and vulnerability—are comprehensible (see Geller, 2002; Goltz and Hietapelto, 2002; and Pfeffer and Salancik, 2003), resistance is easily camouflaged and can asphyxiate strategic change efforts (Cheldelin, 2000). To fully realize transformation, change agents must identify sources of resistance, engage them, and defeat them—or more positively, surmount the resistance (Ford, Ford, and D'Amelio, 2008). Given the turbulence caused by forces pushing for change and the ubiquity of resistance to organizational transformation (Stanley, Meyer, and Topolnytsky,

2005), my study was designed to discover and examine how ordinary people become successful change agents. Specifically: *How do change champions engage and surmount resistance to successfully initiate and accomplish organizational transformation?*

Methodological Foundation

When there is an obvious shortage of empirically based work on a subject, the methodology literature is explicit. Qualitative methods must be deployed before anyone can even think about using quantitative measures to test a theory (Creswell, 2009). Because there has been, at least to this point, no empirically tested theory in the literature that fully explains resistance to change (Goltz and Hietapelto, 2002; Young, 2000), studies must use valid qualitative methods to collect data and thorough analysis to extrapolate and explain the related phenomena (Bryan, 2006). In-depth case analysis can be an invaluable tool in this effort (Waddell and Sohal, 1998). This book, therefore, is based on two studies I conducted using a modified grounded-theory approach (Corbin and Strauss, 2008). The following paragraphs offer an overview of the methodology I used to establish the empirical backbone that supports this book. It is my hope that this initial work will open up several veins of research that yield robust quantitative studies.

Because my research mission was to critically examine resistance behavior and "championship" (the act of championing or advocating), I needed to identify organizations that had recently experienced a major change or were in the process of making transformation happen. All of the institutions I considered had reported instances of resistance. Although it is possible to learn from failure, I intentionally set aside institutions where change efforts failed in order to examine the efforts of ordinary people who succeeded.

To leverage triangulation (Yin, 1994), I collected multiple types of data from numerous sources: (1) internal and external reports and studies related to the specific transformations, including strategy and planning documents; (2) all iterations of mission and vision statements published during the time of the transformation; (3) minutes of trustee meetings; (4) minutes from related committee, task force, senate, and presidential meetings; (5) needs-assessment and evaluative documents (including accreditation and external consultant reports); and (6) press releases and news clippings. I referred to historical documents, including: (1) published histories of each institution; (2) institutional charters; (3) event histories pertaining to the planning and rollout phases; and

(4) responses to requests for proposals (RFPs) and project progress reports distributed to funding agencies. I collected institutional data spanning the time of the transformation from: (1) annual reports; (2) college catalogues; (3) admissions and enrollment reports; (4) fundraising and foundation documents; (5) annual financial reports; and (6) organizational charts.

I conducted interviews using a semi-structured technique that encouraged informants to illustrate the key elements of the transformation processes, identify the forms of resistance they experienced, and describe the approaches that were successful in engaging and surmounting that resistance (see Appendix C). A pilot study was conducted to test the protocol, and the results were used to refine the questionnaire deployed in the full-blown research effort. I conducted, recorded, and analyzed a total of close to seventy interviews, each lasting over 1.5 hours and resulting in hundreds of pages of transcribed material.

Many qualitative theorists believe that the closer the researcher is to the raw data, the better the analysis (Glaser and Strauss, 1999). Having conducted, recorded, and transcribed all of the interviews personally, I agree. It helps to be intimately connected with the data. Once loaded into a software package (I used QSR's NVivo), the transcribed interview data, field notes, and documents contain the contextual resins that fix meaning to the whole analytical process. A more clinical approach, in which researchers get their first brush with the data only after it has been collected, may be "scientific" but does not communicate nuances of tone and tenor. Particularly difficult to comprehend are complex idioms that are meant to convey irony, sarcasm, and strength of conviction and intent when one must simply analyze transcribed texts.

Broadly speaking, qualitative methods are about allowing the data to speak through documents, notes, journals, and interview transcriptions (Creswell, 2009). My synthesis and interpretation of the data began at the onset of data collection (Creswell, 2009; Yin, 1994; Merriam, 1988). A systematic method of collecting and organizing the data in a sequential format facilitated my development of the initial case descriptions. I was able to identify and describe patterns in the data through pattern matching, explanation building, and developing logic models (Creswell, 2009; Yin, 1994).

Utilizing the tools provided by the grounded-theory analysis process, I coded the interviews according to the ideas conveyed in each statement, asking: (a) What is really going on here? and (b) Can I explain what I think I am seeing? (Corbin and Strauss, 2008). The first piece of this microanalysis involved open coding designed to examine the fine-grain detail of the data. I asked questions like, "What is this person saying here?," "Why is this person saying this?," and "What is the range of potential meanings of each sentence?" Individual sentences and groups of sentences that captured a particular idea or the essence of each interviewee's comments were bracketed (Creswell, 2009). These groups of texts were categorized. *In vivo* codes were used as labels for each category when appropriate. I compared, conceptualized, and categorized incidents, events, and activities until saturation was achieved (Corbin and Strauss, 2008; Creswell, 2009).

Next, I used axial coding techniques to examine the major open-coding categories, creating appropriate subcategories. The context and conceptualizations began to take shape through "questions such as why or how come, where, when, how and with what results." The answers "uncovered relationships among categories" (Corbin and Strauss, 2008, 127). At that point I looked for conditions of causality or intervention that, when combined or interwoven, explained the phenomenon. Eventually, it became obvious how subcategories were connected via conceptual threads.

The final step in the analysis was the selective coding of the data for each institution (Creswell, 2009). Although there were many cases of resistance at each institution, I selected three from each to portray in this book's chapters. They richly describe many of the salient properties and dimensions of resistance and championship. Even though only six cases of resistance and engagement are illustrated in detail here, I included all of the identified instances of resistance in the analysis to give each category greater precision and strengthen the explanatory power of the results (Corbin and Strauss, 2008). I then wove the resistance and engagement phenomena together with the transformation narratives to develop a theoretical foundation for understanding them. What emerges from this comparative case analysis using the grounded-theory approach is a robust illustration of how ordinary people champion change and successfully move through the resistance they confront.

Readers should be aware of two factors that affected my research. First, as mentioned above, the studies that are the foundation for this book are based on proven *qualitative* research methods. When I began the studies that undergird this work, there were no empirical works available from which to expand the theoretical constructs with a quantitative approach. Because of this, the qualitative approach made the most sense. Second, the two settings for my study are a college and a university. Unlike in business settings, where profit and loss are powerful drivers of change, in a college, profit is almost completely absent as a motivator. College and university campuses may therefore well be the perfect locations to study resistance to change in its purest form. Without the overlay of profit and loss, individual and group acts of resistance to change are not easily deflated, making them more plain, visible, and robust. Likewise, change champions must deploy tools other than monetary arguments. Thus the findings herein may particularly assist those who would champion change in organizations or other settings where money is not, or is no longer, a relevant driver.

Definitions

Some researchers use small details to differentiate terms such as strategy, strategic thinking, and strategic planning (see Mintzberg and Quinn, 1996). Others use terms broadly, effectively blurring distinctions between concepts (e.g., between change and transformation). I hope that the following definitions of terms as I use them in this book will help to prevent confusion and provide clarity.

Organizational Change and Transformation

Transformation is akin to radical change, a step below full-blown metamorphosis, where the underlying assumptions about the functions of an organization—how it should operate and conduct business, its core values, strategies, structures, and capabilities—are modified to produce an organization that is fundamentally different from its predecessor (Cameron and Ulrich, 1986; Fletcher, 1990; Newman and Nollen, 1998). **Change** is the alteration of a portion or subset of an organization; it may or may not be embedded in or related to a transformation effort (Beckhard and Pritchard, 1992; Bergquist, 1993; Owens and Steinhoff, 1976; Rowley, et al., 1997). To be more precise, to **change** a process or subset of an organization is to alter, modify, or replace it such that the end result is at least in part different from the original. The **transformation** of a large and complex segment of an organization or of a complete institution is the wholesale revision, augmentation, or replacement of all of its pieces such that the end result is fundamentally and measurably different from the original. Transformation alters the culture of the organization by changing underlying assumptions and institutional behaviors, processes, and products; it is deep and pervasive, affecting the whole organization (Eckel, Hill, and Green, 1998).

Organizational change can be thought of as a continuum along which the effort expended will increase in direct proportion to the scope of change (see Exhibit 1) (Burke, 2008). Certainly, changing pieces of an organization does not entail as much work as transformation, which involves the whole of an organization—its parts, their relationship with each other, and the surrounding

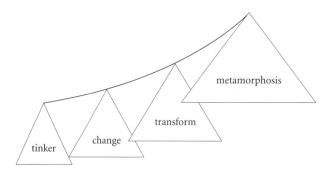

Exhibit 1. Change on a continuum.

environment (Beckhard and Pritchard, 1992). No one will particularly mind if you tinker with routines that involve your daily work pattern. Change may only involve, say, revising a memorandum of understanding between you and your suppliers that produces a different product flow through your supply chain. This is substantially less challenging than trying to effect a transformation, one on the scale of Hewlett-Packard's acquisition of Compaq, for example (certainly from the perspective of those in the Compaq organization). This book does not address metamorphosis, as this involves a complete and wholesale change of an entire operation such that, while the DNA may be similar, outwardly the resulting agency looks nothing like the original (much like the degree of difference between a caterpillar and a butterfly).

Engaging Resistance

The phrase **engaging resistance** is not commonly used in the reviewed literature. Given the sweeping literature-based assumption that transformation efforts naturally produce resistance, agents pushing a transformation agenda will necessarily encounter and need to engage some form of resistance (Judson, 1966). This is not to suggest that all change breeds resistance (Burke, 2008). Tinkering in areas that will have a minimal effect on the whole organization may barely warrant the attention of a sentence in the corporate newsletter.

Although an appropriate dictionary definition of engagement is somewhat violent, the imagery may seem apropos: engagement is "to be involved in battle or conflict." (A more benign and positive image of engagement can be derived from two people betrothed.) By *engagement* I mean acknowledging the existence of resistance and working to surmount it by addressing the resisters and the resistance behavior. I use the word "engagement" because other words, such as "mitigate," suggest that the action has a particular outcome. Whereas the act of engagement may involve minimizing resistance, it can also include the act of embracing resisters, or ignoring them. The action taken to engage resistance can be one or a combination of behaviors based on the sense each champion makes of his or her experience (Weick, 1995). As will become clearer in the later chapters, the more neutral term "engagement" suggests that we think of resistance not always as negative, but as something that could be placed on a continuum of responses to change, from positive to negative (Burke, 2008; de Caluwé and Vermaak, 2003; Piderit, 2000).

Overview

To begin this book, I develop the platform for unveiling the results and discussing my findings by telling the transformation stories of two real organizations. Portland State University and Olivet College were two of the institutions involved in the initial W. K. Kellogg Foundation study mentioned earlier. Both organizations undertook serious, wholesale transformations of their respective general education curriculums over almost exactly the same ten-year period. Through the W. K. Kellogg Foundation project, I gained access to many of the ordinary people involved on both sides of the effort—resisters and champions alike. These two organizations are on almost opposite ends of the continuum of higher education institutions in terms of context and organizational complexity, a fact that strengthens my claim that the findings were derived from an analysis of data gathered in a robust way and are therefore empirically valid. More specifically, in qualitative research, conclusions that are drawn across qualitatively different organizations strengthen the validity of the work (Creswell, 2009). If you examine the websites of both these institutions, you will find them to be dramatically different.

   In Chapter 1, I establish the framework and foundation of the study by beginning the transformation narratives at both institutions. These stories are real; names have not been changed. Almost 100 percent of the participants in this study gave me permission to share their names and details. In the rare instances that informants did not give me permission to use their names or specifics, they did give permission to use their data for research and analysis purposes. In the text I identify most of the people I quote by name or position; if a quotation appears without attribution, it is because that person chose to remain anonymous." Even so, the work has not been sanitized. The stories of these ordinary people, both named and anonymous, as they championed difficult change efforts are just as compelling as the findings and conclusions.

In Chapter 2, I examine the theoretical backdrop for what we know about change and resistance. I also refer to a smaller preliminary study I conducted as an exploration of the act of change agency, in which I interviewed several leaders of a small liberal arts college as it worked to convert from college to university. This study allowed me to identify a previously unrecognized pattern of behavior related to change agency and raised deeper questions that evolved into the larger study that produced this book. The main emphasis of Chapter 2 is on building a theoretical framework for understanding transformation that includes resistance.

In Chapter 3, I expand the narratives to encompass the change actions taken by the people leading change at Olivet College and Portland State University. The reader will see clearly how resistance and change agency are interwoven. When ordinary people decide to make change happen, their championship behaviors permeate their daily existence, and advocacy of those changes becomes their prime directive. Events do not always take place in a logical or chronological order, but often occur simultaneously (Burke, 2008). Change can be messy, but laying out the story chronologically helps to clarify the realities facing both organizations.

In Chapter 4, I explain my findings on the nature of resistance. I do this before unpacking the six specific cases of resistance at Olivet and Portland State in order to provide a foundation for understanding both the forms of and the rationale for resistance. The bulk of Chapter 4 leans heavily on the findings that triangulate from the data gathered at both institutions. So armed, readers should be able to identify the sources, forms, and targets of resistance as they occurred.

In Chapter 5, I end the saga of the transformations at Olivet and Portland State by presenting six specific cases of resistance, three from each institution. These were not the only cases of resistance that occurred at either college. In fact, there were many, but those presented herein best illustrate the main forms of resistance and engagement behavior. These stories represent how ordinary people improvised as they responded to the ever-changing conditions that constitute organizational life. From these cases, a pattern of interactivity among and between resisters and change champions emerges.

In Chapter 6, I present 13 types of engagement behavior that, when juxtaposed with the 10 forms of resistance, shape the nature of engagement behavior

— place or deal with close together for contrasting effect.

over time. I offer a framework for three periods of engagement that defines a new model that can be applied to all types of organizations—not only colleges and universities. Finally, I introduce two phenomena I label "positive pull" and "negative bounce." These concepts are conceptually simple, but because they were not formal results of the study, I present them only as interesting phenomena rather than concrete findings.

In Chapter 7, I conclude the book by drawing lessons about resistance and engagement behavior that change champions can use in their own organizations. I also identify several directions for future research. Besides advancing the scholarship on these subjects the goal of this work is to inform the efforts of ordinary people who are trying to make powerful, positive change happen in their spheres of control.

Although this book is organized in what seems to me a logical order, readers should not feel compelled to read it in the order it is presented. Scholars or students of organizational behavior, change, or development may find the preface and the even-numbered chapters most compelling. Practitioners may wish to start with the narrative case presentations in the odd-numbered chapters. Regardless of the approach you take as a reader, as Weick would suggest, there is no substitute for wading in to see what sense you make of it.

Acknowledgments

I am grateful to the many people who willingly participated in this study. The contributions of all of them, both named and unnamed, amplify its value. Both champions and resisters, ordinary people all, rose up in a time of turmoil to play an important role in improving their organizations. I am grateful to the Olivet College and Portland State University communities for allowing their stories to be told, and I hope their telling will assist others who are working on improving their own organizations.

I would be remiss if I did not acknowledge the scholars who laid a foundation for my work. In particular, four members of the University of Michigan faculty supported my earlier work and encouraged me to press on. Marvin Peterson offered ongoing and steady guidance and sage advice. Jane Dutton kept me focused on the positive, and by sharing some of her earlier work on Positive Organizational Scholarship, inadvertently helped me frame my research. Kim Cameron's perspective was instrumental in my decision to keep the work whole rather than dissect it for submission to various scholarly journals. Finally, John Burkhardt was my main point of contact with the Kellogg

Foundation, which led me to Olivet College and Portland State University. His steadfast practitioner-centered viewpoint kept my empirical ambitions honest.

Last, I would like to thank the good people connected with Stanford University Press. In particular, I thank acquisitions editor Margo Beth Crouppen. In our many conversations her perspective and insights, as well as her editorial suggestions, were clear and spot on. Likewise, the honest perspectives of the peer reviewers strengthened the work in many ways. To those who wish to remain anonymous, I thank you for your time and attention. It is an honor to be considered a colleague.

As many authors before me have stipulated, notwithstanding all of the feedback and input that helped improve this work, it is my own. And despite all good intentions and effort, no work is perfect. This book is no exception. I accept full responsibility for all content herein and any errors.

A Tribute

In early November 2009, academia lost a fine scholar in Eric Dey, who passed away suddenly. His death was a shock to all who knew him, as Eric was not only young, but also a vibrant academic, a gifted teacher, and a great friend. His academic accomplishments were many and varied. For me personally, and for many of his other former students turned colleagues, he was an always encouraging and positive mentor. With this book, I honor his legacy: he was, in his own classy and oft times humorous way, an agent for positive change in our academic industry.

Dedication

As I was completing the data collection for this study, my first son was born. By the time I finished the analysis and a bulk of the preliminary writing, my spouse Darby and I were expecting our second son. Their lives are intricately wound up in this work, and I thank each of them for supporting me as I finished it. I dedicate this book to my boys, Clayton and Jeremy, in the great hope that the content herein leads to improved organizations such that, while my life has been good, their experience in life is exponentially better.

Onward.

Aaron D. Anderson
San Francisco
August 2010

Engaging Resistance

1 Prelude to Resistance

Introduction

Personally, you and I, we know change. We have felt it. It is palpable; sometimes painful. Any parent can describe the extreme changes the first-born brings. In an organization, there is continual fluctuation as a company's reality is punctuated by a variety of forces (Romanelli and Tushman, 1994). Ask any public elementary school principal how she has had to adjust in response to cutbacks in state funding. Waxing or waning resources can bring change across whole industries (Pfeffer and Salancik, 2003). Ask recording industry executives about the effect the iPod has had on their sector. George Orwell demonstrated convincingly that absolute power corrupts absolutely, and reality affirms that the currency of power is a powerful driver of change. The lessons of AIG, Lehman Brothers, and brokers of credit default swaps in the first decade of this millennium prove the point. The calamity of the ensuing economic meltdown has led to change, whether you wanted it or not (Gilgeous and Chambers, 1999).

Change can cause anxiety. Those who have tried to quit smoking or lose weight with the latest product or fitness fad know it full well. If we could reach out and touch it, we would see that the change puzzle has many sharp edges. If we were to draw a picture of change freehand, it would no doubt include an illustration of the friction between two or more abrasive areas. In almost every substantial organizational change equation, there are those who resist and those who push change forward (Burke, 2008). Which one you are will depend heavily on how you expect the change to affect you (Demers, 2007).

In many organizations ordinary people are asked to drive change, and many are able to do so successfully. These champions can motivate positive shifts in their companies as they negotiate the sharp edges of the change process. They understand the abrasive elements and are able to smooth the contact points. They acknowledge their existence and treat them delicately and diplomatically. Indeed, as Margaret Mead suggested, behind every great organizational evolution is a small group of likeminded people who dove into the deep end of the change swamp. Wading through it, they improvised solutions to the known and unknowable problems facing them to successfully reach a new status quo.

The aim of this book is to examine the actions and improvisations that champions of change exhibit as they are knee to neck deep in their respective organizational change swamps, and to discover how they were successful. By identifying the actions and behaviors of ordinary people who, through their daily interactions, became advocates for or resisters to organizational change, we can achieve two aims: (a) to see resistance as one of the many possible responses to change efforts, and (b) to identify strategies and approaches that allow us to work through resistance.

This study of two organizations, examining roughly a ten year period, reveals the strategies and tactics champions deployed to mitigate resistance to their efforts. A critical, empirical examination of these change efforts produces a new framework for explaining the nature of resistance. What does resistance look and feel like? How does it interact with the efforts of champions and cause them to react? How is resistance engaged and surmounted to make lasting change?

Although I am writing as a scholar, the findings herein have merits for a broad audience across a broad set of industries. In the end, you and I may agree that championing change is way more art than science. Even so, my hope is simple: that the new theoretical framework presented in the latter chapters will inform your efforts to conquer the change demons that live in your organizational swamp.

The Prelude

Clearly, not all change is good and not all resistance is bad (Burke, 2008; Ford, Ford, and D'Amelio, 2008; Piderit, 2000; Waddell and Sohal, 1998). The people who promote change or perpetrate resistance can be seen as positive or negative contributing members of an organization depending on one's point of view, perspective, and history with that person (Cutcher, 2009; Ford, Ford, and D'Amelio, 2008; Ford, Ford, and McNamara, 2002). Just as we need gravity to stand, we need resistance to survive organizationally. In fact, well-placed and meaningful resistance to change efforts can prevent an organization's leaders from making harmful and sometimes fatal decisions that could otherwise lead to the demise of the very agency they are working to perfect (Burke, 2008; de Caluwé and Vermaak, 2003; Piderit, 2000). Being open to working through resistance can lead to even better results than expected (Burke, 2008). Even so, resistance is seen by many, and traditionally, as a thing to prevent, avoid, or quash at all costs (Piderit, 2000; Waddell and Sohal, 1998). The multibillion-dollar change consultancy industry is testimony to that view.

Organizational change and transformation efforts are buffeted by a wide assortment of resistance behaviors as a part of the natural response to change (Burke, 2008; Piderit, 2000). Resistance can range from relatively benign verbal disagreements to corrosive measures up to and including sabotage of the organization the resister ostensibly wants to protect (de Caluwé and Vermaak, 2003; Ford and Ford, 2009). Change champions can counter such resistance with actions that range from including potential resisters in the design phases to outsourcing whole segments of a company (Burke, 2008).

Until now, the literature has offered no comprehensive discussion of resistance behavior and corresponding strategic engagement tools (Demer, 2007; Goltz and Hietapelto, 2002). Therefore, with this book I have three goals: first, to translate for the layperson the empirical findings of my research, in hopes of bridging the gap between theory and practice; second, to tell the story of both resistance and champion behavior using real-life examples—case studies that illustrate how successful change champions experience, interpret, and mitigate resistance behavior during organizational transformation; and third, to develop a theoretical foundation for the behavior of change champions in their transformation efforts. My broader purpose is to offer a useful model for those who find themselves, intentionally or not, working to comprehend resistance to organizational change.

The cases offered in this book are stories of real people, with real jobs. They are ordinary individuals, who, through a progression of events and the responsibilities of their positions, became change champions or resisters. By adopting or adapting some of their approaches, you too might be able to lever your efforts to positively change your own organizations. At the very least, the knowledge extracted from a comparative analysis of these case offers a new empirical layer of explanation to what we already know about organizational change and transformation.

With no apologies, the cases provided in this book are taken from post-secondary educational institutions. Given the nature of the higher education industry and the fact that there are very few U.S.-based organizations (educational or otherwise) with a longer history than some of the older colleges and universities, there may be no better place to study change and resistance. When you peel back the veneer of the profit motive, resistance and change championship behavior become visible in their raw form. In that sense, I cannot think of a better place to witness and study more pure forms of resistance than on a college campus. The lessons are arguably transferable to all organizations.

All change begins for a reason.

Olivet College

On the Olivet College campus on a brisk Michigan November day in 2001, windswept leaves brushing past the original stone church and stately library whisper no hints of the ten or so years of turmoil experienced by members of the college's community.[1] Olivet College sits on the crest of a small hill at the top of Main Street in the south-central Michigan town of Olivet; outwardly it appears to be a typical private liberal arts college—small and peaceful. Walking into the warm offices of Dole Hall or the brick 1960s-built Mott Academic Center, one picks up the first clue that something bigger has happened on this campus. Far from any sea or Oakland Raiders fans, the Jolly Roger flies in a number of offices. Scratch the surface with a few probing questions, and a saga emerges of a struggle for distinction, differentiation, and ultimately, institutional transformation dictated by the quest for solvency and survival.

Today, Olivet is rededicated to its original 1844 mission as a college for all, regardless of race, gender, and economic status, embracing the relatively new slogan *Education for Individual and Social Responsibility*. On some campuses, such tag lines serve mainly as brand marketing material for letterhead, brochures, and web pages. At Olivet, the slogan is more than words. It serves as a guiding principle for campus community behavior as well as a vision that shapes and reflects the entire curriculum.

At the outset of the last decade of the twentieth century, Olivet College was a tinderbox waiting for a match. Deep cleavages among and between faculty, staff, and administrators marred the campus culture. In a tradeoff, or "devil's bargain," faculty members had essentially abdicated all responsibility for the college's governance in exchange for minimal oversight and individual autonomy. The subtext of the agreement between the faculty and the administration was: "We won't ask anything of you if you don't ask anything of us." The result was indeed pure academic freedom, but the trade-off was low pay, an ineffectual faculty senate, and no checks or balances on the administration.

Under the fifteen-year direction of the former president (whose tenure spanned 1977–1992), the college effectively isolated itself by retreating from participation in any regional or national conversations about the changing climate and practices in the postsecondary knowledge industry. The administration was leading Olivet College toward insolvency, a prospect that spurred a move for retrenchment. The board of trustees had been hand-selected by the administration and was minimally involved in the operation of the campus. Many were loyal friends of the president.

According to one former faculty member, board "meetings were closed, and no one outside of the executive circle was allowed to call the members. Their phone numbers were not available to anyone—including faculty and staff." Campus visits by trustees were rare beyond official meetings and commencement's ceremonial duties. Yet a small number of trustees caught wind of the grave problems facing the institution and set the stage to act. Before these trustees were able to make a significant move, the match was struck and the tinderbox set ablaze by racial crisis.

The Struck Match

Very few members of the Olivet community have an unbiased recollection, but all point to the events surrounding the incidents of April 2, 1992, as the catalyst for deep and sweeping organizational transformation at Olivet College. While an account of the situation has already been written by C. T. Bechler (1993), a number of interviewees stipulate that the crisis-generated sense of urgency amplified the fear of a pending collapse of the college itself. For some, the incident itself was symptomatic of a larger campus-wide malaise.

Before April 2, 1992, tension between the 56 black and 634 white students had been at a slow boil. Earlier that spring, a white female student had entered the campus judicial process alleging that her African American boyfriend, also a student, had assaulted her. After the young man was found responsible and suspended from the college, a group of 20 to 25 African-American students protested the decision at the vice president's office, claiming racial bias. On Wednesday, April 1, 1992, another white student claimed she was abducted, beaten, and raped by four students on a back corner of the campus. Although no evidence was presented to prove that the incident occurred, rumors swirled that the attackers were African American men. Late that same night—really the wee hours of April 2—trashcan fires were set outside the dormitory rooms of several black student leaders.

The following evening (April 2), an argument arose between a white female student and her white boyfriend. The male left and returned with two of his black friends and began banging on the woman's door. Feeling threatened, she phoned a friend's home where members of a fraternity were living, and soon a group of students mustered to her support. Anger between the white and black students was manifest as racial epithets pitched in both directions. A number of black female student witnesses summoned additional black students in an attempt to "even the numbers." As white fraternity members were leaving the residence hall, their level of intoxication fueled a heated verbal exchange, sprinkled with a few wild kicks and punches, and ended with a fistfight between two students—one white and one black.

The brawl attracted a group of 15 to 20 students and one residence hall director. Within five minutes, two Olivet town police officers were on the scene, as well as officers from the sheriff's department and the state police. By the time the vice president arrived 20 minutes later, the situation had been diffused: two students were sent to the hospital, and Olivet College was changed forever.

In the days that followed, the usually sedate and unknown campus of Olivet College became the focal point for a hungry national and international news media. Black and white students, staff, faculty, and administrators took their respective sides. The Federal Bureau of Investigation and the Michigan Department of Civil Rights began monitoring events. The bucolic campus was thrust under a microscope and every action taken by the administration scrutinized as emblematic of race relations in America. In a defining action, Olivet's black students began to walk off campus. After the president gave permission to all students fearing their safety to complete their courses and exams by mail, 52 of the 56 black students packed their bags and left for home with two weeks remaining in the semester.

The Tinderbox

Alone, the April 2 incident might not have been enough to catalyze a campus transformation. But a number of institutional conditions in conjunction with the ensuing racial tension coalesced to push the transformation forward. Olivet was suffering from a significant drop in enrollment, as were a number of colleges across the country in the late 1980s. The college's annual budget was then, as it is now, inextricably linked to tuition dollars. With a total enrollment of 735 students in 1991, any drop in tuition revenue dramatically affected college operations. A poor reputation in funding circles hindered philanthropic development, and the institution was ignored by a number of granting agencies and foundations.

With most matriculating students hailing from the state of Michigan (96 percent), Olivet College was already suffering from a poor reputation outside the state of Michigan, which was further tarnished by the 1992 incidents. One faculty member reports that they had worn out the "come to Olivet and you get a small school, low student-to-faculty ratio, and it's a nice rural campus" sales pitch. "Basically, there was no real reason why anyone would choose Olivet College over any other small liberal arts institution: we were simply not distinctive in any way." Enrollment had fallen for three consecutive years, and dropped another 4 percent in the fall of 1991.

The people on the Olivet campus felt isolated and fractionalized. Academic stagnation was the norm; most college faculty and administrators had not been to an academic or professional conference in years. Disapproval of the administration was responsible for low morale among faculty and staff, even lower than was usual on any campus. One staff member recalls that "the way that things were run in 1992 was the way that they were run back in the early 1980s." Moreover, turnover among the faculty had been an astounding 20–30 percent per year since 1987.

The overarching force contributing to the general malaise among college faculty and staff was the "culture of fear, suspicion, and distrust" permeating the campus. Clearly, this was propagated by a mismatch between the president's leadership style and the contemporary needs of his institution. One favorable view describes him as a "blue-skies" president simply "not wanting to hear anything negative at all." Much of the faculty saw his administration as imperial. Although regarded as personable and friendly, the president used a "top-down, hierarchical, hands-on" approach to management. Power distribution at Olivet College in 1992 reflected a traditional corporate structure, with the president controlling much of the campus, rather than sharing campus governance with the faculty—a common practice on other college campuses. Moreover, the "devil's bargain" struck years earlier had disempowered the faculty senate to the degree that it was seen by most as allowing the administration to run roughshod over or around faculty in many policy decisions: allowing faculty not aligned with the administration's view to be fired, and banning others from setting foot on the campus ever again.

Fed up, shortly after April 2 several faculty members met with three trustees in Battle Creek to express their concern about the leadership. Sharpening the point, one consultant hired by the trustees to conduct a review of the president's performance "came up with more problems than expected." The president's inability to raise money, or lack of attention to doing so, had led to cuts in many areas. "Creative" financial and budget moves led to suspicions of embezzlement. The outcome of the ensuing 1992 vote of no confidence in the president after the April incidents resulted in the first step in the "Olivet transformation"; the board pushed the president into retirement that summer.

After the 1992 racial imbroglio, Olivet College was barely holding on. In the words of one faculty member there at the time, "It was desperate. Once it started coming out just how bad things were, we realized that if we didn't change then we would all be out of jobs."

Historical Roots

Olivet College entered the business on the cutting edge of the higher education industry. Its roots can be traced back to the anti-slavery movement, and the founding charter made it the first college in the nation to admit students regardless of race, gender, and those who were "not rich in this world's goods." After losing an election to lead the Oberlin Church in 1843, the Reverend John J. Shipherd, one of the founders of Oberlin College, took the loss as a sign from God to start another college. He found himself quite literally lost in the woods, riding in circles around a small hill in south-central Michigan, which he took for another sign from God. After purchasing the property on which the college sits, Shipherd returned in February 1844 with 39 settlers (14 of whom were children) from Oberlin with the mission of building a new college and town as a "harmonious Christian community."

Remembering that the biblical Mount of Olives was a center of piety, morality, and learning, the missionaries named both the college and the village Olivet. Although technically founded as a nondenominational organization with an independent and self-perpetuating board of directors, the campus was first sponsored by the Presbyterian Church and as a Congregational Christian college. In December 1844 the Olivet Institute opened its doors with a group of nine students and three faculty members; its unique mission was outlined in its first catalogue:

> Having no partisan or sectarian interests to subserve, we wish simply to do them [young men and women] good by placing in their hands the means of

intellectual, moral, and spiritual improvement and to teach them the Divine art and science of doing good to others.

The institute's first catalogue listed 72 students, "39 ladies and 33 gentlemen" in residence in 1846. After 15 years of wrangling with politicians, the state finally issued a charter for the institution and the official name was changed to Olivet College in 1858. Except for a brief period of experimentation with an Oxford-style tutorial curriculum during the 1930s and 1940s, a painful communist witch hunt engulfing the campus in 1959, and periodic building campaigns, Olivet College's experience in the twentieth century was unremarkable. A number of notable faculty members, among them Carl Sandburg, Gertrude Stein, Sinclair Lewis, Amelia Earhart, Frank Lloyd Wright, Grace Hall Hemingway, Milton Horn, and William Dole, throughout the century attracted students.

The 1991–92 Organizational Status Quo

Fall of 1991 enrollment numbers identified 735 students (427 male, 308 female), 90 percent of whom were enrolled full-time. Most students were drawn from rural Michigan (96 percent); the 8 percent black student population came mainly from the Detroit metropolitan area. The racial composition was overwhelmingly white: 90 percent, with less than 2 percent either Hispanic or Asian.

Delivery of courses fell into the traditional teaching paradigm. Lectures were a standard format. The college offered two undergraduate degrees—Bachelor of Arts and Bachelor of Music Education—as well as Michigan Provisional Elementary and Secondary Education Teaching Certificates. The curriculum was arrayed around a general education requirement known as "the Core." The Freshman Core consisted of a two-course sequence devoted to reading, writing, and reasoning. The Sophomore Core consisted of a two-course sequence intended to integrate training in research and geography with the study of historical ideas, events, and personalities. The Junior Core also consisted of a two-course sequence that focused on the arts, literature, philosophy, and religions of Western Civilization. Rounding out the Core were three required distribution courses: a laboratory course, a math/science course, and a creative arts course. After completing the Core, a student selected from 24 majors. The most popular, business administration, enrolled 23 percent of the 255 declared students.

Forty-nine of Olivet's 71 instructors were classified as "faculty," with the remaining 22 "adjunct faculty." The majority of faculty members (64 percent) did not hold terminal degrees in their fields (e.g., Ph.D.) and had served the college just over seven years. The faculty was organized by discipline and in departments. The college had a nominal tenure-track system in which faculty came up for periodic review. The remaining faculty held adjunct status and were retained on an at-will contractual basis.

Faculty governance revolved around a longstanding senate. Representation was determined at the program or department level, and senate members served on a number of standing committees, including RTP (rank, tenure, and promotion) and curriculum development. Governance at the college looked traditional in form. However, the autocratic nature of the president's leadership style coalesced with the tacit but understood "devil's bargain," the lack of an organizational chart, and the absence of concrete job descriptions, allowing the administration to construct ad hoc communication lines, circumvent faculty senate officers, and exert direct control over employees. One longtime faculty member recalls the tenor of the dysfunction under the president:

> Everything and everybody was divided from everyone else, and it wasn't competition for resources. Success was killed and failure was rewarded, and I mean that literally. If you succeeded you were criticized, and if you failed, somehow that was success. It was just a perverse system. And it was extremely abusive.

The rumor mill grew more virulent in the days before and after the 1992 crisis. The perceived abusive wielding of power and banning of certain staff from campus also gravely affected faculty morale. One organizational consultant reported gloomy trends (from 1987 to 1991) verifying that (1) only 45 percent of entering first-year students made it to the senior year; (2) the academic climate necessarily emphasized remedial education, implying lower academic and admissions standards; and (3) a higher proportion of males on campus—the opposite of most comparably sized liberal arts colleges.

The solutions to the many confounding problems that coalesced to form the catalyst for change at Olivet College were not obvious. The antidote selected by the college's leaders seemed counterintuitive and equally confounding. When faced with dire fiscal and cultural concerns, what did the college faculty and academic community do? They decided to transform the undergraduate curriculum.

Portland State University

In many respects, Portland State University (PSU) looms large in contrast to Olivet College.[2] Whereas Olivet is a small, private liberal arts college with a church-related foundation and a history extending back to the mid-nineteenth century, Portland State was founded in 1946 in response to demand generated by the GI Bill at the end of World War II. In 1969 it became a "comprehensive public institution," offering mainly bachelor's degrees and a modest number of graduate degrees. Olivet maintains a student population of around 1,000 students and has about 50 faculty members. At Portland State, the English Department alone within the College of Liberal Arts and Sciences (CLAS) in 1990 had similar numbers. Cornfields and woods surround Olivet College at the southern end of the small town's main street. Portland State maintains an urban campus complete with high-rise buildings on the southern edge of the metropolitan city of Portland, Oregon.

As much as Olivet and Portland State are organizationally different, surprisingly, both institutions undertook a significant transformation of their undergraduate curricula at exactly the same time. And they used remarkably similar processes and strategies to achieve their goals. Although different people were involved, the visions they selected were the same: center on students as learners and use curriculum as the lever to modify the climate and culture on campus. Planning for the PSU transformation culminated in the 1994–95 school year with the four-year rollout of a comprehensive thematic model for general education (GE) called University Studies (UNST). The hope was that transforming the curriculum would bolster sagging enrollments, improve a flagging sense of community among undergraduates, and reframe the teaching of lower-division courses.

Implementation of University Studies thrust PSU into the national spotlight as a shining example of how to fix what was wrong with general education and undergraduate education at research institutions across the country. In fact, Portland State was honored as one of the first three recipients of the Pew Charitable Trusts Awards for Undergraduate Curricular Innovation (Toth and Rennie-Hill, 1998). Still, at the close of the millennium, PSU faculty, staff, and students were working to embrace its ten-year-old motto, *Let knowledge serve the City*, and to define the niche carved out by former president Judith Ramaley to become something not readily defined by the Carnegie Classification System—an "Urban One Institution," with an ambition to fully integrate the institution with and primarily serve the City of Portland.

Context and Crisis

In 1990, Portland State was a university of little distinction with a dismal retention rate (between 1986 and 1991, 32 to 45 percent of entering, full-time freshmen did not return for their sophomore year).[3] At that time, PSU "was an institution characterized by instability, lack of identity, and both ignored by and ignoring its community ... although it was situated in the midst of a major metropolitan area, it was not part of the fabric of that community."[4] Students used the university as a way station where they could accrue credits that would transfer to another college or university, or as a place to tie up the loose ends of collected credits from several community colleges. Tension between the faculty and the administration came to a head in 1988 when the president, threatened with a full faculty vote of no confidence, resigned under suspicion of having misappropriated funds, among other things.

During the 1989–90 academic year there were 6,964 men and 7,874 women enrolled, for a total head count of 14,838 students (with undergraduates numbering just over 10,000). The total dropped in the following two years, to 14,758 and then to 14,285. The distribution of students was an inverted pyramid. That is, most students were enrolled as seniors and juniors and smaller numbers were enrolled as sophomores and freshmen. The average undergraduate age was between 26 and 27, and between 34 and 35 at the graduate level. Transfer rates both into and out of the institution were high. Of the entering students, greater numbers transferred from community colleges and other Oregon postsecondary institutions than enrolled directly from high school.

Courses were offered to fulfill a number of majors at the undergraduate level, as well as master's and Ph.D. programs, in about sixty disciplines. By many reports, the typical Portland State student did not fit Astin's (1992) criteria for successful students.[5] Most worked part- or full-time. There was (and is) only one (privately run) residence hall near campus. The majority of students live off campus. Many lived with or provided for their families. Most enrolled in one or a few courses at a time, taking an average of seven years to graduate. The institution suffered from a lack of community connectivity, which is common on many commuter campuses. The major academic units of the university were the College of Liberal Arts and Sciences; the Schools of Business Administration; Education; Engineering and Applied Science; Fine and Performing Arts; Urban and Public Affairs; and the Graduate School of Social Work. The primary mode for delivery of general education (GE) was the "distribution system," typical of most colleges and universities of the day.

When Judith Ramaley was appointed the first female president of Portland State in 1990, undergraduate education at research universities across the country was under serious scrutiny. The public was calling for increased accountability, particularly for better undergraduate teaching. Close to 90 percent of postsecondary institutions in the United States employed a distribution-style GE program similar to the one at Portland State. Existing alternative models were seen as pedagogically unsound, too extreme, or simply not transferable to large research institutions. According to the 1998 Boyer Commission report on undergraduate education, "Almost without realizing it, research universities find themselves in the last half of the century operating large, often hugely extended undergraduate programs as though they are sideshows to the main event" (Boyer Commission, 1998, 37). It is easy to get the impression that the proposed University Studies GE model was designed explicitly in response to the Boyer Commission's report. However, in 1992 when the faculty took up the issue at Portland State, very few institutions were bothering to consider the subject. The fact that the UNST model came five years before the Boyer Commission report makes it both revolutionary and somewhat prophetic. For the PSU leadership, the question whether to transform was simply a practical academic answer to a particularly grim set of circumstances.

The First 40 Years

The College That Would Not Die (Dodds, 1996) is an apt title for the book written to mark Portland State University's first 50 years.[6] Among the colorful descriptors Gordon Dodds used to portray PSU, "From out of the mud" literally describes its origins. "Retrenchment and exigency" characterizes its default budgetary situation, as it has been an impoverished institution for some time. "Embattled wicked stepchild," describes its status within the tertiary state higher education system and with the Oregon taxpayers. From inside its gritty blue-collar wrapper, Portland State University's stakeholders have waged a continuous fight for distinction and its right to exist as an independent and important piece of the Oregon State System of Higher Education.

Quite literally, PSU started "from nothing"—no employees, no campus, and no students. In 1946, with a mission to serve the growing population of World War II veterans in the Portland metropolitan area, Stephen Epler, with a Ph.D. from Columbia's Teachers College, wrangled the wherewithal from the Oregon State Board of Higher Education under the umbrella of the General Extension Division to start an education center. Leveraging the promise of tuition dollars from the GI Bill of Rights and the availability of classroom space in the nearby community of Vanport, Epler began by hiring two employees.

Veterans were moving to Vanport, Oregon, in droves for inexpensive housing and employment opportunities. Comprising the world's largest housing project, Vanport was located below water level between the cities of Portland, Oregon, and Vancouver, Washington. The community was protected by a series of dikes and levees. Flanked by a meat-packing plant, two freight rail systems, a carbide factory, and the Columbia Slough, Vanport residents were periodically bathed in a variety of foul stenches, depending on prevailing winds.

The Vanport Extension Center (VEC) opened in the summer of 1946, operating out of office space and classroom facilities bequeathed by the Housing Authority of Portland. Seventeen faculty members taught 221 students in 14 courses covering 9 disciplines (business administration, chemistry, economics, engineering, English, mathematics, physics, psychology, and sociology). Tuition was $50 dollars per term (nonresidents, $95). Veterans were reimbursed $65/single or $90/married to cover tuition and subsistence. That fall, an astounding 1,410 students matriculated, cramming the classrooms. The standard faculty teaching load was five three-credit-hour courses. Some faculty members taught a sixth course for extra pay. Unlike many colleges and universities of the day, VEC was totally self-supporting in its first two years.

VEC's first transformation was forced quite literally by nature. A heavy snow pack and a warm, rainy spring contributed to an unusually high water level in 1948. On Memorial Day at 4:17 p.m., a railroad dike gave way and quickly opened a 500-foot gap in the protection. No lives were lost in the scramble to evacuate, but all of the campus buildings were destroyed. From out of the river mud, VEC had to begin anew.

With the support of the State Board of Higher Education, but against the wishes of the system's chancellor, who took the opportunity to petition for its closure, Vanport officials capitalized on the availability of space, moving the center to an abandoned shipyard in nearby St. Johns. Although there was no proximate housing, the new campus was blessed with something almost no current campus can boast—acres of abundant parking. Epler welcomed the first students to VEC's "new" campus in 1948 saying, "You will have the experience of turning a shipyard into a college" (Dodds, 1996, 27). The Center later became affectionately known as "Oregon Ship."

Recognizing that Portland was the only major metropolitan area in the West with no "closely available, publicly supported institution" (*Sunday Oregonian*, February 1, 1948, quoted in Dodds, 1996, 32), John Hakanson, an alumnus, suggested that VEC be moved to a permanent downtown location. Oregon State College (in Corvallis) and University of Oregon (in Eugene) officials opposed such a move, fearing redundancy that would result in a loss of students at their campuses and increase competition for limited state funding. After two tries, Hakanson's bill (House Bill 213) passed the state legislature and was signed by the governor on April 15, 1949. The bill appropriated funds to purchase the dilapidated downtown Lincoln High School building to house VEC. Once again, faculty, staff, and students began a new semester in the fall of 1952 by moving: from Oregon Ship to the downtown facility. Although the institution's name was changed to the Portland State Extension Center with the move, the community began to commonly refer to it as Portland State College.

Meanwhile, Epler was working Salem's political channels to introduce a constitutional amendment to allow the four-year college to grant full degrees (bachelor's and master's degrees, rather than just certificates), stressing the growing need to prepare teachers for the baby boom. Again, it took two tries and three long years before a bill was unanimously approved on December 14, 1954, by the State Board of Education to do just that. The governor ultimately signed the appropriation on February 10, 1955. The Portland State community celebrated with a parade of revelers and by taking down the bronze-lettered sign "Extension Center," leaving only the words "Portland State" on the wall for all to see.

Prologue to a Third Transformation

Oregon taxpayers have historically demonstrated an unwillingness to fully fund their postsecondary institutions. Consequently, budget issues plagued Portland State, eventually leading to contract concerns and a crisis in the early 1970s that pushed the faculty to unionize (71 percent of the faculty voted for unionization in 1978). In a move that embittered the faculty, in 1974 the newly appointed president became "adversarial . . . and took an uncharacteristically belligerent position" at the bargaining table (Dodds, 1996, 388). On March 14, 1979, the administration proposed retrenchment measures that usurped the need to declare a fiscal emergency before laying off tenured faculty. No contract had been reached by the close of the academic year in June. Faculty representatives were convinced that the administration was trying to sabotage the collective bargaining process. After 11 months (190 hours) of negotiations, they reached their first tentative agreement on August 3, 1979, at 3:02 a.m.

Still, the financial difficulties never waned. With some advance warning, the president publicly declared a financial crisis on September 16, 1981. Among other solutions, some faculty members took early retirement. Two years later, however, "the situation was [again] grim. In 1983–84, PSU would have to absorb $750,000 of temporary reductions to avoid layoffs . . . identify permanent savings of $748,00 and plan for an additional $1,015,000 permanent savings" (Dodds, 1996, 396). The faculty senate considered closing down the campus for a day, or a month, to make a statement. Some of the more distinguished (read: employable) faculty jumped ship. After 12 years of service, the president retired and a new president was hired in 1986.

The new president's tenure was tainted from the outset and became more controversial over time. Amid rumors that he was not the selection committee's first choice, some faculty members felt that the chancellor of the state system had foisted a personal friend on Portland State. A series of disputes played out in the *Vanguard* (the student newspaper) embroiled the new president in a First Amendment scandal, with faculty members supporting the rights of the newspaper. By early spring 1988, more rumors circulated that the president was misusing funds by somehow secretly funneling money to the university Foundation, resulting in a movement by the faculty in March of that year to vote "no-confidence." Although, a July investigation by the Oregon Department of Justice found no criminal wrongdoing, many longtime supporters of the university in the community viewed the issue as moot—feeling "that only when the President steps down can Portland State begin to recover" (Dodds, 1996, 457). After only two years of service, the president voluntarily stepped down, citing irreconcilable differences and the impossibility of mending working relationships between himself and the faculty.

A New Era

Judith Ramaley began her term in 1990 as PSU's president with a standing ovation at her convocation, before she had said a word. From the outset, President Ramaley had her hands full. Reeling from the 1980s timber industry bust and not yet into the high-tech boom, Oregon voters passed an amendment (Proposition 5) in 1990 to lower property taxes and limit their use in education to elementary and secondary schools. The proposition was phased in over a number of years, subjecting the state's college and university system to yet another series of predictable fiscal crises.

Ramaley quickly earned a reputation with the faculty for being hardnosed but fair by: (1) eliminating the School of Health and Human Performance; (2) promising not to lay off any tenured or tenure-track faculty; and (3) insisting that all positions to be eliminated would come from the administrative, service, and nonacademic classifications. Even so, the president was hit with another round of budget cuts from the state in 1992—this one in the guise of a $138 million dollar cut spread across the Oregon higher education system. Unable to follow the usual committee protocol, the president announced on June 1, 1992, that, in accordance with the collective bargaining agreement, she was going to begin a program reduction process. According to others in the administration, Ramaley refused to be negative, preferring to ask, "What is the 92 percent that is worth saving?"

The 1992 Organizational Status Quo

In 1992 the status quo of general education at Portland State was not by itself enough to start the massive university-wide transformation of the curriculum. Two key forces coalesced to push the initiatives: (1) motivational leadership on the part of the president and the provost, and (2) the fiscal crisis (Pratt, 1998).

First, most of those interviewed for this study identified President Judith Ramaley and Provost Michael Reardon as the instrumental mobilizing forces driving the transformation. Many testify that without their efforts the project would have been a nonstarter. Compelling as leaders, both were engaging and powerful personalities for different reasons. Having been a member of the faculty since the mid-1960s, according to one high-level administrator, Provost Reardon was "part of an old tree of connections" and carried great diplomatic and institutional clout; he knew every skeleton in every closet. President Ramaley had an uncanny ability to lead the campus "to the 'Promised Land' in a sense. So, there was this kind of openness and we believe you." She also defended the perimeter, which had an enabling effect on the other members of the institution.

Second, the university was "genuinely at a point of crisis" with regard to state support for higher education in Oregon. According to one PSU official, "There are a lot of explanations that we can make up after the fact as to why we did it like that. But the fact of the matter was that we just had to do it. We didn't have a choice." The budget situation in the early 1990s was not out of the ordinary; almost all past Portland State presidents had at one time or another been in similar straits. However, the combination of three flashpoints turned what seemed to be a necessary retrenchment at Portland State into a dire need for transformation.

The first flashpoint was the passing of Proposition 5 in 1990 by the Oregon voters. Adding to the budget woes, declining enrollment and a poor retention rate were the second flashpoint. These two issues necessitated the raising of tuition by more than 85 percent over a five-year period and exacerbated the retention issue. Essentially, one faculty member was astounded that "10 percent of the college-going population in the state of Oregon was priced out of the marketplace."

The third flashpoint was not obvious to most of the campus community not involved in statewide political discussions about higher education in Oregon. It is an artifact of the longstanding competition among Oregon State, the University of Oregon, and Portland State. Just before Ramaley's appointment, the governor had commissioned a study on the future of higher education in the city of Portland. A number of ideas raised threatened to divide up and reallocate portions of Portland State to the different institutions. In the absence of a sitting president, with only an acting president from 1988 to 1990, "*It was a feeding frenzy.*" In short, one official reported:

> Proposition 5 was happening; tuition went up, and so enrollment dipped. The college was at the low point of enrollment for a long period of time. We were down one point to 11 percent at the college [CLAS] in terms of faculty positions. In the sciences, it is almost incredible to think about this. In one department we were down 32 percent and in another department we were down 28 percent [from where we] had been about 7 years earlier. It was almost an, "And so, what is our future?" sort of an issue.

As at Olivet College, decision makers and campus leaders at Portland State University were faced with numerous troubling factors that amplified the need for change. Again, solutions were not obvious. When faced with dire fiscal and cultural concerns, what did the administrators and faculty tackle first? The undergraduate curriculum.

Notes

1. Sources for the Olivet College narrative include a number of college general catalogs and annual reports as well as Belcher (1993), McClendon (1999), and several interviewees (cited when quoted).

2. The original writing of the Portland State University case was completed for my dissertation (Anderson, 2003) and is thoroughly documented therein.

3. PSU, Office of Institutional Research and Planning (OIRP), cited in the General Education Working Group Report and Recommendations, September 1993, p. 10.

4. Report to the Kellogg Forum, "Portland State University Report to the Kellogg Forum" (draft), 2000, 1

5. Astin's work on student involvement and success implies that the more a student's social and academic life revolves around the life at a college, the more successful she or he will be. Contrarily, Portland State was largely a commuter campus, with no real residence halls, and many students also worked and had families.

6. Dodds's work was the primary resource for this section.

2 The Theoretical Backdrop

Before digging deeper into the case studies and unpacking the findings, it will be helpful to establish the theoretical backdrop for change and to place resistance within it. Fortunately for scholars and practitioners, a few works offer a substantial exploration of the related organizational change theory. For a comprehensive set of the change theory ancestors and an overview of the seminal works to date, look no further than Burke, Dale, and Paine's (2009) edited volume, *Organization Change: A Comprehensive Reader*. For a reworking of modern theories, see Demers's (2007) *Organizational Change Theories: A Synthesis*. Burke's (2008) *Organization Change: Theory and Practice* provides a bridge between the two. Cawsey and Deszca (2007) offer a *Toolkit for Organizational Change* that practitioners may find handy. Rather than replicate the good efforts of these authors, here I elucidate the frameworks and theory that informed my study.

The Intangible Plan

Traditionally, authors and change consultants have steadfastly proclaimed that leaders, or "change champions," should have a solid vision for the end result they seek, as well as concrete plans in place well before they pull the change trigger (e.g., Kotter, 1996). My research suggests this is fine in theory, but difficult to make happen in practice. The institutional leaders I interviewed indicated, without exception, that while they indeed held a strong vision of the final outcome, they had no concrete notion about the path a change effort should follow; nor did they attempt to plan their change effort from beginning to end. Their plans and actions evolved over time, and the process of change was ambiguous and arduous (Burke, 2008). At best, these leaders grasped the change tiger's tail only loosely. They were able to articulate a sense of urgency that change needed to happen, but were less specific about which way the effort would take them and how their organizations would shift as a result of their efforts.

The ambiguousness of the early planning phases reduces one's ability to anticipate resistance, but counterintuitively may be beneficial to the overall aims of the change effort. This became clear in a preliminary study I conducted, separate from the Olivet and Portland State larger research effort, to explore the processes employed by one administration to convert their institution from a small liberal arts college into a comprehensive private university (Anderson, 2000). My analysis of the data yielded findings that help explain why many people may be wary of change.

The most surprising and perhaps even paradoxical aspect of this smaller study was the uniformity of the opinions shared by the interviewees. When asked, all indicated that there had been no plan for executing the transformation. Even the top-level administrators said that their efforts were "more of an evolution than a planned process." Even though none of the change leaders had devised any semblance of a strategy or plan for their organization's transformation, the words they used in the interviews mirror many of those used by those who recommend intentional strategic planning and change efforts.

Specifically, although the champions of organizational change stated that they did not use a concrete plan or strategy to make change happen, retrospectively, a plan emerges from examination of what they said and did (Weick, 1995). Although not overt, their change strategy was intricately woven into the culture of the organization.

Absent the design assistance of a hired team of consultants, plans for change are invented, and unfold, on the fly. Ask anyone experienced with nonconsultant-led change efforts if a model or theory for change was deployed to assist and enable the process. Almost no one will say yes or be able to describe it. Even so, quixotically, as they move through change, much of their work follows established change models.

I call this the **intangible plan phenomenon**. While moving through what may be thought of as an "organic" change effort, change leaders and participants are not readily able to articulate the process, but the process is apparent in hindsight—which is perfectly logical if you follow Weick's (1995) sensemaking principles. This phenomenon adds clarity to Burke's (2008) strategic planning paradox that the action of change agency does not fit a linear model, although stepwise models are often used to describe change. My study shows that change processes are not something that institutional leadership can or must clearly articulate before undertaking them. Transformation efforts appear to be explainable as a gradual, evolutionary process, not wholly tangible. Yet some elements of the process must be readily available, clearly articulated, designed to motivate people and foster loyalty and to serve as an underlying strategic foundation for any transformation (de Caluwé and Vermaak, 2003).

Having an intangible plan rather than a concrete change agenda may in fact be entirely beneficial. An intangible plan is malleable, thereby tacitly amenable to outside influence, which can engender more support for the overall change effort. The nature of intangible change plans allows for a constantly customizable set of processes that foster innovation and creativity. But saying that change plans are amendable and actually amending plans based on criticism are two separate concerns.

One can think of this intangible plan phenomenon less as an approach to change efforts and more as the point where change efforts become a fundamental cultural element of the organization. Resistance, as a natural part of organizational life and an expected response to change efforts, should be considered valuable feedback in shaping the effort (Bovey and Hede, 2001; Ford and Ford, 2009; Geller, 2002). It is not enough for change leaders to suggest that others embrace change. Change leaders must prove the point by modifying and adapting plans on the fly. The early cementing of a change plan and an unbending mindset may make the whole endeavor excessively fragile. Without the flexibility to change course or amend plans in response to feedback, champions risk interrupting the change effort or stopping it altogether.

With an intangible and thus malleable plan, change agents can adapt to resistance. As to when such plans become too permeable, that is best left for another study. Suffice it to say that an intangible plan provides opportunity for the organization to be flexible and spontaneous, open to new paths, able to incubate many ideas, and more difficult to criticize and resist; and it allows for many voices to operationalize transition in an entrepreneurial culture through an organic process.

Because a plan is intangible does not mean the process is or should be secretive or covert. Simply put, change champions will find that, even though they may have a strong vision for the effort, it is difficult to articulate a plan when (a) internal and external constituents are empowered to influence the direction, (b) numerous ideas are being incubated at all times and there is no telling which will emerge a winner, and (c) the plans must follow the resources. Instead of causing anxiety, an intangible approach may help to engage resistance and thereby increase the strength of the change effort. A number of propositions that remain to be proven, but can be instructive nonetheless, were a byproduct of the smaller study.

Transformation is fostered in organizations where leaders maintain a clear vision and cultivate an organizational mission that clearly supports evolution, where the end result is left open and no strategic guide is documented (Geller, 2002; Lbianca, Gray, and Brass, 2000; Pardo del Val and Fuentes, 2003).

Fiscal stability and independence provide a solid foundation for and freedom to move transformation efforts forward (Pfeffer and Slancick, 2003). Even so, times of crisis and financial difficulty can also present opportunities for dramatic change (Schein, 1992). It is debatable whether it takes a crisis to spur large-scale change or transformation. But when a crisis does not lead to the demise of an organization, it can instead intensify the sense of urgency and increase the organization's readiness to undertake change (Jansen, 2000).

Although there may be no need for a fully mapped grand transformation plan, transformative actions must be thoroughly thought through, justifiable, well designed, and competently executed because all actions have consequences (Weick, 1979). Change champions must foster ongoing, symbiotic interactions by seeking and paying attention to diverse opinions and working to build constructive relationships.

Because an organization's board often bears legal responsibility for a whole organization, cultivating a supportive board comprising individuals with complementary skills and connections is essential to a transformation effort. Trustees can become actively engaged in the planning process through committee work. Often, critical decisions that are ratified at board meetings provide high-level support for change efforts. Board members can provide vision and reinforce the culture as they demand performance from an institution's leaders. Therefore, getting board members' perspectives on elements of resistance may be a practical part of the change equation (de Jager, 2001).

Last, uncontrollable internal and external factors may foster, stall, or stop a transformation process (Demers, 2007). Like the forces of nature, not all aspects of a transformation process are controllable (Burke, 2008). When it rains, one can put on a raincoat or use an umbrella. Of course, one might also choose to dance naked in the puddles. Either way, the rain affects your decision. Societal shifts, broad economic swings, and revolution can also affect the strategy of a transforming institution (de Caluwé and Vermaak, 2003). Being flexible in moving resources to meet demand is the mark of an entrepreneurial institution. Although demand is not controllable, institutional leaders can adjust as interests wax and wane for particular programs or products.

If a transformation process is not fixed, but evolutionary and ongoing, milestones become important, even if an end point is never reached (Quinn, 1996). Intangible or not, planning or the absence of it will not lead to a long-lasting sense of organizational change nirvana because resistance is a natural byproduct of championship and may well be the proof that a transformation is taking place (Bovey and Hede, 2001; Oreg et al., 2008). Just as rock climbers stipulate that you are not climbing if you are not falling, perhaps if you are not generating resistance you are not transforming (Burke, 2008).

A Synthesis Framework

To begin a conversation about change and resistance, I often conduct an exercise to remind people why change is difficult. Try this right now. Put this book down. Stand up. Cross your arms. As swiftly as possible, switch the position of your arms. The arm that you had on top should now be on the bottom; but maybe it's not. Was the task challenging or easy to accomplish? If it was difficult, why?

Conducting this exercise in a large room full of people usually produces mixed results that reflect all possible permutations of the experience. Invariably, it produces a visceral reaction. Some find it overly easy, a "no-brainer" if you will. Some find it a difficult but surmountable challenge. Still others are stymied, unable to even move their arms.

The exercise mirrors the trouble with any change effort. The responses to change efforts vary (Burke, 2008; Piderit, 2000). In every organization undergoing change, some will say that the proposed change is easy to comprehend and will immediately buy in. Others will require more explanation or guidance before signing on. Still others, because of their natural predilections, simply won't be coming along for the ride. What the exercise makes plain is that champions who find a change to be simple, rational, and reasonable may have to work with others who approach it from the opposite end of the spectrum. Although you, the champion of change, may have been thinking through the change for a great while, the people you are expecting to help you through it have, through no fault of their own, spent less time with the idea. Regardless of the size of your organization, its members will range from being completely accepting of change to being steadfastly against it. But do not mistake an unwillingness to change for an inability to change. The two types of resistance require different approaches.

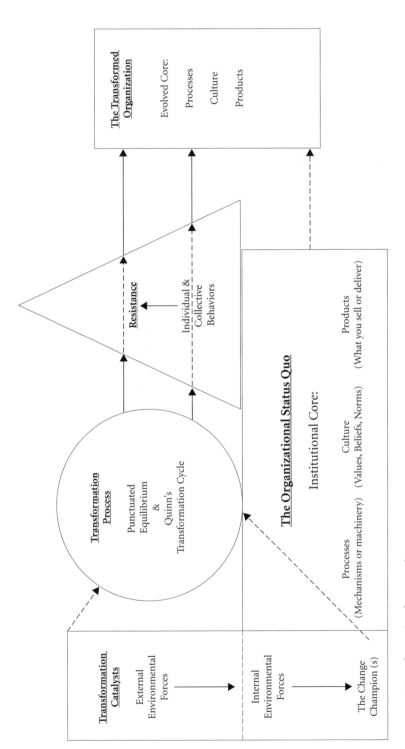

Exhibit 2. Transformation framework.

While there are many models or stepwise frameworks offering recipes for undertaking and responding to change, it is challenging to find an encompassing, empirically based framework that conceptualizes the process as ordinary people experience it (Burke, 2008; Demers, 2007). Everyone has had some kind of experience with change, and much of it is memorable because it was painful in some way, but most of us do not think about change from the macro level. We become distracted as we wend our way through the change thicket, hindered by the brambles and briars. To fully grasp the change process, particularly an intangible one, it is helpful to place our personal experiences within the context of a broader framework. As you read the next paragraphs, think about a powerful experience with organizational change that you have had. This should help you determine whether your experience matches or diverges from the model.

In a Darwinian sense, scratching for organizational survival means continuously transforming goals, mission, and operating structure (Crane, 1963). Some scholars suggest that transformation occurs as a process managed by the leaders of an organization. Quinn's (1996) model is one of a large number of models constructed since Lewin (1947) crafted his unfreeze, change, refreeze paradigm. Combining key portions of the literature, I developed an a priori model (Exhibit 2) that captures the salient elements of organizational transformation and helped shape the methodology for my study. This synthesis, described below, provides a framework for understanding transformation and places resistance in this context.

Transformation Catalysts

Inseparable from the environment organizations transform as a direct result of shifts within their milieu (Chaffee, 1985; Baldridge, 1975; Klimecki and Lassleben, 1998). Thus my framework begins with **transformation catalysts**. Transformation efforts are composed in concert with a wide array of fluctuating, sometimes paradoxical, internal and external forces (Chaffee, 1985; Christenson, 1982; Levin, 1998b; MacTaggart, 1998; Peterson, 1997; Rowley, et al., 1997; Sporn, 1999). As internal and external forces coalesce, members react to anything they sense is amiss, and one or more change champions decide to act (Weick, 1995).

While change or transformation can happen organically, most often there is a catalyst. A sense of urgency, up to and including a threat to survival, is necessary; otherwise there is no identifiable impetus for breaching the status quo (Collins and Hill, 1998; Klimecki and Lassleben, 1998). The importance of quality leadership in a transformation effort cannot be overemphasized (Hipps, 1982; Peterson, 1982). Whether they are newly arrived executives (Kraatz and Moore, 2002), or rank-and-file personnel who see an opportunity (Clark, 1997) or are thrust into action by crisis, ordinary people become change champions and the standard-bearers of vision, strategy, and empowerment (Astin and Astin, 2000; Atwater and Atwater, 1994; Bensimon, Neumann, and Birnbaum, 1989; Cameron and Ulrich, 1986; Kotter, 1999; Green, 1997). Such individuals must shoulder the power and authority to move initiatives forward (Bryson, 1995; Keller, 1997; Koteen, 1989; Nadler, 1998; Winstead, 1982). As essential catalysts for transformation, champions can be individuals or a collection of likeminded stakeholders (including front-line players) from throughout an organization (Rhodes, 2000; Senge, 2000). Ordinary people who are contemplating championing a change effort should be careful to obtain permission from the requisite authorities. Without it, their efforts will inevitably be painful and burdensome.

Although champions are essential to the transformation process, they are not its only possible leaders. Indeed, people in the pool of resisters may have powerful leadership capacity, but with different goals in mind (Zoller and Fairhurst, 2007). Resistance leaders are a critical part of any change story.

The Organizational Status Quo

Because the forces that cause champions to feel the need to initiate a change process rarely subside during the effort, there is a dotted line from the top of the first block pointing to the change cycle represented by the circle in the model. Once a person decides to act, the champion targets the organizational status quo, which includes the culture and other core elements of an operation, the processes and products that form the basis for every operation. The organizational status quo is placed at the bottom, constituting the foundation for the model.

The decision to initiate transformation necessitates a hard look at the status quo. Most organizations are built to maintain the status quo, and people are often either indifferent to or against change of any kind (March and Simon, 1958; Burke, 2008). People's natural inclination is to achieve permanence and stability, not change and transformation (Bainbridge, 1996; Kraatz and Moore, 2002). Organizations are built to support a state of equilibrium in order to maintain coherence and consistency for those working within them (Romanelli and Tushman, 1994). The routines of organizational life protect a collective identity, which further inhibits change (Argyris, 1985; Brown and Starkey, 2000). As such, change champions face the challenge of targeting an organization's cultural foundation—all of its people, processes, and products (Alfred and Carter, 1999; Cameron and Quinn, 2006; Galpin, 1996; Peterson, 1995).

The Institutional Core

Any transformation must be clearly linked to the core (the central functions) of an organization; otherwise its members may perceive change objectives as peripheral and unnecessary (Nadler, 1988). Regardless of type, every organization consists of a set of competencies and rooted processes that are a part of the core business operations (Hamel and Prahalad, 1994; Sporn, 1999; Senge and Sterman, 1992; Wilson, 2000). For example, teaching, research, and service constitute the central business of most postsecondary institutions (Brinkman and Morgan, 1997). Emphasis on the three varies; research is the focus at prestigious state and private universities, whereas teaching is emphasized at small liberal arts colleges and community colleges. The faculty and staff embody the emphasis of the institution by carrying out the duties of their positions and engaging in the processes that yield its products (Birnbaum, 1988). Shaped by tradition and history, the organization informs the values, norms, and beliefs (culture) that guide its members' behavior (Clark, 1991; Kuh and Whitt, 1988). Learning and knowledge generation are the result.

In the for-profit sector, industrial processes vary greatly, but always serve the same end: to construct the products (or services) that are sold to their customers. One may be in the business of modifying genetic codes to produce cancer treatment drugs; another may offer tax consulting services. Corporations' processes and cultures may be different, but the end result is typically a good or service that is sold to sustain the operation.

While many can readily identify an organization's core processes and products, the third element of a company's institutional core deserves special attention. Culture, if left out of the change equation, can stall or kill a transformation effort, but is the most troublesome to decipher and change (Cameron and Quinn, 2006).

Organizational Culture   The tendency of change agents is to deal indirectly with culture during transformation efforts because it is easier to focus on concrete, tangible processes (Atwater and Atwater, 1994; Cameron and Ettington, 1988; Galpin, 1996). Yet failure to address culture will almost certainly lead to failure (Cameron and Quinn, 2006). Culture is socially constructed as a group adapts to external forces and develops internal ways of behaving; its culture is taught to new members as the correct way to perceive, think, and feel (Schein, 1992). Kuh and Whitt offer this encompassing synthesis of culture:

> [Culture is a] persistent patterns of norms, values, practices, beliefs, and assumptions that shape behavior of individuals and groups in an organization and provide a frame of reference within which to interpret the meaning of events and actions. . . . Culture is described as a social or normative glue based on shared values and beliefs that holds organizations together and serves four general purposes: 1) it conveys a sense of identity; 2) it facilitates commitment to an entity, such as the organization or peer group, other than self; 3) it enhances the stability of a group's social system; and 4) it is a sense-making device that guides and shapes behavior. In addition, the culture of an organization defines, identifies, and legitimates authority. (Kuh and Whitt, 1998, 9–27)

Subcultures   Subcultures are defined as "subgroups of an institution's members who interact regularly with one another, perceive themselves as a distinct group within the institution, share a commonly defined set of problems, and act on the basis of collective understandings unique to their group" (Kuh and Whitt, 1988, 37). Depending on the type of organization, there could be a sales force subculture, a research subculture, a technology subculture, professional/academic subcultures, and so on. Like tribes and territories, functional units within the same organization are interconnected, but not necessarily part of a tightly interlocked operation (Clark, 1997; Weick, 1976). The existence of subcultures within an organization adds another layer of complexity to any transformation (Schein, 1992; Overton and Burkhardt, 1999).

The Transformation Process   The line from change champions through the organizational status quo to the **transformation process** element of the model is dotted because the attention paid to the status quo by change agents on their way to initiating some kind of process varies. It depends on the scope and scale of the transformation, as well as the attention to detail paid by the champions. Regardless, champions taking action (even the very act of planning for change can trigger resistance) to transform an organization can be explained with two models; Quinn's (1996) transformation model and Romanelli and Tushman's (1994) punctuated equilibrium theory. Therefore, the transformation process element is depicted as a circle to reflect Quinn's model, which will be explained after a brief discussion of punctuated equilibrium theory.

Punctuated Equilibrium Theory   There is much anecdotal evidence that organizations improve in an incremental, serendipitous, and evolutionary way (Dill, 1999). A primary mode for institutional change in over two centuries of higher education has been additive, witnessed in "almost archeological layers" (Duderstadt, 2000, 3). This is not surprising if one conceptualizes the common state of a postsecondary institution in the way that Romanelli and Tushman (1994) suggest. Their punctuated equilibrium theory states that organizations evolve over long periods of stability and incremental growth (equilibrium periods) that are punctuated by short bursts of fundamental change (revolutionary periods), which substantively disrupt established activity patterns and install the basis for new equilibrium periods. Further, radical and discontinuous change of all or most activities of an organization is required to break the strong grip of inertia during a stable period (Cameron and Ulrich, 1986; Farmer, 1990, Godkin and Allcorn, 2008). This type of change becomes organizational transformation when it involves core values, strategies, structures, and capabilities (i.e. the institutional core). During these revolutionary periods, deeply embedded routines are disrupted and reinvented, and behavior and outcomes become less predictable (Newman and Nollen, 1998).

Quinn's Transformation Cycle   Even within the equilibrium phase, organizations evolve to some degree. This process happens in four distinct phases, as described by Quinn (1996) (see Exhibit 3).

1. **Initiation**—Spurred by some catalyst, a group **desires** to change and improve. The group develops a **vision** of a future state. Because it is difficult to tell if the vision is illusory or sound, there is a danger of acting on a vision that cannot be implemented. Fear of failure at this point can cause stagnation.

2. **Uncertainty**—Despite an uncertain outcome, participants begin by engaging in intensive, intuitive **experimentation**. The failure of an experiment could send the group into panic. But by persisting through

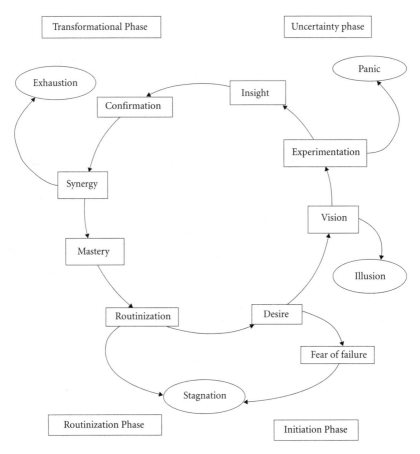

Exhibit 3. Quinn's transformation cycle. From Quinn, R. E. (1996). *Deep change: Discovering the leader within.* San Francisco: Jossey-Bass.

the discomfort, the group gains **insight** that guides them through to the transformation phase. Through intuitive, experimental learning, the elements of the problem may be assembled or reframed, and a new theory or paradigm may emerge.

3. **Transformation**—A new paradigm integrates the previously contradictory elements of the system, **confirming** positive movement and resulting in **synergy**. Relationships change. Exhaustion could cause the group to deviate from the cycle.

4. Routinization—When the new vision is achieved or **mastered**, opera-
    tions become **routinized**, and the situation moves once again to equi-
    librium. Here again, a group (or person) could depart from the cycle
    and stagnate in the new status quo.

Quinn concludes that as long as a system keeps circulating through these
phases, it remains healthy. However, it is not easy to keep moving. The transformation process continues when there is ongoing evaluation, reinvention, and
realignment. But the group that falls into any of the four traps (illusion, panic,
exhaustion, or stagnation) may quickly reach organizational death. Quinn ex-
pands on these four traps, but his model lacks a comprehensive exploration of
resistance to transformation efforts.

Resistance

Because the phenomenon of resistance is the focus of this book, I leave a more
thorough discussion of this component of the model for later. I use a triangle
to depict this area because it is the mathematical symbol for change. Think of
the transformation process as a circle that rolls along as change champions
deploy whatever strategy that serves as a fulcrum to guide the action they have
designed. Members of an organization try to anticipate the barriers to transformation as they engage and surmount resistance. Resistance can comprise any
combination of individual or collective behaviors. Thus, as champions allow
the levers (tactics or approaches) to be applied during the transformation process, they must follow the arrows to move through resistance to arrive at the
end result: a **transformed organization**.

The Transformed Organization

The effort involved in undertaking a transformation is great, whether one ar-
rives at the planned destination or at one that is different than expected. Any
transformation should result in an evolved organization with a comprehen-
sively and measurably different set of values, beliefs, or norms, lashed to those
pieces of the institutional core deemed worth keeping (the dashed line from
the status quo to the transformed organization in the framework in Exhibit 2
represents those elements of the old status quo retained in the new) (Green
and Hayward, 1997). The transformation is complete when the goals of the
transformation process become embedded within new, evolved core processes,
values, beliefs, norms, and products (Kotter, 1996; Nadler, 1988).

A Turning Point for the Theoretical
Understanding of Resistance

In his classic encapsulation of the sensemaking conundrum at the micro-behavioral level, Weick is famous for asking, "How do I know what I think until I see what I say" (personal communication, September 1998)? We may be able to capture the essence of resistance to organizational change and trans-formation by adding three words to that query thusly: *How do I know what I think until I see what I say about your actions?* If organizational life consists of a set of interrelated, improvised actions and reactions—the classic Weickian (1979) double interact—which we make sense of and use to determine our next moves, it may be best to conceptualize resistance as an organic response or reaction to change agency rather than as rudimentary behavior that is invari-ably negative and inherently damaging to change efforts (Burke, 2008; Ford, Ford, and D'Amelio, 2008; Piderit, 2000; van Dijk and van Dijk, 2009; Waddell and Sohal, 1998; Weick, 1979). This is indicated by the dashed lines that go through rather than around the resistance triangle in Exhibit 2.

Traditionally, resistance to organizational change has been thought of as something to be anticipated, minimized, and quashed (Ford and Ford, 2008; Hultman, 1998; Piderit, 2000; Waddell and Sohal, 1998). Fortunately, at the close of the previous millennium, some scholars were questioning the dominant conceptualization by recommending a positive approach to un-derstanding resistance (e.g., Waddell and Sohal, 1998; Piderit, 2000). Waddell and Sohal (1998) suggest that thinking of resistance as only doing harm is misguided at best, and possibly detrimental to a full understanding of orga-nizational life. On the continuum of possible responses to change, resistance behavior is just one of the many identifiable reactions, from completely sup-portive to vehemently against (Burke, 2008; de Caluwé and Vermaak, 2003). Piderit (2000) helps us all the way around the theoretical corner by strongly suggesting that the old paradigm for understanding resistance is flawed. Scholars and practitioners should better view resistance as integral and pos-sibly helpful to every change effort.

Others since Piderit have dedicated themselves to carving out new under-standing about resistance from this positive conceptualization (e.g., Burke, 2008; Ford et al., 2002, 2008; Ford and Ford, 2009; Goltz and Hietapelto, 2002). Because the literature had not turned this theoretical corner at the time I final-ized the design and executed my study, the research that serves as the basis for this book may be imperfect. However, to paraphrase former U.S. secretary of defense Donald Rumsfeld, we all conduct research with the theory we have, not the theory we wish we had.

There is, however, an enticing synchronicity between my findings and this new theoretical direction. Perhaps my colleagues and I wrestled identical theory demons at precisely the same time. My hope is that the model building in the later chapters will fill in many of the gaps identified by those writing in the field at the start of this millennium.

A more complete discussion of the nature of resistance is presented in Chapter 4. Let us now return to the transformation narratives of Olivet College and Portland State University.

3 From Planning to Implementation

The discussion of theory development in Chapter 2 becomes more concrete when placed amidst the action of the real transformations of Olivet College and Portland State University. As the story unfolds in the ensuing pages, the ambiguous, intangible, yet interwoven natural facets of the change process should be apparent.

The Olivet College Transformation Narrative

The dire circumstances of 1992 threatened the existence of Olivet College. With an international media whipping up a frenzy over the racial tensions, several other forces also pushed the need for transformation. The campus's psychological climate, organizational structure, perceived abuses of power, and relative isolation coalesced to shape a malaise exacerbated by a culture of fear, suspicion, and distrust. Morale was low among the professionally stagnant faculty. High faculty attrition resulted in a mix of very young staff and seasoned veterans. Faculty members were disengaged from any responsibility for governance of the college. Many felt disempowered and were reluctant to take the necessary steps to improve the situation for fear of reprisal.

The board of trustees had begun conversations about the college's situation before April 2, 1992, but the events that followed, including a faculty vote of no confidence in the president, spurred them to action. It was reported that the board chair, a longtime friend of the president's, had "graciously negotiated" his departure. On May 1, 1992, the college's president resigned.

The board of trustees hired Gretchen Kreuter, then president of Rockford College in Illinois, as interim president on June 30, 1992. Kreuter's "no-holds barred" approach to ferreting out and terminating "troublemakers" quickly turned the faculty and staff against her. She was viewed as someone hired to "clean house." Kreuter's dismissal of two senior administrators just days before Christmas 1993 put most personnel in survival mode. By the spring of 1993, the college faced a million-dollar deficit. A June 1993 external survey found that 85 percent of faculty and staff "disagreed or strongly disagreed" that their experience at Olivet had been a rewarding one.

Meanwhile, the board commissioned a committee of faculty, staff, and students to conduct a national presidential search. The team was charged with finding a "turn-around president," bypassing traditional candidates in favor of "a mad scientist ... an inventor ... a critic of traditional higher education practices, and [someone] willing to take risks and to experiment" (Olivet College Narrative Summary).

A Breath of Fresh Air

Michael Bassis, then a 48-year-old provost at Antioch College, emerged from a pool of over 100 applicants as a person capable of turning the college around. When asked why he wanted to work at Olivet in the capacity of president, Bassis answered, "I wanted to be president of this college at this time, because of the potential for the growth of the college and the chance to put my abilities to good use." While Although he presented no detailed strategy or process for turning the college around, he did have "a broad vision of how to change, and articulated a way of involving everyone by giving a certain degree of responsibility and authority to the faculty" (Dole interview). On July 15, 1993, Michael Bassis assumed the presidency of Olivet College. In a series of surprising and uncustomary moves, he deferred his inauguration for a year, rolled up his sleeves, and called an immediate campus-wide emergency meeting to start the institution toward massive transformation.

Having visited the campus before accepting the presidency, Michael Bassis deduced that the Olivet turnaround would be "more than a transformation, it was a culture war!" (Bassis interview). The past practices of campus leadership had created a hostile environment in which those being led were largely suspicious of anyone leading. Fortunately, Bassis's leadership style was the antithesis of both prior administrations and was described by many as a "breath of fresh air."

Bassis reports that he did not at any time have or portray a vision for how to reshape the institution beyond a desire to simply empower the faculty to be the

principal drivers of the transformation. The responsibility was great. Bassis recalls being deathly afraid that he might well be the last Olivet College president.
Amidst the turmoil and the need to keep the college open, one gets the feeling
that the president was acting on intuition.

> There was so much to do that I was going to just roll up my sleeves and do it.
> And I didn't have time to think everything through, and for the most part in the
> first six to eight weeks I was operating pretty much on instinct. There is some
> real value in doing it that way. A lot of the time you make a plan beforehand and
> you get to step three and it doesn't work, or you get to some different circum-
> stances that are different in step three. And if you are really dumb, you continue
> with the plan even though it doesn't fit. And so, making up the plan as you go,
> there is some wisdom to that. (Bassis interview)

For the first time in recent memory at Olivet College, a president began
his administration by asking the faculty members for their opinions and empowering them to make decisions about the direction of the college. Michael
Bassis spoke early and often about the need to transition the culture of conversation from one mainly about "wages, hours, and working conditions" to one
where the primary concerns were "What do 'Olivetians' share in common?" and
"Given the range of alternatives open to them, why should a student choose
to attend Olivet College?" (from his inaugural address, September 24, 1994).
Bassis's first step was to ask the college to shape its academic mission by asking
directly, "Is there a common vision we can forge for Olivet?"

Premeditated or not, his actions were quick, decisive, and concrete, symbol-
ically establishing the tenor of his presidency. The charismatic leadership of the
president and his willingness to shift authority and responsibility to the faculty
sparked forward movement. In an astonishingly quick-paced set of maneuvers,
Bassis turned the Olivet community 180 degrees from a culture of nonparticipation in institutional governance by initiating a participative transformation
agenda that empowered the faculty to take full responsibility for their own future. His main strategy was to simply ask them to become engaged in finding a
solution to Olivet's problems.

Initiating Steps for Transformation

The transformation process comprised a series of related and interlinked ad
hoc decisions based on the sense that the people leading the effort (the change
champions) had about the right way to proceed. It was messy, but the first steps

were based on one clear strategy: to engage and include as many of the faculty as possible in the design and implementation of the transformation.

> We tried to keep the door open at all times for anyone to join the process. And perhaps more importantly, we went back and repeatedly asked people to step up and take on a role even if they were continually complaining about one thing or another. (D. Tuski interview)

Conducting another of many "firsts" for Olivet College just two months after his appointment, Michael Bassis convened an all-faculty forum to consider the situation. Reflecting the urgency that most felt, remarkably, the faculty senate suggested that they meet Saturday during the Labor Day holiday weekend of 1993. Reminding the faculty of Olivet's unique history, the new president introduced the first of several metaphors describing the predicament and process. Likening the tangled mess of academic programs to a bowl of spaghetti, Bassis presented two choices: (1) either untangle the given plate in a process that would no doubt mangle many strands, or (2) toss out the whole lot and create a new batch. In favor of the latter, Bassis encouraged the faculty to start from scratch with a new academic vision.

In what became the script for future meetings, Bassis charged the faculty with setting the parameters for operation and unleashing the community to do the work. In this instance, Bassis outlined two parameters beyond setting the charge for a new academic vision for the whole college: (1) the faculty were to elect six peers to form a commission to develop the vision (the Vision Commission); and (2) the vision was to adhere to a set of six principles that he defined. As the commission developed new ideas, they tested them on other faculty members in breakout sessions and departmental meetings across campus. The members returned with feedback, and through an iterative process the work began to gel.

While the Vision Commission acted quickly to complete its work, the faculty senate continued as usual. Believing that the work of the senate should be to focus on the "normal" business of the college, the senate president firmly stipulated it was inappropriate for any senate time to be used as a vehicle in the change process. Welcomed at the time by President Bassis, this decision established that all transformation work would take place outside the confines of the senate.

> We did two things on the senate at that time. We set aside the standing committees of the faculty except for the Rank, Tenure and Promotion, the Performance

Committee, and the Academic Policy Committee . . . because of the amount of work and time constraints on people [working on the transformation]. . . .

The second thing we did is, rather than having proposals come through the Policy Committee and the senate . . . they were brought directly to the faculty . . . essentially setting aside the normal governance process in terms of policy setting and decision-making. . . . And that allowed us to . . . move very quickly. (Homer interview)

By October 6, 1993, the Vision Commission had completed the bulk of its work and published an executive summary. On December 6, 1993, President Bassis convened a second full faculty forum to discuss, debate, and vote on the commission's new vision, which it called *Education for Individual and Social Responsibility* (see Appendix A). The assembly vigorously debated the statement after the formal presentation. Ultimately, the new academic vision was approved by 88 percent of the faculty and referred to the board of trustees.

In a rare occurrence, at its meeting on December 18, 1993, the board of trustees opened its doors to a team of faculty members to present the vision statement. As the day was coming to a close, one lone trustee stood to comment, characterizing the vision as "spectacular," and he began to applaud. Soon, every trustee did the same. The team was "blown away," according to one trustee. Never before had a faculty-driven proposal received such acceptance and praise. At their January 26, 1994, meeting, the Olivet College board of trustees voted unanimously to adopt the new vision.

Putting Teeth in the Vision

At the outset of the spring 1994 academic term, Michael Bassis attended the January 14 faculty senate meeting to present a list of the semester's priorities. At the top of the list was implementing the new vision statement. On January 22, Bassis convened a third faculty forum to outline the work of the Vision Commission, congratulate the faculty on their progress, and issue the following charge:

Okay. This is terrific and great. We've got a new vision, and this is important. But, we need to be able to specify in fairly precise terms what students should be expected to have attained by graduation. In other words, what does the new vision really mean? (McLendon, 1999, X,7)

As with the development of the vision, President Bassis placed full responsibility for constructing learning outcomes squarely on the shoulders of the faculty. Along with the charge came two broad guidelines. First, the learning outcomes must be consistent with the newly adopted vision statement. Second, the learning outcomes must be consistent with the North Central Association's accreditation standards.

Key Vision Commission members took up the new charge by serving as the core of the newly formed Learning Outcomes Group (LOG). They and Bassis encouraged other faculty to participate in the process. One month after its formation, the LOG presented its work at the February 21 whole faculty forum. The product was debated, modified, and approved with a supporting vote of 84 percent of the faculty.

Even with a new vision and a comprehensive set of learning outcomes for each major and department, much work remained. The next step occurred at yet another special faculty forum held in late March 1994, where President Bassis issued another charge to the group:

> You've got a new vision, and you've got some new learning goals for students, but what specific form will the new educational program take? How are you going to deliver this new academic program? You need to go find the answer. (McLendon 1999, X, 10)

Now used to the format, faculty members knew exactly what to expect. Bassis had the faculty self-select into four "working groups" that would search out and identify best-practice models and develop plans for how those models might be employed at Olivet. In another first, Bassis was able to secure funding from the W. K. Kellogg Foundation to support the work of these groups over the summer in the form of a $15,000 planning grant. Selecting four chairs, 24 individuals served in the groups—about half of the full-time faculty. Each team conducted site visits to other institutions (for example, Colorado College and Alverno College) to discover as much as possible about innovative undergraduate education delivery models.

Faculty members were called to participate in a two-day working retreat before the beginning of the semester, over the Labor Day weekend. On Friday, September 2, 1994, each working group presented proposals for transforming the Olivet curriculum and answered questions from the whole faculty. The story of this component of the transformation is further described as a case of resistance in Chapter 5. Suffice it to say here that, by the end of the retreat, the group had developed what some said was a "powerful and comprehensive" vehicle that became the foundation for the Olivet Plan.

Planning Ends, Implementation Begins

With board approval the Olivet community turned its attention to refining the details of the Olivet Plan. Phase one was to design the elements that would fit under the Plan rubric. The second phase involved the integration of these elements into the curricular and co-curricular fabric of the college.

Primary coordination of these two phases fell to James Halseth, the institution's new vice president and dean. Under the dean's leadership, the Olivet Plan was refined by eight temporary volunteer task forces and the college-wide Implementation Planning Group (IPG), comprising the task force conveners, the president of the faculty senate, a trustee, and a student. Each team was to: (1) devise an objective or purpose within the context of the larger Plan; (2) link that objective to the previously developed student learning outcomes; (3) identify course requirements ; (4) suggest class sizes; and (5) identify any academic and administrative support needed to support the objective. With astonishing speed, the Olivet Plan was fully designed and approved by the task forces, the Implementation Planning Group, and the faculty senate by spring 1995.

Dean Halseth was concurrently engaged in a sweeping review of the entire Olivet curriculum. The catalogue listed a number of courses and programs that had rarely, or never, been offered. Some had so few students registered that it was difficult to justify their existence. In the end, 15 majors, 15 minors, and 75 courses were eliminated.

Meanwhile, President Bassis turned his efforts toward larger issues, including raising the funds necessary to support the Plan's refinement and implementation. From 1994 to 1997, Bassis worked hard to mend old relationships and build new ones with a wide array of foundations, garnering grants totaling just over two million dollars for the college.

Cementing the Transformation

Although the Olivet Plan had been polished and approved, the transformation was far from complete. In 1995, the first class entered the college under the new curriculum. Shifting the Offices of Associate Vice President for Academic Affairs and Dean of Community Life to the purview of Dean Halseth, the administration set about installing a new set of student life programs and policies. The college established an African American Culture Center, overhauled the alcohol policy, and tried to rein in the Greek society system (which were all independent, local organizations). Theme houses were established to start the integration of curricular and co-curricular learning on campus.

Although aimed at transforming the campus climate and culture, these initiatives were not enough to shift the Olivet community toward the ideals of the newly espoused vision of *Education for Individual and Social Responsibility*. On April 2, 1997—five years after the racial incident that launched the transformation—using a now standard format, President Bassis convened another all-campus forum. His intent was to formulate a set of principles that clearly defined what was meant by responsible membership in the college community. Over two hundred faculty, staff, and students, along with the administration and four trustees, worked through the day to develop seven guiding principles. These became the "Olivet College Compact" (see http://www.olivet college.edu). The following month, the faculty, staff, and student senates all ratified the Compact. In June 1997 the board of trustees endorsed the document.

A New Status Quo?

Michael Bassis resigned the presidency just as the fourth class was about to enter Olivet College under the Plan and the new Compact. At that time, much of the planning and infrastructure building was complete. In place was a vision emphasizing the college's roots; a set of faculty-designed learning outcomes; a unique and distinctive delivery system that made room for "service learning opportunities" in the form of community service and other pro-bono work with agencies outside the college; and a mechanism to evaluate and account for this service in the form of the portfolio system, which housed a student's deliverables for final evaluation at the conclusion of her or his program. The nature of decision-making on campus had been fundamentally altered, empowering faculty, staff, and students to take responsibility for the direction of the college. The Compact gave all members of the community the leverage to confront inappropriate behavior and guide responsible behavior. Communication and relationships among and between everyone—students, staff, faculty, and administration—were greatly improved. Said one faculty member:

> We all now see each other as a lot more important. . . . We all want everyone to be involved and to feel like a part of the system. There is a stronger sense of trust. I now feel extremely comfortable talking to people because there isn't the fear of repercussions . . . the whole responsibility idea has really changed a lot of people's mindsets. In terms of wanting to do things, it seems like more faculty and more staff are wanting to be involved in what is going on and people are just friendlier. . . . It seems like we are doing something important now instead

of just going to teach our classes and collecting our paychecks. . . . It is so much better, unbelievably better. (Knapp interview)

Enrollment hit a record high of 918 in 1998. Retention was up to 60 percent from around 30 percent five years earlier. Ethnic diversity on campus in all areas of the community had increased. In the fall of 1998, 16.2 percent of Olivet students were African American and 6 percent international. The institution was showing a modest surplus in 1998 as opposed to the almost one million dollar deficit it had in 1993. The first class to graduate under the new Olivet Plan was set for commencement in 1999.

The Olivet transformation continued in the wake of these gains and Bassis's resignation. The board of trustees emphasized the desire to retain a new president who was able, capable, and willing to follow through. Dean Halseth donned the interim president mantle in the fall of 1998. Yet, because of growing acrimony among the community and under the duress of a potential no-confidence vote for the second time in less than ten years, Olivet's trustees negotiated Halseth's departure. In an unprecedented move, the board asked the newly selected president, Federico J. Talley, to begin his tenure early in the wake of the June 1999 resignations of interim president Halseth and his academic dean. The Talley administration lasted for about a year and a half before the trustees asked him to step down because of an inability to raise extramural funds. In the fall of 2000, Donald Tuski—a graduate of the college (class of 1985) and longtime member of the community (first as a student, then serving his entire academic career at Olivet in administrative and faculty roles)—assumed the job of acting president. For many reasons, the board of trustees declined to conduct a national search for the permanent position and Don Tuski was officially appointed as Olivet College's twenty-fifth president in the spring of 2001.

The Portland State University Transformation Narrative

Similar to the transformation at Olivet, the PSU transformation can be broken into three eras. The Planning Era encompasses preplanning and planning periods, 1992–1994). This era began after the hiring of President Judith Ramaley and the promotion of Michael Reardon to the position of provost. The era culminated with the November 1993 faculty senate vote to approve the transformation plan and ended as the first class entered PSU under the new plan in the fall of 1994. The Rollout Era began in 1994 with four-year rollout of each component of the plan, culminating in 1998 with the graduation of the first class with a complete University Studies experience. The era ended with the retirement of Michael Reardon as provost in 1999. The Post-rollout Era began with the hiring of Mary Kay Tetreault as Reardon's replacement.

1992 Campus Climate

The climate on the Portland State University campus in 1992 was much like that in many research institutions across the country. Faculty work in both research and teaching was mainly individual in nature. Departments operated in relative silos and answered to appropriate deans. Budgeting practice placed "every tub on its own bottom," where dollars followed student full-time enrollment equivalents (SFTEs). Disciplinary loyalty ranked higher than departmental collegiality. Faculty rarely discussed pedagogical issues, and conversation barely went beyond cordial hallway banter and department meeting discourse. Outside their own disciplines, Portland State faculty had very little interest in, exposure to, or involvement in national conversations related to issues or research in higher education.

The school's constant fiscal struggle and mediocre reputation within the state fostered cynicism and instability within an already demoralized campus population. A traditional faculty governance structure in the form of a senate worked slowly and methodically, "tending toward the phlegmatic and cautious," according to one faculty member. Except for a few individuals in leadership roles, faculty tended not to become involved in campus-wide issues. When it came to making difficult curricular decisions, often there was a "hulking majority of faculty that either had no opinion, or were just going with the flow" (Crawshaw interview). Only a small number of faculty members were critical observers of the administration.

General Education circa 1992

According to the 1992 PSU catalogue, the purpose of the general education requirement was to "develop a student's breadth of knowledge and appreciation for subjects different in content and method from the one in which the student majors" (see also Dodds, 1996). Students were allowed to self-select the proper number of courses to reach a 63-credit-hour total (180 credits were needed to graduate). The catalogue specified the departments and categories from which students could assemble the appropriate number of credits. Some of these courses also served as an introduction to a student's major. Transfer students were given GE credit for courses approved by their departments. Some saw the curricular requirements as a smorgasbord; one longtime academic adviser lamented:

> It was kind of like a formula for playing a game of chess where it didn't matter where the pieces landed—just as long as you ended up with the right number of credits. Someone could, say, take the introduction to sociology course and one other sociology course, and that would fill at least two of the three courses in that domain. But there really wouldn't necessarily be any kind of coordination between the two. And it would be whatever fit with their schedule. They might not take the 100-level courses until they were juniors. There was really no coherence to it. It was just hit or miss as to what the students were doing. (Wolk interview)

Planning Era Action

Michael Reardon tried numerous times over the years to get additional faculty members to address, or at least consider, his concerns about general education. The response was usually bored indifference. Reardon had repeatedly mentioned his desire to transform the GE curriculum while interviewing for the provost position. He doubts anyone believed him. Even so, President Ramaley was pleased to learn that Reardon wanted to proceed with the reform and gave him permission to do so in 1992. Leaving him to it, Ramaley turned to developing a broader vision for the renaissance of the university as a whole. Together with a small committee of faculty and staff, Ramaley worked to declare a separate identity, comparable in potential, but different in both design and expected interpretation, for what they would call "research, teaching, and service in an urban setting." More specifically, the group felt that Portland State was best described as an "urban grant university," or in the parlance of the Carnegie Foundation, an "Urban One," freshly minting a corresponding motto: *Let knowledge serve the city.*

Provost Reardon leveraged this new mission as a means to push the faculty toward rethinking the PSU undergraduate experience. Firmly believing there was no way to rationalize the distribution system, Reardon often stated that the faculty could develop a GE "program that has coherence and rationality" (Toth interview). First he convened two all-campus faculty forums to suggest the need for transformation, discuss related issues, and solicit volunteers to serve on exploratory committees. At the same time, Reardon asked the faculty senate to address several related questions: "What was the nature of liberal education at PSU? What was their understanding of it? How did they view the faculty responsibility toward undergraduate teaching? And what did they think the meaning of a baccalaureate degree was at PSU?" (Reardon interview). Certain the senate would discover they could not negotiate the answers and would therefore support the special task forces, Reardon reasoned:

> I wanted the planning to not get bogged down in the normal destructive process of faculty governance. I didn't trust the governance process itself to produce a good product. And I didn't want to hear arguments that were based on the autobiographical thought process often used by faculty to make those kinds of decisions. I always insisted that these things had to be discussed as issues based on research and scholarship. And I would do everything that I could to get something to a point of approval outside of the governance process. When it got done, then I was perfectly happy to have it go into the governance process for approval. (Reardon interview)

From these forums, the provost hand-selected several faculty to serve with other faculty volunteers on two exploratory administrative committees. These ad hoc task forces reported directly to Reardon and were not affiliated with the faculty senate. Professor Michael Toth (sociology) agreed to chair the Interdisciplinary Committee. Professor Charles R. (Chuck) White (political science) agreed to chair the General Education Committee. They began their work in the fall of 1992. Beyond the idea that these two committees should develop some kind of plan, there was no active management strategy for transformation. Reardon's approach was intuitive and inventive. According to one champion, "This is not a clean picture of the wonderful strategist coming in with a playbook and introducing it. This was every single day figuring out what to do next in the face of considerable turmoil."

Initially, the GE Working Group (as it later became known) comprised eight faculty members. In the end, total membership expanded to 16. Acting for the first time in an administrative capacity, Chuck White explains, "I used an Amway approach. When people would call with issues, I would say, well, you better come join us" (White interview). As a trained political scientist and member of the faculty, White broke the committee work down as he would any research project. "The first thing that Chuck said was, 'I don't know why we need general education at all.' And the next thing he said was very interesting. He said, 'but let's research it.'" Meeting twice weekly, members recall the conversation as very positive, rich, and all were happy to have White "do the leg work and coalesce ideas into a concrete plan" (Latiolais interview).

As a result of their extensive review of the higher education literature and based on their collective experience, the working group came to believe that there was essentially no support, empirical or otherwise, for the existing distribution system. Simply put, "There seemed to be a certain sense that, at its core, the distribution requirements were bankrupt" (Wollner interview). The committee reported that it saw no established rationale for the structure and requirements: "We finally concluded that we could not state with conviction that the current distribution requirements are meaningful" (PSU, 1993, 1). One committee member expressed the extreme view that "the distribution system was inefficient, it was irrational, it wasted time, it wasted money, but for me the most cogent argument [against the distribution system] was that it was intellectually damaging."

As luck would have it, the 1992 meeting of the Association of American Colleges (later to include "Universities" in its name) was moved to Seattle so as not to conflict with the presidential inauguration in Washington, D.C. Leveraging the proximity to Portland, Reardon provided professional development funds to send all members of both committees to the conference. No committee member had ever been to such a meeting, which was dedicated to national issues in higher education. Keynote speaker Alexander Astin presented his work on success factors for undergraduates. His words resonated deeply with the PSU attendees. In a crucial conceptual turnaround, committee members began to think quite differently about PSU's problems. They stopped asking "Why do we have a poor retention rate?" Instead the question became "How can you produce student success in an environment that doesn't have the features normally associated with success?"

Reardon funded a second professional development opportunity in the form of a retreat dedicated to setting an agenda for the two committees. The Council of Deans (all deans on campus) and all committee members attended the meeting at a facility on the Oregon Coast. There, it became clear that the GE Working Group was moving in the right direction, but the interdisciplinary committee was foundering. Recognizing an overlap in their interests, the two committees were merged.

As the GE Working Group shaped its proposal over the course of the winter and spring of 1993, it solicited feedback from the broader PSU community in three forums open to faculty, staff, and students. "The first two were not particularly well attended at all. The faculty basically stayed away in droves" (White interview). Then the committee initiated a two-day faculty symposium attended by close to four hundred faculty, staff, and students just before the start of the fall term in 1993, following the circulation of an updated proposal. The majority of the time was spent discussing the proposal in a roundtable format. The passing of the proposal (See Appendix B for the proposal highlights) through the senate led to the first substantial case of resistance at PSU. This portion of the narrative is presented in full in Chapter 5. Suffice it to say here that the proposal passed in the faculty senate in November 1993 with a vote of 37 for and 9 against.

The Rollout Era Begins

Once the proposal passed, the GE Working Group was quickly replaced with a new task force headed again by Chuck White. The proposal that passed the senate was a broad statement that mapped a major shift within the curriculum. The new group was charged with immediately designing and putting in place the infrastructure to support the program. To begin, the group gave the new program a name—University Studies (UNST)—for two reasons: (1) to reflect that the whole institution was responsible for general education; and (2) to signify that this was a wholesale replacement for the old distribution system. The program was set to commence with the fall term 1994 first-year phase-in of Freshman Inquiry (FRINQ), less than a year later. A tremendous amount of work needed to occur before the first class of students could take a single UNST course.

A model "inquiry"-style course had been developed in 1990 by a group of science faculty and was taught with the support of an NSF grant (Becker interview). Still, the GE Working Group developed the first UNST course from scratch. With the support of grants from the Pew Charitable Trusts and the W. K. Kellogg Foundation, five faculty members from different departments (English, Physics, Mathematics, Anthropology, and Speech and Communications) labored over the summer of 1994. In a modified summer-long colloquium, they shared disciplinary knowledge and pedagogical practices, and created the first FRINQ course, commonly referred to as "Einstein's Universe."

The course was first offered in the fall of 1994. Each design team member taught one of the five sections serving almost 200 students. What made "Einstein's Universe" different from the usual GE course was that students remained in the same section for the full academic year (three terms in the PSU trimester system) for a total of 15 credit hours. Faculty members were expected to teach subject matter spanning several disciplines. Occasionally throughout the year, team members would guest-teach in each other's courses to address special topics. In the following years, more sections of "Einstein's Universe" were added and other courses developed and taught by other faculty members or adjunct faculty. Those who taught FRINQ courses report working very hard and remember the experience as superlative: "It was the best faculty experience with relation to pedagogy that I have ever had. And I have been teaching in colleges and universities since 1959. Everybody brought stuff to the table. We made consensus decisions about it [the syllabus]" (Reece interview).

As PSU's new general education program, University Studies was "required for incoming students, but volunteer, or optional for the faculty. Although all CLAS departments offered GE courses in the old system, there was never any kind of decision or formal agreement of how much each department owed to UNST" (Patton interview). Departmental and individual faculty cooperation to develop and teach FRINQ courses was difficult to obtain for four widely reported reasons.

1. It takes an enormous amount of time to construct a course, teach it, and coordinate with a team of five professors. Rough estimates are that FRINQ faculty spent about twenty hours per week on a single course; the time commitment was particularly high for those developing and teaching courses outside their own disciplines.

2. The time required pulled faculty members away from teaching required major courses. It also diminished the time available to do high-quality research and publish.

3. Participation in UNST was not rewarded or recognized in the tenure and promotion process.

4. By its nature, the very existence of UNST pulled students out of the introductory courses in academic departments, thereby deflating departmental budgets as dollars typically follow SFTEs in university budget cycles.

Simultaneous Developments

A number of important background developments took place just before and during the first-year rollout of UNST (1994–95). Whereas academically the approved plan was broad but thorough, there was no plan for building a corresponding management infrastructure. Negotiating with Provost Reardon, the newly hired dean of the College of Liberal Arts and Sciences (CLAS), Marvin Kaiser, was granted control of UNST as a condition of his employment. Dean

Kaiser successfully argued that since the CLAS had previously been primarily responsible for delivering the GE program, it should also lead the UNST (Kaiser interview). Significantly, Provost Reardon retained exclusive control of the UNST budget. Doing so effectively disconnected the authority for the new program from those responsible for carrying it out. Both Dean Kaiser and Provost Reardon came to regret this move.

In January 1994, Chuck White was given the title of associate dean, told to report to Dean Kaiser, and given the responsibility to direct the UNST program. (More details are presented in Chapter 5.)As direction of the project required more attention, White began to farm out different UNST elements to other faculty members. For example, the responsibility for Sophomore Inquiry (SINQ) and Junior Cluster (commonly referred to as SINQ/Cluster) program was shifted to Michael Flowers (English). As more courses were added to the FRINQ program, the faculty made sure that they were represented in administrative decisions by creating the "FRINQ Faculty Council" with a representative from each course team. The council then elected a chair as liaison to White. As the Sophomore Inquiry courses were developed, a similar "SINQ Faculty Council" was formed and liaison elected.

Responsibility for developing the Senior Capstone portion of UNST dovetailed with the establishment of the new Center for Academic Excellence (CAE) in January 1995. Devorah Lieberman (Communications), one of the first FRINQ faculty members, was appointed the CAE's first director. With offices located around the corner from each other, the two groups began to develop joint faculty retreats, skill-building workshops, and the community outreach that would constitute part of the Senior Capstone portion of UNST. In the minds of the faculty, the CAE's goal of UNST faculty development inextricably linked the two. In fact, because UNST faculty used the CAE services so frequently to deal with their new challenges, "some faculty thought that the CAE was for UNST faculty alone rather than open to all" (Wetzel interview).

From FRINQ to Capstones

As students progressed through the first year of Freshman Inquiry, a number of faculty members were hard at work creating and defining sets of courses to constitute the Sophomore Inquiry component of UNST. Although the original intent was for SINQ courses to "continue to include small group, mentored sessions to assist students to improve upon the foundation provided by the freshman core" (PSU, 1993, 49), there was a notable disconnect between the freshman and sophomore components. "The real weakness is in the middle and always has been in SINQ/Clusters" (White interview). Unlike FRINQ, which kept a group of students together for a full year in one interdisciplinary course, SINQ courses were shorter three-credit courses, and were linked thematically with Junior Cluster courses. The responsibility for continuity and connectedness fell to the professors. The courses, however, were not altogether different from the regular courses offered by each department. A "U" at the end of the course number in the catalogue indicated that it qualified as a SINQ or Junior Cluster course. A number of departments, such as the History and the Philosophy Departments, so designated virtually all of their courses. According to the director of the program, the SINQ/Cluster sequences were

> more like piles than they were clusters because we had to put clusters together very rapidly, and because there were neither the resources nor the will I think, and certainly not the time, which we would have needed to build courses from the ground up. That would have been like, good god, conceiving a third of the curriculum all over again. It meant gathering together previously offered courses that sort of fit together in piles . . . like gathering together courses from Poly Science, and some from elsewhere, and ultimately linking them together by some thematic link that we saw among them. And ultimately, from the get-go, these kinds of courses sort of served other needs. They were double-duty courses mainly serving the majors. (Flowers interview)

Many of the faculty who detested FRINQ found the SINQ/Cluster courses more acceptable because they were similar or identical to what they were used to teaching. But much to the surprise of the administration, a group of very vocal faculty dissenters built their own high-quality SINQ/Cluster set.

During the 1995–96, the first year of the Sophomore Inquiry program, UNST received a grant from the Corporation for National Service to pilot, or test, five Senior Capstone projects. The money was given directly to the CAE because the office already had people working on community partnerships. It ran the program until 2000, at which time authority shifted to the UNST director.

In practice, Capstone projects are led by senior faculty and involve interdisciplinary teams of students working within the local community in a year-long service capacity. Ironically, some UNST planners felt that the Senior Capstone would be a disaster. As it turned out, the program was and is the most widely accepted and uncontested portion of University Studies. The fact that faculty teaching Capstone courses receive $4,000 for supplies and expenses may feed the positive perception. And response from the community agencies has been uniformly enthusiastic. The first full-blown Senior Capstone program was offered during the 1997–98 academic year, with 25 options.

More Simultaneous Developments

Throughout this transformation, no new UNST course was approved through the usual faculty procedure. Because UNST "was experimental, a lot of things were done quite ad hoc, gestational, and last-minute. Therefore, it didn't really fit with the traditional review process, which was as long, cumbersome, and bureaucratic as one would expect" (Gelmon interview). In 1996 the University Curriculum Committee (UCC) began institutionalizing UNST courses by customizing an approval process. Initially, the courses were approved as they were designed. Now the UNST office works with faculty members to generate new courses and then submits outlines to the UCC for review on a regular schedule.

Assessment of UNST was and continued to be a challenge. Because the program was novel, traditional assessment methods were not wholly applicable. Some attempts to evaluate the program were stopped midstream due to complications and confusion. Most formal evaluations were conducted as a subset of grant reporting requirements. Faculty became frustrated with the disjunction between all the national attention and recognition the program was receiving and the perceived lack of objective assessment. This prompted the faculty senate to order an evaluation of the University Studies program in February of 1998. Ironically, for those hoping for a scathing review, the results submitted to the full senate in June of 1998 were rather benign.

The integration of University Studies into the fabric of the institution was not yet complete when Judith Ramaley resigned in 1997 to assume the presidency of the University of Vermont. Daniel Bernstine, then the dean of the University of Wisconsin law school, took the helm at PSU. Looking forward to retirement, Provost Reardon agreed to stay in his position for only two more years to provide continuity for the new president. Bernstine immediately commissioned a blue-ribbon faculty committee to conduct a climate assessment of the entire institution. Among other things, the commission strongly recommended that the institution "needed a Vice-Provost for undergraduate education, and that UNST needed to report to that person" (Miller-Jones interview). It was thought that doing so would stimulate faculty participation in UNST because it would no longer be perceived as just another unit within one of the colleges.

In the final year of Michael Reardon's tenure as provost, the budget responsibilities for UNST were shifted to Marvin Kaiser, effectively consolidating the program under the CLAS. In August 1999, Mary Kay Tetreault, then the vice president for academic affairs at California State University at Fullerton, was hired as provost. The lingering question was where to permanently house UNST. Provost Tetreault first created the position of vice provost for curriculum and undergraduate studies and conducted a national search to fill it; next she removed UNST from CLAS and gave it a home under the new vice provost. Although Chuck White applied for the new post, the position went to Terrel (Terry) Rhodes, from outside the PSU community. Because personnel decisions are private, it is not possible to know exactly why Tetreault did not hire White. After being denied the promotion, White predictably resigned his position as director of UNST. Chuck White's story as the primary champion of the UNST effort constitutes a case of resistance and is therefore further elaborated in Chapter 5.

Before we move to the specific cases of resistance, it is important for the reader to have a broad understanding of the nature of resistance, which is the topic of Chapter 4. This understanding will provide insight into the six cases presented in Chapter 5.

4 The Nature of Resistance

With the preceding chapters in mind, readers should be ready to delve into the resistance phenomenon in greater detail. The analysis presented here provides a platform for discussing the key elements of resistance and engagement behaviors that emerged in the transformations of Olivet College and Portland State University. (An overview of the method that undergirds the research for this work is provided in the section in the Preface entitled "Methodological Foundation.")

The purpose of this chapter is to paint an empirical picture that illuminates the nature of resistance to organizational change. A deeper understanding of resistance goes beyond intuitive or gut reactions to specific behaviors. From the analysis of the data collected for this study I have identified nine reasons why people resist change efforts and ten forms of resistance. Before describing these and further elaborating the nature of resistance, it is important to deliver on the promised robust definition of resistance.

As mentioned at the close of Chapter 2, researchers may have collectively turned a theoretical corner in thinking about resistance. The research and analysis I present here is consistent with this paradigmatic shift. I hope that my findings will contribute to cementing the validity of this shift and help to classify resistance behaviors among the full array of natural responses to change efforts.

Reconceptualizing the Resistance Metaphor

Before the turn into this century, scholars often suggested that resistance was analogous to two fundamental principles of physics (Burke, 2008). Specifically, (1) every action has an equal and opposite reaction; and (2) a body set in motion will remain in motion until acted on by another force, shifting in accordance to the vector of that force (Azároff, 1996). As in physics, it was suggested that the motion of transformation (the action) naturally produces a reaction. Using properties of physics to explain resistance was less a red herring than it was a metaphorical crutch to support thinking about resistance in general. Lewin (1947) pushed us well beyond the simple physics metaphor with his force-field model, which numerous scholars have advanced to explain change. Specifically, there are forces that work to advance change efforts and those that work against change; together they can produce a kind of organizational inertia. The job of the champion, according to Lewin's model, is to overcome this inertia by weakening the restrictive forces and strengthening the enabling ones.

Defining resistance using the reaction-to-change imagery contributed to our understanding of resistance at the close of the twentieth century. But perhaps this imagery has "taken us as far as we can go" (Piderit, 2000, 792). Even more damaging, the analogy may have misled us to believe that all change is resisted and to the wrong conclusion that resistance is inherently negative or at least a detractor to any change effort (Burke, 2008; Piderit, 2000).

A small number of scholars are now advocating that we replace the basic physics allegory with a more organic, perhaps even biological view. That is, it may be better to think of resistance as a natural, fundamental, and useful part of the change process (Burke, 2008; Burke, Lake, and Paine, 2009; Piderit, 2000). At least one organizational development (OD) professional suggests that organization change is akin to a virus or bacterium attacking the body as the necessary blood cells swarm and remove the threat (Jennifer Selby Long, personal communication, October 2009). In this case, resistance behavior operates much like white blood cells attacking the germ.

Perhaps there is an organizational equivalent. Viruses and bacteria, which like change efforts are unequal in potency and inherent value to a system, require different levels of responses. Some bacteria and viruses are good. Some are bad. More specifically, when change—of whatever variety—is introduced, the resisters—white blood cells—swarm and assess the change. If it is deemed good and healthy, the change is left alone, adopted, or adapted to improve the whole system. If the assessment leads to the opposite conclusion, resisters attack and try to kill it, all the while steeling themselves for the next infection/change.

You can see how this analogy may lead to the introduction of any number of medical-based diagnostic tools into the scholarly lexicon of organizational behavior. All manner of organizational dysfunction may be diagnosable as this or that illness. But let's not get sidetracked by discussing what might be the proper dose of change to effectively inoculate organizations against resistance. Remember that change in this illustration is the "infection," (though it is not always bad). Correspondingly, and contrary to earlier thought, resistance may be viewed as a necessary and healthy part of a corporation, something to be fostered and strengthened in the name of building a healthy organization. Taking this analogy just a bit further, it may be reasonable to suggest that change and resistance behaviors work in symbiosis to strengthen the whole organizational corpus. Before we get to far down that road, let us examine some facts.

The strength of this book is in offering empirical findings that describe reality. What we know is that the act of transforming or changing an organization threatens the status quo. People naturally react deeply and viscerally to change because it means "giving up certainty for ambiguity, security for risk, stability for instability, and predictability for opportunity" (Cameron and Ulrich, 1986, 17; see also Chaffee and Jacobson, 1997; Duderstadt, 2000; March and Simon, 1958). Simply put, whenever one initiates a change processes, resistance of some kind should be expected (Backer and Porterfield, 1998; Burke, Lake and Paine, 2009; Cameron and Ulrich, 1986; Cheldelin, 2000; Farmer, 1990; Hermon-Taylor, 1985; Hultman, 1998; Likert, 1961).

Building an Organizational Definition of Resistance

Although the dictionary offers a practical definition of the term resistance—"to strive or work against; oppose actively"—resistance can be enigmatic. In the eyes of the change champion, an individual's actions may appear to be "resistance." But the perpetrator of the resistance may see his actions differently. Indeed, truth is a slave to perception, not vice versa. The danger inherent in organizational change agency is that perception is sometimes substituted for reality; people act on beliefs that they perceive to be true. Taking action based on either a false negative or a false positive can have dire consequences.

According to the old physics metaphor, resistance can be thought of as the opposite reaction, as an opposing force, or as a force that shifts the direction of a particular change initiative (Lewin, 1947). Lewin's force-field model is extremely helpful in conceptualizing how to get past the inertia inherent in any organization. In line with the conceptualization suggested by Piderit (2000), Burke (2008), and others, and in harmony with the new metaphor roughed out above, resistance may be more aptly thought of as a subset of a constellation of individual or group behaviors that emerge as a natural response to the organic introduction of change, which can be plotted on a continuum, from completely benign to entirely hostile. We must be cautious to not view resistance as inherently negative because, on occasion, resistance can prevent change agents from making serious mistakes (Hultman, 1998; Judson, 1966). As perpetrated by individuals, resistance within organizations reflects their unwillingness or unreceptiveness to change, and is manifest as either active opposition to, or at the other end of the continuum, an attempt to escape or avoid a transformation effort (Hultman, 1998). Increasing the magnitude of the transformation can incite stronger resistance (Bain, 1998; Hermon-Taylor, 1985; Syer and Connolly, 1996).

Reasons for Resistance

The very reasons that people organize also fundamentally thwart change efforts. People do not typically join organizations to be continuously tossed into change-driven chaos and turbulence. Individuals tend to join organizations for consistency, role congruence, and the comfort of belonging to a group that sustains their self-image, sense of worth, and goals, not the least of which is sustaining the organization itself. Consistency, routine, and a predictable agenda of activities and responsibilities are what people seek. Organizational change, by its very nature, threatens a person's comfort zone, and simply talking about change may spur resistance. This is because most, though not all, resistance stems from fear (Judson, 1966). As transformation efforts threaten the values, beliefs, behaviors, and jobs of the individuals within an organization, their fear motivates them to protect and defend themselves; the greater the fear (and often the larger the scope of the change effort), the larger the resistance.

At Olivet College and Portland State, the people involved in the change efforts—either instigating or responding to them—may at times have been ambivalent about them, but they were never apathetic. Invariably, interviewees who self-identified as resisters in my study had a strong desire to explain the rationale behind their actions. Likewise, change champions were able to identify why they felt the resisters acted to try and stop the transformations. While there are almost as many reasons for resistance as there are people, we should not mistake an inability to change for resistance (Hultman, 1998). There is a sincere qualitative difference between not wanting to change and not having the skills or technology to do so. For example, a car manufacturer may decide not to switch from building machines that run mainly on fossil fuels to building only electric- or hydrogen-burning automobiles, although the technologies exist to make the switch possible. But only in science fiction can an airplane manufacturer decide to transport people with particle beams instead of airplanes.

To advance the theory and explain why people may be inclined to resist change efforts, my analysis of the data I collected at Olivet and PSU revealed nine sources of resistance. There may be more. For example, I found some evidence that racism was a source of resistance. Racism, while interesting to report, was not strongly represented in the cases nor did the evidence of racism triangulate from other data sources. For scholars, the following nine robust reasons why people may resist change could serve as the foundation for a survey protocol leading to a broader understanding across industries. For practitioners, they offer a broader explanation for why people respond in certain ways to organizational change efforts.

1. Inherited Culture

Both the Olivet and PSU transformations were initiated by new presidents hired by their respective boards. Such practice is common in business as well. When boards recognize a need for sweeping change, the first step is often to replace the CEO in hopes that the dominoes fall accordingly. As in for-profit industries, even though a new president can bring in new upper-level administrators, the faculty and staff (or rank-and-file employees) largely remain the same. The previous longstanding administrations at Olivet and Portland State had established a particular climate and culture. Because faculty do not usually leave when a new president takes over, they continue to operate according to the customs and traditions with which they are familiar.

As a new administration brings a different leadership style, expectations, and vision, one source of resistance is the established culture of the prior administration. For example, the faculty members at Olivet College were not accustomed to an enabling leadership style. This was a byproduct of the "devil's bargain" struck long ago between the faculty and the administration: they paid little attention to the college's governance in exchange for autonomy within their own departments. Moreover, poor treatment of some faculty members by the prior administration and the tenure of the interim president had left a large number of people justifiably traumatized. The result was an inherent culture of mistrust. Said former president Michael Bassis, "It was like people were hiding behind rocks and trees and people were very wary of sticking their head up" (Bassis interview).

2. Reluctance to Take on New Work

When it comes to fostering change, there is commonly a subtraction, not an addition problem. That is, new initiatives are heaped on top of old without any regard for removing antiquated responsibilities or proper realignment of reward and remuneration policies (Lewin, 1947b). Simply put, people are expected to continue doing what they have always been doing while also tackling new priorities. Rarely is organizational capacity generated by the temporary subtraction or outright elimination of longstanding practices. A common view is that change "is like fixing a plane while flying it" or "building a bridge while crossing it."

It is, therefore, no surprise that the largest reported cause of resistance was faculty reluctance to take on the amount of new work either implied or imposed by the new initiatives. They took this stance even before the transformations were set in motion, in deciding not to join voluntary planning committees. Already carrying full academic loads, faculty members understandably hesitated. They began to see how much additional work these new programs might entail as the programs materialized through the development and approval process. If, during the planning effort, there had been a complementary effort to subtract responsibilities, capitulation and embracement of the initiatives might have occurred more swiftly (Lewin, 1947b). Unfortunately, the subtraction of responsibilities is typically left out of the change equation. Likewise, one of the biggest mistakes a change champion can make is keeping old reward and remuneration structures in place while expecting new or changed behavior (Pfeffer and Slancik, 2003; Burke, 2008).

At both schools, resisters' concern about more work was not altogether unfounded. Faculty members working in the University Studies program at PSU report that teaching one Freshman Inquiry course (FRINQ) required a minimum investment of about 20 hours per week. This is substantially more work than a typical course—particularly if one had been teaching, say, Anatomy and Physiology for 10 years. Complicating the situation was the fact that the corresponding promotion and tenure requirements were not altered to fit the new paradigm. Many faculty members stated outright that they would not teach in the Freshman Inquiry program because, (a) "it takes me away from my research agenda," (b) "it is a lot more work," and (c) "there is no recognition for it." When a person's responsibilities change, but the rubrics for measuring quality performance (or for awarding bonuses) do not, you have another reason for resistance.

3. Status Quo Protection

The argument against more work is one component of the larger umbrella source of resistance, status quo protection. "Not only did faculty members not want to have to do more, they didn't want to have to think about new ways of doing things" (Dole interview). Simply put, asking people to do more work or to work differently pushes them to resist. Status quo protection involves preserving two fundamental aspects of organizational life: working in the way one was trained, and being able to demonstrate expertise (Cameron and Quinn, 2006). The sense that one has of being good at or excelling at one's job keeps people working with the method they know.

The proposed transformations of the curriculums at Olivet and PSU are excellent examples of shaking up the status quo. Before the transformations, the main pedagogical practice for delivery of course content was the lecture, commonly referred to as the "teaching paradigm." At both institutions, the transformations asked faculty to depart from their usual practice by using discussion and other formats in the classroom—referred to as a "learning paradigm." Asking faculty to shift from a teaching to a learning paradigm made some traditional faculty members uncomfortable. One PSU faculty member summed up the argument:

> There are several things. One is that it takes an enormous amount of their time. And the other is that it is not what they are trained to do. We are all trained in a certain discipline, and we know how instruction in that discipline goes. When you step out into something way more general, we don't have any guideposts, we make it up as we go. And, that is hard work, and it is likely to be unsatisfying because you really can't be confident that you are doing it right, and it is not in your field, so you are not doing the intellectual work that you set out to do, when you became say a physicist, or a mathematician. (Moor interview)

4. The Implication That the Current System Is Broken

As transformation is instigated, the subtext is that the current system is broken. The message inferred by those who developed or who support the status quo is that they may have gotten it wrong. The suggestion that transformation is necessary may not only imply that the old ways of working are flawed, but also cause people to feel like inherently bad components of any "new status quo." One PSU example shows how emotionally attached people can become to the status quo. Early on in the development of the new curriculum, one faculty witness reported:

> I was walking up the stairs behind one of the people who was an opponent from the Geology Department. And somebody made sort of a mild crack that, "Well,

I guess that [the vote to approve the University Studies plan] was a successful effort" And this guy turned around, practically on the verge of tears, and he said, "Yeah, it has pretty much trashed 20 years of teaching in the distribution system," as if the distribution format were some sort of sacred artifact of the curriculum.

5. Culture Clash

While culture is the glue that holds an organization together (Kuh and Whitt, 1988), organizational transformation shreds the very fabric of the institution by snipping the cultural fibers of tradition. Contemplating change without considering the cultural implications of that change almost certainly condemns an effort to failure (Cameron and Quinn, 2006).

Beyond the threats to academic freedom and the "frightening feelings" of loss of control and autonomy, the nature of the transformations at Olivet and PSU struck at the heart of the traditional academy by mandating fundamental shifts in the undergraduate curriculum, which is usually the purview of the faculty. Interestingly, the most intense forms of resistance in both institutions came from faculty in the hard sciences. Their refusal to participate or to change stems from how these faculty members were acculturated into their disciplines, which attracted them to these disciplines in the first place. The nature of the transformations, which were inherently more humanities based, was, according to one faculty member, "anathema to the scientific method because it questions the notion of objectivity and broader philosophical issues." To suggest that these faculty members conduct their courses under a new pedagogy was like asking the faculty to "eat my mother's liver":

> They will just chew on it and chew on it and never swallow it. I was trained, and I am a clone of my graduate professors. I was lectured at all those years. We didn't do any of the interactive group crap. We sat in class and took notes, the old Carnegie thing. And so I like lecturing. And here we were [with the Olivet Plan], taking out all that made us comfortable and why we bought into the system and it looked like we were taking it up and turning it on end. But [the resisters said] why should we worry about pedagogy? We already had a perfectly good one. Why should I be worried about learning when my business is to teach? I don't know how to do group processes stuff. Nobody in my education did that for me, so why should I? So, there were all these kinds of things that constituted change. I think that the set of activities that a professor had gotten used to and had gotten them into the business from the time that they were an undergradu-

ate looked as though it were changing. And they just said, "I can't accept this. This is an old dog having to learning new tricks, and the paradigm has shifted" And they just resisted. (Homer interview)

6. Fear

Another root cause of resistance is fear. At Olivet, threat of job loss, uncertainty, and confusion were all sources of fear. For example, Olivet faculty saw administrators deal with resisters by encouraging their departure or pushing them out and hiring replacements from outside.

Uncertainty and confusion about new initiatives, new teaching methods, and new processes also generate fear. Often faculty members genuinely did not understand how a proposed program would work. Moreover, because the plans were fleshed out in the open, they tended to change regularly. Those affected did not always have enough information to see the bigger picture:

> The process of change creates uncertainty, muddiness, cloudiness, confusion, and that is very discomforting to people. And that causes resistance. You are reestablishing standards, the canon, the curriculum, and how you interact with students and . . . with each other. And so, while you are trying to be more inclusive and democratic, at the same time you are being a little bit more confusing and uncertain with what you are doing. And that just drove some people crazy. (D. Tuski interview)

7. Legitimate Concern

Some resistance is generated by legitimate concerns about a process or a product. Crafting change initiatives is never easy. Problems with change designs and plans, and mistakes made by the champions themselves, can cause grave and genuine concern among employees. Moreover, employees may reach their own well-considered conclusions that the plans, as proposed, simply will not work.

One legitimate concern about the change initiatives at both schools was that there would not be enough money in the budget to cover the costs. Resisters at both institutions would crunch the numbers, even bringing calculators to planning meetings to demonstrate that there was not enough money to support such labor-intensive, expensive initiatives. Some of their arguments were based on worry that their departments would lose funding. In addition, the act of consolidating the money for the new programs presented a unique situation.

Whereas before the proposed transformation no one had bothered to calculate how much was spent for general education, post-transformation it became painfully obvious how expensive the new GE was (e.g., $2.4 million for UNST at PSU). Both schools were already in difficult financial straits.

8. Hypocritical or Unfair Champion Behavior

Resistance occurs when champion behavior is construed, accurately or not, as hypocritical or simply unfair. Such perceptions are based on actions that are or could be interpreted as unequal treatment or simply "not walking the walk." In other words, when champion behavior is not in synch with the espoused values of the transformation initiatives or collegial decorum, trust erodes. Trustworthiness is an important part of the change equation. Asking others to change and not changing yourself will likely be construed as hypocrisy.

The perception of hypocritical leadership is sometimes the result of honest mistakes perpetrated by the leadership and interpreted differently by followers. At other times, the perception may be valid, the result of blacklists or coercion in response to resistance. The burden is on the champion to behave appropriately and ethically. Even the most minuscule action can be used as fodder for resistance. When people feel that any portion of a process is inequitable they tend to "fight back a lot harder" (D. Tuski interview).

A good example of this at PSU was the use of deal making. Because some departments were rewarded for participating in the new program, there was an uneven distribution of soft money, which caused some faculty to perceive that the champions were playing favorites. Even seemingly benign behavior from one perspective can be construed as hypocrisy and thereby justification for resistance. After Michael Bassis left Olivet College and James Halseth took over as interim president, Don Tuski reported:

> They wanted me to go to the senate meeting and tell certain people to get off the senate. They wanted me to say that one person [a resister] or another should be fired or not tenured. They told me that I "needed to get more adversarial with the faculty," and you can quote me on that! We were meeting one day in the blue room [presidential conference room], and while we were sitting in the blue room, Jim Halseth was smoking (and you can't smoke in the building!) and telling me . . . that I have to move over to the Mott building, that I have to be more adversarial with the faculty. *And here he was sitting in the blue room smoking?* (D. Tuski interview; emphasis reflects astonishment on the part of the interviewee)

9. Damaged Relationships and Personality Clashes

Because organizations are composed of people, all transformations must take into account personal values, beliefs, and personalities (Cameron and Quinn, 2006; Cawsey and Deszca, 2007). Simply because people are members of the same organization does not imply that they will be collegial or that they will even be tolerant of one another. To be sure, members of a community are interdependent, but our capitalistic culture promotes an individualistic approach to work. With differing languages and modes of practice, siloed departmental structures reinforce differences between disciplines and the natural propensity for people to associate with others who share their interests and values (Bergquist, 1992).

The nature of intergroup relationships was, for example, soured by such things as the "top-down, administration-driven" flavor of the initiatives at PSU that caused some on that campus to resist. At a more micro-behavioral level, damaged relationships and subsequent personality clashes also spurred resistance. Some resisted because they did not support hiring a particular person. Simply suggesting the need for transformation can ruin relationships with people who stubbornly oppose change of any kind. Some people resisted change simply because they did not like particular champions: "There were certain personalities, that whatever they suggested, no matter what it was, there were [other] people that were not going to like it" (Rowe interview).

In the latter stages of the plan development and implementation at both campuses, the separation between those planning and those resisting was exacerbated by a perception that those who championed change felt themselves to be superior. An "enclave culture" emerged amidst a sense by resisters that those doing the planning were "untouchable" or were "circling the wagons." Such a perception by those not doing the planning can sour relationships and raise tensions between the players. Resisters may resist simply because they feel excluded.

Resistance in Practice

Now armed with nine reasons why people may resist change efforts, our task is to describe resistance as it occurs in practice. Piderit (2000) points out that many of the studies around resistance examine behavior, emotions, or beliefs. I chose to look more deeply at behavior, in particular three different aspects of resistance behavior—intensity, source, and focus, as identified by Hultman(1998). Intensity, source, and focus are theoretical axes on which champions assess and interpret the actions of others responding to change. My research reveals that people's subjective assessment of intensity, source, and focus is the foundation on which they make sense of what is happening and then act.

Comprehending the nature of resistance amidst the complexity of ongoing organizational change is somewhat less challenging from the reverse angle—that is, by looking at the level of complexity, from less to more. In particular, it is not terribly difficult to identify the focuses or targets of resistance. It is more challenging to decipher the intensity, and even more demanding to identify the sources or causes of resistance. As the ensuing discussion drills down from the less to the more complex elements of resistance, it is important to keep in mind that these variables are inseparable. They are connected and embedded within the larger, messier context of the organizational transformations themselves.

Although the design of this study emphasizes the champion's perspective, the perspective of resisters is equally valid, and future researchers may wish to examine change from their point of view.

Focus of Resister Behavior

The least complex variable is champions' assessment of the **focus** of resister behavior. Although Hultman (1998) points us to three focuses of resistance behavior (the self, other people in the organization, and the organization itself), my research supports only the second of these: the people. In addition to the people—the champions leading the transformation—resisters are focused on the process and the products. The process refers to how the plans and implementations are designed and carried out. The products are outcomes resulting from initiating and carrying out the plans.

The Process   From the Olivet and PSU cases, we see resistance behavior focused on each target at various times, and sometimes on all three simultaneously. Many resisters believe that they are being excluded from planning and implementation processes. Although both Olivet and Portland State champions intentionally conducted the planning phases outside the rubric of standard faculty governance procedures in the faculty senates, interviews and documents indicate that both institutions tried hard to be inclusive. All planning committees were run and staffed by faculty members. Even vocal resisters were approached, invited to participate, and placed on key committees.

"Regular" faculty members may not have been inclined to volunteer because it is hard to know that a change initiative will be transformational before it is full-blown. At PSU, some saw the first plans as just more in a long string of changes that required attending boring administrative meetings. One PSU resister points out the lack of inclusion of a biology course in University Studies as a fault of the process, but freely admits that both he and his department colleagues did not participate in any of the planning after attending the initial open forums.

Ironically, the one group with a legitimate complaint, Olivet College staff members, did little to resist. At both Olivet and PSU, staff members were intentionally left out of the planning processes because the schools' initiatives were originally seen as strictly academic concerns. It was only when the idea was introduced in one component of the Olivet Plan that "*everyone is an educator*" that staff members became genuinely concerned about the transformation. Even so, staff members at both institutions expressed little resistance.

The Products   About midway through the planning phases, the initiatives became tangible and quite visible as the champions at both institutions held forums to share proposals and solicit feedback from all campus stakeholders. For a wide variety of reasons (nine of which I described above), from this point forward, the proposed products were under attack. At times, people complained about the poor quality of the products simply because they felt left out of the design process. Others argued that the programs lacked rigor and watered down the curriculum. In the main, three arguments against the products were used to resist the initiatives. First, the most heavily contested issue was the question of affordability. Resisters at both institutions argued unceasingly at a wide array of meetings that the initiatives were too costly, not possible to staff given the available faculty, and on several occasions were armed with calculators and spread sheets to prove their point. Second, resisters also argued that the Olivet Plan and University Studies were pedagogically misguided at best, and at worst, failed the majors and could not possibly deliver what they were promising academically. Finally, resisters claimed, rightly, that no data supported the notion that the old system was broken. Before the transformations, little to no evaluation or assessment of the existing general education programs was conducted at either institution.

The People   The champions of transformation are naturally the most visible of its proponents, essentially in the direct line of fire. At both institutions, there was a point at which some resisters began to associate the people leading the initiatives with all of the problems they were facing. Some champions earned that focus by behaving unethically or hypocritically. Champions became the objects of extreme scrutiny; they were insulted in meetings, yelled at, maligned behind their backs, discredited to outside agencies, said to be fools, vilified, occasionally seen as evil or operating with spurious motives, and, at PSU, denied promotions. Such attacks can reach a level of intensity that turns the situation from honest professional critique to personal criticism. This leads naturally to a discussion of the second resistance variable: intensity.

Intensity of Resistance

The intensity of resistance behavior can be thought of as a subjective assessment of the gravity of resister behavior along a scale from latent, awaiting a trigger, to extreme. The nature of postsecondary institutions ensures that resistance of some intensity will confront any transformation effort. As discussed in the opening chapter of this book, resistance should be considered a natural part of the change process, but it is not always evident, depending on the scale and scope of the changes offered. More than one champion stipulated that if you are not experiencing some form of resistance, you are not transforming. Essentially, there is nothing to resist until the change is initiated. When people become aware of change as something that will affect them, they react. Territorial, resisters operate according to the classic NIMBY (not in my back yard) scenario:

> As long as transformation and change affects everything except me, it is a great idea. But the minute that we [champions] dig into those elements or areas— however you want to describe them—where people live, for which people have ownership, their job or their office, then all of a sudden, transformation is a bad idea. (Rutledge interview)

My research shows that resistance intensity, if it could be measured, would be a register of the vector and power of the opposing force, ranging from one end of a scale as dormant, to passive, to active, to aggressive, and finally, at the other end, as intense and personal. Before the start of a transformation, one could be tricked into thinking that resistance is nonexistent. In reality, it is latent, awaiting the start of some planning process. Once a proposal exists, resistance moves from dormant to passive and shows up "in a willingness to talk about problems, but a lack of willingness to 'do' [anything] about problems" (Rutledge interview). Intensity at the passive level could be considered minimal resistance, such as "doing what normal faculty do: sitting around a cup of coffee and complaining" (Reardon interview), or simply ignoring or not participating in the process. People are "ambivalent or lethargic about the whole thing, which is a certain kind of slow, non-action resistance" (Wertheimer interview).

Passive resistance can also be internal to the planning process. At times, resisters are encouraged to join planning teams and may express their opinions during meetings. Wise champions listen to these concerns and use the feedback to augment and create a more effective plan for transformation.

Once plans become more concrete, resistance intensity escalates because there is now something to directly target, rather than a vaguely defined product leveraged through an intangible plan. At this time, a sense of good will may still permeate the process. There is an honest desire to hear out the proposals, even if some demand evidence that they will work. People begin to espouse their opinions and argue more vociferously in meetings: "The people who are most honest about it and candid will tell you right to your face. They will stand up in a meeting, or they will tell you in a hall, 'I don't agree with this, I don't think this is workable'" (Rowe interview). Operating under the rubric of academic freedom, active resistance at both institutions "was very vigorous in faculty meetings. And you had to have a lot of respect for people who spoke up like that because they debated some of those issues in the face of a large number of people who were favoring" the initiatives (Hubble interview).

As concerned faculty members began to meet in groups to discuss strategy both on and off campus just before and during the rollout phases, resistance became aggressive. Beyond badmouthing the program and the people, "it started to get nasty" (Knapp interview).

> It didn't get intense until the president changed and then the provost changed a year later . . . and that was when it got really serious. Because these guys [resisters] felt that now they had an opportunity to really open the door on this and to have some conversation. But unfortunately, that conversation didn't happen the way that they felt it should. And it got snuffed very quickly. And that made them louder, and that is when the debate got into the *Chronicle of Higher Education.* (Latiolais interview)

As resisters saw their efforts ignored or have little effect, benevolent concern gave way to negative opinions, genuine conviction, hard feelings, and real anger. Any strategy to resist became fair game. Faculty members started to involve students by raising their concerns in the classroom. They contacted the media, spoke to accreditation teams, and began to attack individuals outright.

To some champions, as the intensity escalated, resistance began to look more like sabotage. Strong disagreements among colleagues escalated into personal animosity. Rational discourse slipped into the realm of emotive thrusting and parrying. According to one PSU faculty member who was present during these meetings:

> The intensity of it was extreme and almost unrestrained, to the point that the normal level of civility and decorum that ought to attain in any kind of discussion of ideas, no matter how antagonistic one's particular viewpoint might happen to be with the paradigm that was given, was completely dismissed. I mean, I have seen, and I am not exaggerating, I have seen shouting matches on both sides . . . vilification being slung back and forth across tables. The level of it was indeed very extreme.

Only a small number of individuals engaged in resistance at the highest levels of intensity. The time and emotional energy necessary to sustain such aggressiveness is beyond the capacity of most people. But for those who had the capacity, the strength of their convictions occasionally pushed them over the edge. Relationships became emotionally charged; trust was violated; communication broke down. In some cases, hatred and animosity led individuals on all sides to unbecoming and unethical conduct. People begin to take the whole transformation very personally and "essentially decided to resist with all their might" (Wollner interview). "It was sort of like, 'if you push me, then I am going to push back harder.' And what started out more as a questioning of things, got uglier and uglier over time, in a sort of snowball effect" (Knapp interview). According to Olivet's interim president:

> You know, he [faculty member resister] was giving it out and I was giving it right back. You are not going to push me. I don't like to be that way, but I am not going to put up with that. If you are going to hit me with a brick, I am going to hit you with a bigger brick. (D. Tuski interview)

At the extreme level of intensity, the interchange of resistance and engagement behaviors is so charged that individual resisters may resign or be forced out. Although there was intense resistance at both Olivet and PSU, only at Olivet did people actually leave the college. Problematically, at this level of intensity, emotionally charged perception often is substituted for truth or fact. Again, the views of Tuski:

> When it comes to feelings, it is not a matter of right or wrong. But just because I am able to share my feelings, does not mean that I am right. It is what I feel. People get it wrong when they are honest with their feelings and then they

think that they are right about the whole situation. They might be partially right, and they usually are, but they are not completely right. Unless I as a president can absorb and process what the person is saying, [I'll get myself] in trouble, and that is when resistance really gets built up. (D. Tuski interview)

The Ebb and Flow of Intensity   As noted earlier, when the size of the force (or the area targeted for change) increases, the force of the opposition will increase to match the forward movement. This was largely the case at Olivet College, where the ultimate expression of resistance culminated with the resisters' sabotaging the North Central Association (NCA) accreditation review and coincided with the rollout of the Plan. In contrast, at PSU the intensity of resistance was dynamic and at times did not match the champions' behavior. In fact, resistance intensity can be purposely elevated to exceed the level of action taken by change champions in an attempt to overcome a transformation initiative. Such interplay between resister and champion behavior is similar to one's body sometimes over- or under-reacting to a virus. In the PSU and Olivet cases, we can witness the ebb and flow of resistance intensity.

Except during the early attempt at PSU to pilot the University Studies transformation in 1993, resistance subsided, percolating beneath the surface for the bulk of the rollout duration. By 1998, the initiation efforts were long over, and the University Studies (UNST) program had been woven into the fabric of the university. But resistance was still strong, and it culminated with a faculty effort to survey students and other faculty in the 2000–01 academic year about their views of University Studies. By then, however, the transformation was largely complete, a new set of leaders for University Studies was in place and heading the institution, and according to the catalogue UNST was the university's only general education requirement. Perhaps the outcome would have been different if the same intensity of resistance had been played out earlier or at the outset of the transformation.

To be fair, the intensity of champion behavior can also exceed the force necessary to surmount resistance. In the latter phases of the Olivet transformation, a number of resisters indicate that they felt the aggressiveness of the administration was out of line. Rumors of a "blacklist" circulated. But whether one really existed was of no concern to the resisters because it was only the perception that mattered. When resisters were asked about the tactics used by champions at Olivet, they replied that it was simply not possible to match the level of intensity of the change champions because the actions of the administration were "unethical, immoral, and illegal" (Schroth interview). True or not, the belief that there was a blacklist may have been one reason why so many faculty and staff ultimately left Olivet, in contrast to PSU, where no one resigned. The perception may not have been altogether off base, according to the current Olivet president, who was a key champion of the transformation:

> It got to a point when he [Jim Halseth] was interim president, that he wanted to do some stuff to some of the resisters that I didn't think was ethical. And he wanted to use me in some ways that I felt was unethical. After Michael [Bassis] left … there was a threat of a pseudo no-confidence vote on Jim [Halseth] and the administration. But in the aftermath, there were five or six sort of resisters and Jim wanted to go after them. [I had just become] associate vice president, and to me the gang war was over. So I started to reach out to some of these people, and that is when I got blacklisted. Because I said enough was enough. Now, I was treated pretty poorly, and Louise [Tuski] was treated pretty poorly by some of these same people. But I wasn't going to keep this cycle of academic political violence going. And there really was some trench, hand-to-hand combat going on to get a lot of this stuff passed, but I know politics at Olivet … and I sincerely reached over to some of them [faculty members] who were saying no earlier on, or were part of the resistance. It didn't make any sense to keep beating on them, or to fire them. And they [the administration] were going down that road. And they were telling the board that they really needed to do this to keep this thing [the Olivet Plan] going. And you didn't need to do that, you didn't need to slash and burn, and that was what they [the administration] were trying to do. And I said no and there was some confidential stuff that I won't tell you, but I said no to two or three things, and that is when I got onto the blacklist. … And so we came to blows and we have not talked since … but my allegiance has always been to the College. I don't care if you are a board member, president, staff member, student, or faculty member. If I feel that you are doing something that I believe in my heart and gut and mind [will] hurt the College, it's no holds barred. (D. Tuski interview)

Sources of Resistance

Finally, we turn to the more complex variable that forms the final axis for understanding how people interpret the resistance behavior they are experiencing. This section draws on Hultman's (1998) work, in which he provides a set of criteria for understanding the sources of resistance. These criteria helped me construct the questions that constituted my interview protocol (see Appendix C).

Sources of resistance emerge from discrepancies between reality and facts, descriptive beliefs, evaluative beliefs, and values. People can use **facts** to counter a transformation effort by carefully disputing the champions, skillfully presenting opposing facts, or neglecting to relay all the facts. **Descriptive beliefs** involve perceptions about organizational realities; they are not facts, but subjective interpretations that define for someone what is true or false. Whether a person's beliefs are true depends on what is regarded as evidence. Descriptive beliefs become the basis for resistance when they lead to any of three fallacies (deductive, inductive, cause-effect). A deductive fallacy occurs when someone bases a belief on the assumption that an original premise is true but turns out to be false; or when someone uses an accurate premise to make an incorrect deduction. An inductive fallacy occurs when a general premise is incorrectly taken to be true based on a series of descriptive beliefs. Again, the original beliefs or the induction could be false. Last, the cause-effect fallacy occurs when a person mistakenly concludes that one true belief causes another. All three fallacies can lead a person to jump to conclusions that activate resistance behaviors.

Whereas descriptive beliefs assign meaning to experience, **evaluative beliefs** assign judgment of value (good versus bad) to them. Resistance arises when a person believes that a proposed change or transformation is flawed and assigns value to facts or descriptive beliefs. These beliefs are often stated in conjunction with one another, as in, "The vice president always protects the chemistry department and gives us the short end of stick on budget issues." The assumption that the vice president favors one department over another is a descriptive belief. The assumption that the chemistry department is always favored is an evaluative statement. While it is difficult for individuals to assess which beliefs are true, these beliefs form the basis for resistance to what they view as unfair treatment.

Predictive beliefs are interpretations about what is going to happen based on fact, descriptive beliefs, or some combination thereof. That is, a person makes a prediction about the future state based on his knowledge or beliefs, or lack of knowledge or awareness, about the past and the present. Asking "what if we . . . ?" or "what if we don't . . . ?" can lead individuals to predictive fallacies based on faulty descriptive beliefs or misconstrued notions about conditions in the future. These can lead to assumptions that a particular initiative will fail or that current practice will not continue to succeed in the future, thereby prompting resistance.

Values are also beliefs, but center on what people view as important in life more than on what is happening in the organization. They influence people's

Individuals resist when they believe that:

1. Their needs are being met already (descriptive belief).

2. The change will make it harder for them to meet their needs (predictive belief).

3. The risks outweigh the benefits (predictive belief).

4. Change is unnecessary to avoid or escape a harmful situation (predictive belief).

5. The change process was handled improperly (evaluative belief).

6. The change will fail (predictive belief).

7. The change is inconsistent with their values (fact/descriptive belief).

8. Those responsible for the change cannot be trusted (descriptive belief).

Exhibit 4. Common causes of resistance. From Hultman, K. (1998). *Making change irresistible: Overcoming resistance to change in your organization*, pp. 143–46. Palo Alto, Calif.: Davies-Black.

criteria for making decisions and play a gate-keeping function for motivation. A person may resist transformation because an initiative goes against her values. Moreover, initiatives that threaten cherished values will likely yield more resistance than those that go against less important values (as defined by the individual).

Hultman's eight common causes of resistance, are based on his 20-plus years of consulting experience (see Exhibit 4). These, in combination with the nine reasons identified through my data analysis above, provide a comprehensive picture of "why" people resist change. A change champion must be careful to identify both cause and symptom, as one without the other may lead to an improper diagnosis and thereby an ineffective strategy for engaging and surmounting the resistance.

Forms of Resistance

Because of the confounding vagaries of how individuals may self-identify (i.e., from "antagonist" to "protector of the institution"), my study was not designed to explicate the complete psychosocial origins of resistance. The above discussion should be sufficient to help people comprehend the primary reasons why people might resist change. The study did focus on the very palpable manifestations of resistance encountered by change champions. In other words, what does resistance to transformation look like as the champion encounters it? Specifically, I set out to identify what individual or collective actions as experienced by change champions might augment, shift, or altogether stop the action of a transformation.

The literature suggests a large array of behaviors that we can expect when walking through a change or transformation. At the individual level, resistance may emerge as anger, defensiveness, emotional outbursts, and psychological withdrawal. Psychosocial enactments such as fear of the unknown, lack of trust, language barriers, and threats to a person's positional power amplify the fear of pain that is a basis for resistance. Pain and fear are dangerous byproducts of transformation in that they can lead to personnel loss, stress, conflict, and revenge or sabotage (see Exhibit 5).

As people are presented with transformation initiatives, they may begin searching for less painful solutions, or they may undertake strategic initiatives of their own (Quinn, 1996; Rhodes, 2000). Vitriolic attacks against change agents are attempts by those who built the present to protect the status quo (Duderstadt, 2000; Hamel and Prahalad, 1994). Threats to the status quo, as well as orders to transform, can be ignored, rejected, and reinterpreted, all of which are easy resistance mechanisms to hide from a champion's plain view as individuals seek to maintain both individual and organizational identity (Backer

Variable	Form of Resistance
Demonstrated behavior	Vitriolic attacks and emotional outbursts
	Defensiveness and attempts to preserve the status quo
	Ignoring or avoiding initiatives and directives
	Psychological withdrawal
	Searching for less painful solutions
	Undertaking separate strategic initiatives
	Disengagement or retreat to the classroom or laboratory
	Using language and jargon to reinforce separation
	Disagreement, including rejecting or vetoing initiatives
	Discounting the legitimacy of others
	Power grabs
	Stirring conflict
	Revenge or sabotage
	Political game playing
	Noninvolvement and avoidance
	Participation in rallies or protests

Exhibit 5. Possible forms of resistance (from the literature on organizational change). Sources: Chaffee and Jacobson, 1997; Green and Hayward, 1997; Heydinger, 1997; Overton and Burkhardt, 1999; Nadler, 1998; Pfeffer, 1994; Judson, 1966; Trice and Beyer, 1993; Quinn, 1996; Likert, 1961; Backer and Porterfield, 1998; March and Simon, 1958; Pfeffer, 1994; Syer and Connolly, 1996; Ryan and Oestreich, 1991.

and Porterfield, 1998; Bergquist, 1992; Brown and Starkey, 2000; Hearn, 1996; Reponen, 1999). Retreat to the classroom, the laboratory, or the office can be seen as avoidance and disengagement from the process (Rowley, et al., 1997; Ryan and Oestreich, 1991; Syer and Connolly, 1996). The use of technical language and jargon can reinforce separation and be used to maintain barriers between departments (Overton and Burkhardt, 1999).

Divisiveness between faculty and staff (or managers and employees) on some campuses prevents the building of genuine partnerships; faculty members have been known to discount practical know-how, viewing staff as inherently less important than faculty and strategic planning as less important than research (Adams, 1973; Senge, 2000). Some may stir up conflict, inflate arguments, and attempt to persuade members of the organization to subvert change initiatives by asserting power (Eckel, 2000; Greiner and Schein, 1988; Kriegel and Brandt, 1996; March and Simon, 1958; Mets; 1997; Pfeffer, 1994; Pfeffer and Salancik, 1978). From a political perspective, as individuals coalesce on the different sides of an issue, each faction works to accumulate and exercise power to tip the advantage in their favor (Nadler, 1998; Pfeffer, 1994). Some opponents of change may even seek out leadership roles as a way of increasing

An individual resister may:

- Flood you with detail or unnecessary explanation
- Request more detail
- Express confusion
- Delay or cancel meetings
- Remain silent
- Offer easy and unexpected compliance
- Say "nothing is wrong" or "everything is fine"
- Press quickly for solutions
- Intellectualize the issue
- Attack, undermine, or sabotage
- Express anger
- Withhold information, data, or documentation

Exhibit 6. Individual manifestations of resistance. Source: Scott, B. (2000). *Consulting on the inside: An internal consultant's guide to living and working inside organizations*, p. 69. Alexandria, Va.: American Society for Training and Development.

Resistance behavior	Description
R1. Attacking champions	Any movement by individuals or groups to defame, detract from, or undermine the individuals leading a transformation.
R2. Building a case against	Using research, statistics or other evidence to prove the effort has either failed or will fail.
R3. Criticizing in the media	Using internal or external media (e.g., television, newspapers) to generate opposition to or publicize arguments against the transformation.
R4. Using students (customers) as pawns	Representing student (customer) viewpoints or exposing students (customers) to counterarguments to leverage them as pawns.
R5. Leaving a post or the institution	Removing oneself from the process by resigning from a particular post or leaving the institution entirely.
R6. Not participating	Refusing to or opting not to participate in any aspect of the planning for, implementation of, or established elements of the transformation initiative.
R7. Offering contrary alternatives	Making proposals or suggestions, or offering solutions or alternatives, not in line with the proposed transformation objectives.
R8. Sabotage	Working behind the scenes in what may be interpreted as unfair, unethical, or illegitimate ways to stop the progress of transformation.
R9. Voicing disagreement	Expressing disagreement in formal or informal meetings with individuals or groups.
R10. Voting in opposition	Voting against initiatives or a transformation action during any formal or informal voting opportunity.

Exhibit 7. Forms of resistance demonstrated at Olivet and PSU.

their power and influence over an initiative (Bergquist, 1992; Koteen, 1989; Pfeffer, 1994; Rowley, et al., 1997; Zoller and Fairhurst, 2007). Some additional resistance behaviors are listed in Exhibit 6).

While it was important to broadly identify all possible significant forms of resistance to establish a baseline for study, those not seen in both institutions do not figure into the subsequent discussion. More specifically, the data from my study triangulate to support the reporting of only 10 forms of resistance (see Exhibit 7), which are explicated more fully in the cases discussed in Chapter 5.

We are now armed with a thorough understanding of why people may resist change, how it is directed, how to decipher the intensity of resistance, and 10 empirically derived forms of resistance. In Chapter 5 we turn to six illustrations of resistance in the context of real transformation.

5 Six Cases of Resistance

There were numerous instances of resistance during the transformations at both Olivet College and Portland State University. Likewise, the change champions at both institutions used a wide variety of strategic tactics and tools to engage and surmount the resistance they encountered.

While the focus of this book is on resistance to change as experienced by those who championed the efforts, I also interviewed several of the key resisters. In the main, the resisters' perspectives support the results. However, there are times when, juxtaposed with the viewpoints of the champions, resisters' experiences show up as confounding or outlying, or even provide conflicting evidence.

The six cases offered in this chapter dig deep into the Olivet College and Portland State University transformation sagas. Although robust, the cases are not the full story. Because the data collected for this work encompass a ten-year span of transformation efforts, the findings go well beyond those clearly identifiable in the cases. The primary purpose of this chapter is to demonstrate how resisters and champions interact. In order to provide a full appreciation for the natural interplay—the organic symbiosis—among and between resisters and champions as they are spurred by organizational change—I describe how ordinary people operating on each side of these efforts engaged one another.

The six vignettes presented here illustrate the circumstances surrounding resistance and engagement action. At the conclusion of each one, I identify the forms of resistance and engagement supported by the data. A full exposition of my findings on engagement behavior is presented in Chapter 6.

Resistance at Olivet College

The Olivet College transformation can be divided into three eras. Era one encompasses the planning and approval process (1993 to 1995), which began at the outset of the Bassis administration. Infrastructure building (e.g., the Compact) and implementation occurred simultaneously (1995–1997) during era two, which began when the first set of students matriculated at the college under the Olivet Plan. Era three was the subsequent two-year period, during which the Olivet Plan was modified on the fly with the primary focus on implementation (1997–1999). Era three concluded as the first graduating class under the Olivet Plan marched at commencement. Even though the transformation continued past era three, under three subsequent presidents, this study covers only these three eras.

Olivet Case 1: The Block Plan

Our first example of resistance occurred in 1994, during the development of the Olivet Plan and culminating at the Labor Day weekend retreat/working meeting convened by President Bassis for all faculty members. On this occasion, resisting faculty members were able to assert their position and stop the integration of a block system—an academic calendar based on students taking one course at a time—that would have required the retooling of every course in the college's curriculum to fit within a three-and-a-half-week cycle.

Earlier that year, in March, President Bassis had challenged the faculty at an all-faculty forum to figure out how to deliver on the promise of the recently designed learning outcomes. Unlike with prior initiatives, the president imposed a structure and specified a timeline because summer was swiftly approaching. The faculty self-selected into four prescribed "working groups" that would search out and identify best-practice models, conduct site visits, and construct proposals for implementing the models at Olivet. As in the past, the group consisted primarily of volunteers; additional members were appointed, encouraged to participate, or asked to take leadership roles. In this instance, two faculty members identified by the administration as resisters were specifically encouraged to participate. Capitulating, one mathematics instructor and the chair of the English Department joined the working group researching the Block Plan at Colorado College as "resident skeptics."

Supported by the $15,000 dollar W. K. Kellogg Foundation planning grant, the working groups toiled separately over the summer, developing independent proposals to restructure Olivet's undergraduate education curriculum and delivery systems. By August 1994, the working groups had completed extensive research and site visits and were writing their proposals. Over the summer, both the Block Plan working group "convener," Louise Tuski, and President Bassis came to believe that a model based on Colorado College's one-course-at-a-time system was the solution Olivet required. Believing so strongly that the Block Plan, coined the "Engaged Curriculum," could deliver transformation to the college, Bassis said to the faculty at one point, "If I could give you one gift, it would be this one-course-at-a-time option" (Bassis interview). In her quest to prove that the proposal could be a solution, Louise Tuski absorbed a fair number of direct and indirect attacks from those who opposed the Engaged Curriculum.

The main argument against the Engaged Curriculum stemmed from the belief that subjects such as mathematics and foreign languages would suffer in such a structure. For example, if a student takes French 101 in the first three-and-a-half-week term, and then does not take another French course for several months, the French 101 learning may effectively need to be replicated. The two skeptics, who were also part of a small number of faculty members likening themselves to the *Star Wars* Rebel Alliance, felt "a little bit of coercion to go along and make a positive report of the things we saw in Colorado, even though we didn't think that it would work here" (Scott interview). The math instructor felt so strongly that the Engaged Curriculum would not work that he split from the working group and partnered with one of the science faculty members to develop an alternative proposal.

For the first time in recent memory, faculty members were called to participate in a two-day working retreat before the beginning of the fall semester. On Friday, September 2, 1994, the working groups presented their proposals and answered questions in front of the whole faculty. An external consultant facilitated the process. After all the proposals were delivered and questions answered, each participant was given a set of gold stars and asked to place one star next to each point in the proposals that they supported. Following a brief frenzy, the jovial atmosphere subsided as it became apparent that no clear majority supported one proposal or another. Votes of the 40 faculty members present were dispersed unevenly across the proposals, receiving 13, 12, 11, and 4 votes respectively. The Engaged Curriculum received the most votes. One administrator recalled:

> The [atmosphere in the] room was really heavy. We had come to the end of this long process, and we were so close, but there was no solution—we couldn't

agree on what to do. People were tired, frustrated, and hungry, and we were wondering how we would get out of this logjam. And, we only had one day left. (McLendon, 1999, Y, 13)

President Bassis adjourned the meeting at about 4:00 p.m., encouraging participants to enjoy the cookout that followed at his home. A cloud hung over the festivities as faculty lamented the situation, dreading the work facing them the following day. One faculty member recalled that even the children at the picnic recognized that something was amiss. He said, "People were milling around the yard and everyone was sullen-faced. It was just a depressing atmosphere" (McLendon, 1999, Z, 1). In a fateful move toward the end of the picnic, President Bassis wrangled the leaders of each working group, several other faculty members, and the newly hired vice president [Halseth] into the study of the president's house. One surprised participant recalls:

He called us into his study, locked the doors, and said, "No one's getting out. Nobody is going home until this thing is done. We have come too far for this to fall apart. We are going to stay here until we reach some agreement." Then, we settled into a huge argument for the next three hours. (McLendon, 1999, Z, 1)

The members of each working group had seriously invested themselves in hammering out what they believed to be winning proposals and answers to Olivet College's problems, and now "the different groups were at each other's throats" (Rabineau interview). Bassis's strategy was to encourage discussion, but essentially to listen. He did just that for about two hours.

From the perspective of some of the participants in the smoke-filled room of the president's house, the Engaged Curriculum was the lynchpin of the whole transformation. But moving to the one-course-at-a-time system would have been a massive curricular and scheduling undertaking. The author of an alternative proposal presented earlier in the day, a stalwart resister, was also present at the evening meeting. He had been collared earlier at the picnic by other faculty members who implored him to help them stop the block plan. To do so, he was advised to unite with another proposal leader against the Engaged Curriculum.

Conversation in the evening meeting was deadlocked. Arguments pertained mainly to pedagogical differences about how to effectively present course sequences and the need for students to be exposed to certain subjects over an extended period of time in order to synthesize the material. While the block plan might work well for those in the arts, hard science faculty members found it beyond comprehension how to conduct, say, a lab course in a similar fashion. It seemed to detractors that those who supported the Engaged Curriculum were in favor of it because it would work well for them. The corresponding perception was that they were not listening to some of the people who were saying, "Hey, this is not going to work for me" (Schroth interview). Moreover, there was more than one department that anticipated difficulties adjusting to a block plan. Eventually, enough people were of the mind that the Engaged Curriculum was such a radical departure from the status quo that it would be difficult to implement.

The turning point occurred around 8:00 p.m., as the Engaged Curriculum Working Group convener, Louise Tuski, left to put her children to bed. When she walked out of the room, those who opposed the Engaged Curriculum moved to take a vote. Returning to find the plan defeated, Tuski was furious, feeling that the decision had been made behind her back. After substantial argument that abandoning the plan was necessary, she conceded.

Demonstrating what the resisters classified as genuine leadership, "Bassis backed down from something he really wanted because it just wasn't going to meet with the full approval from the full faculty" (Bolman interview). Perhaps President Bassis could have forced the proposal, but he felt that it would have been politically unwise to do so. In fact, letting the Engaged Curriculum go may have saved the whole transformation. According to the vice president:

> It seemed to me that one of the ways to get the result we wanted was for Michael and me to . . . lose one. It wasn't that we contrived to lose something, but it was that we really did lose something—that in order to effect a compromise, in order to really come out of that retreat with a plan, the block plan really had to go. And my sense of it . . . is that the defeat was really a kind of a victory. (Halseth interview)

Once the group got past the block plan issue that evening, they began discussing a delivery system for everything that they were trying to do at the college. Decisively, President Bassis, who had said very little during the debate, got up and started circling elements of each of the plans that had received the most support by faculty earlier that day. In effect he was pulling ideas from all the proposals into something that he felt could both work and that everyone could stand behind. At the end of the meeting Bassis said, "It looks like we agree on these things, essentially setting up the guideposts for the plan" (Homer interview). The moniker "Olivet Plan" was suggested by someone at this meeting as a way to identify the set of objectives for the transformation.

Out of the Engaged Curriculum came a compromise in the form of an Intensive Learning Term (ILT). Without specifying the logistical details, the next day Bassis described the evening's events to the whole faculty. He concluded by calling the Olivet Plan a "powerful and comprehensive" vehicle for transforming the work of Olivet College in five innovative elements:

1. A "first-year experience," which would provide students with a rigorous introduction to the college and its distinctive vision of individual and social responsibility.

2. A "portfolio program," which would require students to take responsibility for their education by developing an individual portfolio of educational self-assessment.

3. A "service learning" component whereby students would develop an ethic of social responsibility through service to the community.

4. A "senior experience," which would help students integrate what they had learned throughout their education.

5. A "learning communities" component, which would allow students to take thematically linked courses. (McLendon, 1999, Z, 2)

Although the Engaged Curriculum had been stopped in its tracks, these amalgamated elements would also necessitate an overhaul of the curriculum, as well as a corresponding redesign of the general education core to bring it in line with the new vision. After presenting the broader concepts, Bassis stressed to the faculty that the retreat was not the time to debate the details. They had not yet been worked out. Still, he pushed them to decide whether they were supportive of the overall concepts. Astonishingly, 90 percent of the faculty supported the proposal. The remainder of the day was dedicated to fleshing it out. At their October 1994 meeting, the trustees unanimously endorsed the Olivet Plan.

Olivet Case 1: Findings

Three forms of resistance and five approaches to engaging resistance are apparent in this case. The first approach to engagement was proactive. Specifically, from the outset, President Bassis worked to involve others in the planning, in part to identify potential resisters in hopes of bringing them on board. Also, it seemed to him that if the initiatives were planned by large numbers of faculty members, other members might be more likely to accept rather than resist the proposals.

A second approach was to coerce support for some of the initiatives during the planning process. Resisters perceived this intention, whether the champions intended them to or not. Given that the pending proposals were contrary to their pedagogical beliefs, some resisted by presenting an alternative proposal at the Labor Day meeting. When it became obvious that there was no clear majority supporting one plan over the other, several resisters at the picnic appealed to two faculty members in the president's ad hoc meeting to at least stop the Engaged Curriculum from going forward.

Bassis's third and fourth approaches were to lock people in his study (another example of coercion) and listen to all sides, and then settle for nothing less than a consensus about what to do. The resisters expressed their strong objections to the block plan during that meeting. Seizing an opportunity to defeat the Engaged Curriculum when its key proponent left the room, the resisters called for a vote and won. In retrospect, Bassis realized that unintentionally losing the fight on the Engaged Curriculum allowed him ultimately to win the approval of the whole package.

Olivet Case 2: Burying Alternative Program Proposals in Committee

Olivet College had a broad but thin curriculum when Michael Bassis assumed the presidency in 1993. It appeared as though the college "wanted to be all things to all people" (D. Tuski interview). There was a sociology and anthropology major, as well as a biological anthropology major, for example. The college had added an average of 1.2 majors every two years for close to 20 years. Even so, many programs listed in the course catalogue were dormant. In addition to developing curricular and co-curricular components, a necessary part of the transformation strategy was to streamline and integrate the existing curriculum into the Olivet Plan. To achieve this, the president charged his academic dean with consolidating and eliminating some degree programs. One thought was to combine the anthropology and sociology majors. A young anthropologist named Donald Tuski accepted the challenge and took the lead. Looking for support, he asked the only other anthropologist on campus to work with him. The other faculty member indignantly declined, saying "If you want to go do that, you do it yourself" (D. Tuski interview).

Going it alone, the lone anthropologist worked to build a combined program proposal despite the rebuff. Because the proposal was not directly linked to the Olivet Plan, it had to travel through the standing process for introducing new programs under the purview of the faculty senate. Oversight and initial review of such programs was the responsibility of the faculty senate Policy Committee. The chair of the Policy Committee, Mary Schroth, was also the chair of the Mathematics Department. She also considered herself to be a part of the dissenting "rebel alliance" and happened to be a good friend of the opposing anthropologist. Whether the opposing anthropologist encouraged Schroth to block the proposal is not known. But the proposing anthropologist sensed, based on the actions taken, or more concretely not taken, by the chair that his submitted proposal was buried "at the bottom of the pile behind some other mundane proposals that were little micro-changes of policy or courses in the departments" (D. Tuski interview).

Because there were no set rules or guidelines beyond common sense and courtesy, the chair of the Policy Committee was free to raise or not raise proposals for review. Customarily, proposals were dealt with in the order in which they were made. In this case, Tuski felt that "some people were doing some very dishonest things in terms of procedures" because his proposal was not handled in a timely fashion. Frustrated, the anthropologist sought the support of a senior faculty member who was president of the senate, and together they "called her [the chair] on it" (D. Tuski interview). The anthropologist went so far as to threaten to file a formal grievance, forcing the proposal to be reviewed by the full committee late in the spring semester.

The chair's perspective was somewhat different. Interestingly, her answers to probing follow-up questions reflected only committee actions rather than her own behavior and focused on why the proposal was rejected, not on the delay. In no uncertain terms, she stated that the committee never buried any consolidation proposal. From her perspective, the committee simply rejected the consolidated major and asked for revisions because the program proposed a major that required significantly fewer credits than any other major on campus. In addition, the low credit total comprised several of the courses offered in the general education curriculum. "Well, we didn't agree with that. And we turned it down and asked for revisions" (Schroth interview).

Later in the semester, the anthropologist brought a revised proposal back to the committee on the same day as the last senate meeting of the academic year, hoping that it could be passed and presented on the faculty floor for a vote. Schroth said, "We turned it down again," citing low credit totals. At that time, however, nothing in the college's governance procedures prevented faculty members from going directly to the faculty floor with a proposal. Because waiting until after the summer for another shot at committee approval would set the initiative back a full year, the anthropologist, with support from some of the faculty, presented his proposal at the faculty meeting himself. This was essentially an end run around the committee. Ultimately, the faculty senate approved the proposal on the condition that credits be added to constitute a major. The proposal would then go back through the Policy Committee for approval without having to be presented again on the floor.

Olivet Case 2: Findings

This case illustrates how individuals can both resist and champion change. One form of resistance and one approach to engagement are apparent. Again, perception was a proxy for the truth in this case. Because the two sides interpreted events so differently, it is difficult to be certain of the facts. From the champion's perspective, the resister could have been working to sabotage the initiative. Also from the champion's perspective, beyond persistence, the resister's main mechanism for surmounting the resistance was to build a coalition in support of his initiative.

Olivet Case 3: Sabotaged Accreditation Review

One strategy used to leverage the Olivet Plan through the faculty was to conduct separate, full-faculty votes on each piece as it was finalized. Periodically straw votes were used to give the administration an idea of who needed convincing and how successful they might be in the official vote. Four faculty members regularly contested each piece of the Plan. Depending on the proposal, an additional one, two, three, or four others would also dissent. Not surprisingly, there were usually eight or so votes against each proposed element. Even though some votes were conducted using secret ballots, the administration was often able to deduce who the opponents were based on who was most vocal as the proposals were debated:

> They were outspoken at meetings, but more often, they were outspoken about it behind closed doors. At every turn, the same three or four people would speak up at overt and covert meetings and just basically rip the Olivet Plan to shreds or just get nasty . . . saying "this is a ridiculous idea. This is terrible and we shouldn't be doing this." (Homer interview)

Publicly, resisters argued that the Olivet Plan was fiscally irresponsible. Given the dire financial situation at the college, many wondered how it would pay for all the new courses. Another concern was that the existing curriculum was not altogether broken and would be unnecessarily altered in favor of an unproven program. At times, such arguments were made during completely unrelated segments of meetings. One resister was a young math professor who wore red sneakers like a trademark. Because he was initially supportive of some parts of the plan, some informants felt the more senior dissenting faculty (including his department chair, who was also the chair of the senate Policy Committee) used him as a pawn:

> They exploited him because he was good with students. He would really do some Olivet Plan–like kinds of things with his students, doing things outside of class, having a math team, and integrating curriculum. But ... they really used him as the point person to resist the change. (D. Tuski interview)

The math professor admits that he was the most vocal resister. Eventually, his view of the entire college soured as he and his four allies came to hate everything about the Plan. According to one witness:

> It was like his whole vision became colored and he became absolutely obsessive ... because he wasn't being tactful, people tended to react to him more aggressively. It was sort of the, "if you push me, then I am going to push back harder" [approach]. And what started out more as a questioning of things got uglier and uglier over time. As he got more resistant, he got more aggressive in terms of asking and answering questions. The more pushback, the more adamant he got about it. ... Some other people got pulled into that kind of thing. There were several faculty members that became the core resistance to all of it. It became personal for them. (Knapp interview)

Despite the vitriolic protestations of a minority, most decisions were made via consensus, and at no point did the majority dip below about 80 percent in favor of each segment of the Plan. Recognizing that their critiques, debates, and votes were having no effect, the group of dissenters took another approach. A pending visit by an accreditation team gave the rebel alliance an opportunity to voice their concerns externally. According to the red-shoed math professor, "There was a certain amount of hope among the dissenting faculty that an outside accrediting agency [the North Central Association] might call some attention to what was going on in a way that we could not from within" (Bolman interview).

In the fall of 1995, the NCA review team arrived on campus minus their chair, who was ill, with the intention to conduct a thorough review with "a heavy emphasis on personal contact with members of the campus community." The three reviewers held an open meeting for the faculty on the first day of their visit, attended a faculty senate meeting, and held "a final open meeting for faculty, staff, and students who wanted to drop by with issues on their mind" (NCA, 1995, 3, 4). Fearing the worst before the NCA visit, one mid-level administrator stressed to some identified resisters

[that they should] not air our dirty laundry, that we needed to be working together in our accreditation, and that you really don't care about the college itself if you are using NCA visitors as a tool to try to get back at the college or to try to get your agenda heard. It hurts everyone at the college. It hurts our students, it hurts our chances of getting finances. . . . I remember talking with the faculty about needing to find the right place to air the dirty laundry and that they needed to be respectful to the institution and not air any dirty laundry when we have visitors here. (Rabineau interview)

Despite that sentiment, the dissenters proceeded to denounce the Olivet Plan at all review team meetings they attended. The four faculty members argued intensely that the Plan was not working, that it was not a good idea to begin with, and most important, that there was not enough money to hire sufficient faculty to execute the Plan. The math professor went so far as to suggest that there "were some problems with the administration . . . that Bassis had added four administrative positions in the four years and had cut four full-time faculty positions" (Bolman interview). A number of the opposition leaders had actually pulled together documents that identified the polarized views of life on campus between the faculty and the administration. Another dissenter admits to sharing dirty laundry simply because "there was a lot of dirty laundry!" (Scott interview).

The Math Department was using that opportunity to beat up on the administrators at the college and a lot of what we were doing with the Olivet Plan. Basically they were saying that we were not going to be able to afford this, this is just smoke and mirrors. . . . And they used it every way that they could. No matter what the discussion was about, they turned it toward the negative side. . . . It was the manner and the venue and the tone that turned it . . . from being just constructive criticism . . . to "we're not going to go along with this whole thing and we are going to kick holes in the boat if we can." (Wertheimer interview)

One Plan supporter reports that a trusted faculty member who was supposed to take one of the NCA members back to the airport passed off the responsibility to the chair of the Math Department, an avid resister. Others also believe that the math chair bent the ear of the committee member during the 45-minute drive to the Lansing airport, perhaps even influencing the outcome of the review. When asked directly, the Math Department chair said, "No. It wasn't me, and I don't know who did it."

Regardless whom you believe about the return airport trip, there is no doubt that the review team heard the voices of dissent. It was manifest in their final report and recommendations. The college was reaccredited, but on the condition that the accreditation team return for a focused visit in 1997. The following points from the NCA report undoubtedly reflect the arguments delivered by the resisters:

1. The team was clearly able to verify the accurate statement of the Olivet Plan, and note the definite improvement in the educational program that the changes indicate. What the team could not verify, however, was evidence of the results of this new academic plan. . . . there is no way to ascertain the impact of this proposed educational program.

2. The college has an unacceptably high rate of attrition. . . . However, the Olivet Plan and Vision will not attract students to the campus program until there is evidence that it delivers what it says.

3. The plan makes provisions for training faculty members to prepare and evaluate portfolios. However, it is not clear that the college can actually afford the sorts of staffing commitments this requires. Nor is it clear that the support of the faculty will be broad enough to ensure that a sufficient number of faculty members will be willing to participate.

4. The faculty has approved the new General Education program. . . . However, the general education program is not yet fully designed. Several courses still need to be developed.

5. The resources aren't available to provide the kinds of remedial help required by the nature of its current student body. . . . It is not clear that the college will be able to recruit a student body that matches the requirements of the new program.

6. The faculty is working at a level that it cannot reasonably be expected to continue without undermining the quality of the education provided by the college. Existing programs are understaffed, and the faculty is spread over a number of different majors.

7. Faculty morale is a concern and the faculty feels that it is overworked. . . . There are perceptions of inequities in salary workloads. Much of this seems to reflect a lack of faculty access to information and the lack of well-developed structures for faculty involvement in planning, decision-making and budgeting.

8. Given the fragility of the college's financial position and the lack of well-developed decision making and planning procedures, it will be a challenge to effectively organize and allocate resources to support the Plan.

9. The College assumes that the Olivet Plan will increase enrollment and retention and thereby additional revenue. Untested in the market, it will be some time before the college can count on the validity of that assumption. (NCA, 1995)

Apparently, the "confidential" NCA faculty meetings were not altogether confidential. The math professor suspected one or two specific individuals, but there is no denying that information about what happened at those meetings was leaked to the president and the dean. Upon learning about the work of the math professor and his cohort, the dean was livid. A faculty member characterized both the president and dean as "beyond rage." A number of the transformation leaders felt that the action of the four resisters was tantamount to sabotage. They believed that the resisters had every opportunity to participate in the process yet chose not to, preferring to wait until the NCA meeting to air the college's dirty laundry. The administration collectively felt the resisters' action reflected a blatant disregard for the welfare of the college and held them responsible for the NCA team's decision to make a follow-up visit and the short amount of time before the next full review. Although the president indicated that he did not take the situation personally, he was obviously "extremely disappointed that these people would use the ears of the NCA team to vent their frustration and anger toward the administration" (Dole interview).

The initial response to the NCA report from the dean's office was to call in the dissenting individuals for some frank conversations. Within a year, all four of the faculty members had left the college, having been encouraged by the administration to do so. Two had been denied tenure, and the Math Department head had been asked to resign her chair. Rather than step down, she resigned from the college. The fourth of these faculty members had a negative experience.

The red-shoed math professor, who had received the college's teaching award a year earlier, was told that his service was no longer required and was relieved of all teaching responsibilities the following semester. The official reason for this move was his lack of a terminal degree. Initially, he was offered a package of money and support equivalent to an assistantship to return to graduate school. Frustrated, the professor consulted an attorney, who recommended that he renegotiate the severance deal. Fearing a lawsuit, the administration capitulated in accordance with the faculty handbook—requiring a year's notice before terminating a faculty member. Effectively, they handed the math professor a year's salary and benefits as a severance package. Eventually, the math professor landed a faculty post at another small, private liberal arts college in South Central Michigan. Interestingly, at commencement that year, several students and some faculty wore T-shirts with red sneakers silk-screened on them underneath their robes as a sign of solidarity with the terminated professor.

Olivet Case 3: Findings

This case demonstrates several of the forms of resistance and championship identified in the two prior cases. Again, faculty members resisted by voting in opposition to particular initiatives, voicing dissent, building cases against particular initiatives, and using sabotage. The championship approaches included: coalition building, coming to a consensus, and using straw votes to determine who needed to be reasoned with. Four additional forms of resistance and three different championship approaches are apparent in this case.

By forming a coalition, the strongest resisters voiced their opinions directly to the visiting accreditation team, bypassing the administration. In advance of the NCA team arrival, some administrators tried to reason with the faculty to prevent the airing of dirty laundry. While reasoning had sometimes been successful, it did not succeed in this case. Resisters used every opportunity to discredit the Plan and went so far as to attack the credibility of the administration, creating uncertainty among the NCA team that the transformation would succeed. The administration was furious, believing that these resisters had abdicated their right to complain. It is true that the resisters had been given every opportunity to participate in the planning and implementation process and had simply decided not to. Escalating the response, the dean encouraged the departure of those who had, in his view, sabotaged and discredited the institution. In the end, the remaining resisters came to believe they had been put on a sort of blacklist. The former dean denies this. But once again perception became a proxy for the truth.

Forms of Engaging Resistance Not Illustrated in the Olivet Cases

As mentioned earlier, the findings in this chapter are based on all cases of resistance documented at the two schools, not just the three illustrated above. At Olivet College, members of the college community demonstrated two additional forms of resistance and six approaches to surmounting resistance.

Because of the very public nature of the 1992 racial incident, Olivet College faced substantial media scrutiny over the ensuing years. Resisters periodically used the media presence to voice their objections to a plan or proposal to get some kind of reaction from the administration. Also, faculty who resisted and disagreed with elements of the transformation sometimes engaged students to assist in protesting the initiatives. For example, certain faculty members occasionally shared their negative views of one or more portions of the Plan with students, who in turn circulated them around campus, influencing other students' views.

The first strategy for engagement is not obvious, but is implied in the cases. Plan supporters often presented counterarguments in planning meetings in hopes that they could sway the opinions or change the behavior of others. At times, they cut deals with individuals to gain support as well. Many times, resistance was simply not addressed in hopes that the situation would resolve itself. Another strategy was to hire new faculty after the model had been put in place, thereby shrinking the number of resisters. Particularly during the planning phase, the administration was able to get funding from granting agencies to send people to conferences and provide them with professional development opportunities that might sway their thinking. Finally, at Olivet College some faculty members were rewarded monetarily or in other ways for changing their thinking about the Plan.

Resistance at Portland State University

As at Olivet, the PSU transformation saga can be broken into three eras: (1) Planning; (2) Rollout; and (3) Post-Rollout. Multiple forms of resistance were perpetrated during all three eras. Throughout, students and staff were largely silent on the University Studies (UNST) issues, placing the burden of resistance mainly on the faculty. Three cases described in the following pages stand out, one per era. Again, the findings presented in this chapter are based on all instances of resistance evidenced at PSU, not just those apparent in these three cases.

PSU Case 1: The Push to Pilot the University Studies Program

One of the hallmarks of the PSU transformation was the swiftness with which the University Studies (UNST) proposal was developed. Working group members were energized by the new program's potential and met at least twice weekly. Most faculty members were otherwise occupied and therefore paid little attention to the process and ignored requests for volunteers to assist in the planning: "Everyone was so beaten down at the time by these continuous budget changes. We were kind of just surviving, worrying about if you would get cut" (Patton interview). One key resister admits, "I am sure it is true that I was offered a chance to go to some planning kind of meeting, but I didn't" (Crawshaw interview).

Awareness of the proposed transformation expanded only slightly as public forums were held in advance of the fall 1993 colloquium. For many faculty members, their first exposure to the proposal came when the full document was circulated just before the colloquium. Even so, most faculty members acquiesced or were supportive. A small number were shocked, outraged, and offended by the implied criticisms of the distribution system:

> Apparently a group of faculty had met with the provost on and off campus to come up with this program. And all of a sudden, there it was. Chuck [White] gave quite the impassioned speech [at the colloquium]. *I came out of there just absolutely angry because I knew what was going to happen.* They were talking about pulling people off of upper division and putting them into freshman courses. (Crawshaw interview)

Based on feedback received at the colloquium, the committee added a "revisions and clarifications" addendum to the original proposal. These revisions included changing: (1) the name of the "freshman core" to "Freshman Inquiry" (FRINQ); and (2) the working group title to the "General Education Committee" to reflect the continuation of its role in design, structure, planning, and oversight of the new program. Also appended to the original proposal were two supporting letters from outside sources and examples of potential course syllabi. The whole package was submitted to the faculty senate for consideration in November 1993.

Going into November, said former provost Michael Reardon, "It was one of those rare sets of meetings where there was something meaningful going on. Before it came up to the senate, I met quite a bit with Chuck [White] and with [President] Judith [Ramaley]. Essentially, we were at the point where we had to talk about a strategy" (Reardon interview). Retrospectively, a four-pronged strategy was realized from their action. The first could be called the "transformation as scholarly work" approach. That is, the proposal was grounded in a rigorous review of the literature and participation in the national dialogue on general education. The second was to sell it as an "up or out" proposal. Previous attempts to change the GE at PSU had been foiled by debate over content. The administration worked to prevent a similar fate by encouraging people to vote for the whole proposal, firmly believing and espousing that the faculty should "either vote it in, or don't vote it in . . . , but don't begin to alter it. We had already gone through an entire process where there were all kinds of opportunities for input and making suggestions about the proposal" (Reardon interview).

Also from history, they knew that the project could get derailed if questions about the administration of the program sidetracked the conversation from the proposal's educational merits. Therefore, a third strategy was a promise: to return to the senate with proposals about how it would be administered. But this would be done "only after and if it was approved. We didn't want to talk about how it would be administered until we knew that it was something that we all wanted" (Reardon interview). Last, they worked to build a coalition of support, particularly from the deans. "Like most things, officially, it is interpreted through the deans, and the deans ask departments to participate. And there were a series of meetings where we were asked to contribute" (Farr interview). And they were not afraid to spend some political capital to get this kind of support:

> Michael Reardon was not only an old-timer—he and I came here at the same time—but also he was very savvy. He knew everybody around here. And he knew what people would be inclined to do and say. And he didn't direct the committee. He didn't have to; he chose the right people for the committee . . . and the support was found. The beans were all lined up and it was brought to the senate then. (Moor interview)

Feelings about the proposal among the faculty were mixed. The administration had done such a good job selling and fighting for the proposal that many felt the decision was a fait accompli. One philosophy professor recalls:

> That was a realistic estimate of the situation. I had mentioned to people at the lunchroom table then that I was going to make this motion [to pilot, or test,

the program]. One of the guys who was chair of the department and had been around looked at me and said, "I thought the decision on that had already been taken." (Moor interview)

At that time, some faculty argued that the distribution system was not broken and that there were no compelling data validating the need for change. Other resisters did not suggest that the new program was without merits, but did say that it should at least be piloted before being implemented wholesale. From the science perspective, said one professor:

> You should never do something without conducting some sort of a pilot. *You always run a pilot project.* No matter how wonderful it seems in your head, until you have run it from start to finish, you have no clue how it will play out. It would be kind of like me building a huge experiment without collecting data. (Crawshaw interview)

In 1993, those who were unsure about or offended by the proposal did not coalesce in the face of a vigorous campaign to pass UNST:

> I just didn't know to what extent the people in science were really opposed to it. And the senate doesn't represent them to quite the same degree. And I think that scientists tend to be hidden away in labs more and so they are less likely to be elected to the senate. I think it was a political matter. The people who favored it though, let's put it gently, fought vigorously. They regarded it as a moral issue. Opposition to the whole thing was seen as an unwillingness to treat the students respectfully. It really seemed to them to be a moral issue. And so they campaigned real vigorously. And I didn't. I knew that there was a guy in the Psychology Department whose expertise is rational decision-making. I knew that if I asked him to come to the senate to talk about that, that it would be pretty effective, but I didn't want to do that. I thought in this case, "let me just make the motion, argue my case, and let the chips fall where they may." (Moor interview)

The remainder of the action in this case is documented by minutes taken during the faculty senate meetings of November 1 and 8, 1993. The material is presented as a dialogue in order to highlight relevant portions of the discourse. I have eliminated the irrelevant portions, such as formalities of parliamentary procedure. To reflect the drama, the discourse presented here illustrates only this one case of resistance and the responses from the champions, even though there was more than one item on the agenda.

Faculty Senate Meeting, November 1, 1993   The presiding officer called meeting to order at 3:05 p.m. Fifty voting members were present, and seven absent. Nineteen additional ex-officio members were present, as well as a few others not listed in the minutes, including Chuck White. Formal answers to a set of questions about the University Studies proposal raised by the Office of Academic Affairs were entered by the GE Working Group into the minutes. Also included in the minutes was a letter from an English faculty member and director of writing urging adoption of the new program and pointing out some reservations:

> It seems paradoxical to us that, as writing becomes more central to undergraduate education, writing faculty risk becoming more peripheral. Still, no major change is without risk. The many benefits of your proposal make those risks worth taking. (Letter from Duncan Carter, dated October 29, 1993)

After the approval of the minutes from the previous session, and a reminder about a memorial service for a faculty member, President Ramaley was the first to speak:

Ramaley: We now have a few years in which to demonstrate the effectiveness of our institution, in an attempt to continue receiving these monies. However, we are not out of the woods. But we should be proud of the fact that we are becoming a national model, identifying the nature of the campus and its faculty, and the relationship of PSU to the community and other educational institutions.

Prof. D. Johnson: Now, I rarely speak at these meetings, but I move in the strongest possible terms to accept the report written by the working group.

Prof. Moor: On behalf of Professor Forbes and myself, I offer the following substitute motion. The senate should approve in principle the adoption of a pilot program wherein the general education program proposed by the working group would be made available to entering first-term freshmen as an optional alternative to the present requirements, and that the proposal be referred to the appropriate faculty committees for their review and recommendations.

Presiding Officer: I'd like to turn this meeting over to an informal consideration of this question to all those present. This would ease some of the parliamentary rules.

Prof. A. Johnson: Are we going to be voting on this today?

Presiding Officer: One possibility is to vote on this at the November 8th meeting.

Prof. Franks: Given that we have not seen the data of the Office of Academic Affairs and won't be getting it until mid-week, I would like to ensure that no vote be taken before we have that information.

Presiding Officer: Are there any objections to moving to an informal session? Seeing none, it is so moved.

Chuck White (a nonvoting member of the faculty) began a detailed explanation of the program and included an aside referencing how the Intensive Writing Course pilot program proposed by Professor Carter would fit. He also described the modifications to the proposal, announced the new members of the working group, and thanked the committee for its hard work. He continued:

Prof. White: The question of whether to have a pilot program is important. Now, phased implementation is required by the current proposal over a four-year time period. The GE committee argues that the pilot concept is vague, complex, confusing, costly, and uncertain. It would also be unclear about when to end the pilot.

Prof. A. Johnson: I have a question. Is the working group constitutional?

Provost Reardon: Keep in mind, the UNST implementation will necessarily be considered by the appropriate faculty senate bodies.

Prof. Bowlden: What makes the use of a pilot desirable?

Prof. Moor: There are significant concerns that I have about full-scale implementation of the program. It could presumably direct resources from underfunded departments. Will the benefits be worth the costs? What are the academic benefits? A pilot would enable us to determine whether the approach actually works and would also allow us to determine what the outcomes are.

Provost Reardon: The new program might actually help resource allocations, and might give the university better assessment methods. Many other benefits might accrue to the university.

Prof. White: Even if the program were optional, I expect that most students would elect to take the new program. Keep in mind that current freshmen can graduate under their old catalogue or any newer one, so the old plan would be required for seven years also.

Dean Toulon (ex-officio): Remember, we needed curricular reform. The current proposal is as good as any that I have seen. And a pilot program would lead to confusion. Also, a pilot program would preclude any educational objective from being achieved. We as faculty are here to make crucial educational decisions for the students. Moreover, we would not be able to have an appropriate control group in a pilot because it would be biased toward student selection based on adviser or student perception.

Prof. D. Johnson: I agree. A pilot would not meet either educational or cost objectives. We should be reminded that course content is based on faculty control; this proposal would restore faculty positions on the basis of majors.

Presiding Officer: Are there objections to moving back to a formal session? Seeing none, it is so moved.

Prof A. Johnson: I move to adjourn.

Faculty Senate Meeting, November 8, 1993   The senate reconvened on November 8, 1993, at 3:00 p.m. Forty-nine voting members were present, seven absent. Again, 19 ex-officio members attended. Several other nonvoting faculty members not listed in the minutes were also present. Midway through the meeting, the group returned to the general education issue. Two motions were raised from the floor. The first was Professor D. Johnson's motion to accept the proposal as drafted. The second was Professor Moor's motion to substitute a pilot program. Again, without objection, the session was made informal so that all could contribute.

Prof. White: (In response to a number of questions) Keep in mind that not every course must be interdisciplinary—specifically in the sophomore and junior years—but courses in a cluster must fit together. Also, for courses listed as four credits, the fourth credit constitutes the writing/communication requirement. Those courses, of course, will go through the Curriculum Committee. And keep in mind that all new courses must go through a screening process with the General Education Committee and we will work to ensure that clusters fit together.

Provost Reardon: The real key is to provide a mechanism to allow faculty to respond to general education needs. We cannot anticipate what every course would look like before it is moved into place. The important process is to keep general education from drifting once it began. A mechanism to foster this is needed.

Prof. Beeson: Now, are there mechanics to force students to take math and science in this proposal?

Prof. Latiolais: As a working group member from the Math Department, I can assure you that courses are being developed that have numeracy, elementary statistics, and algebra. The basic foundation will exist.

Prof. Wineberg (ex-officio and chair of the Academic Requirements Commit-tee): For the record, I'd like to read a statement that I have prepared.

I am troubled by the fact that the faculty senate is being asked to vote on a general education working group proposal that, if approved, would completely overhaul the undergraduate curriculum. Yet there is nothing in the proposal about how to implement the curricular changes.

I find it incomprehensible that the proposal eliminates the diversity re-quirement. The Academic Requirements Committee [ARC] spent two years evaluating the merits of a diversity requirement, including how to imple-ment such a requirement. The diversity requirement has been in effect for only one year and already there is a move to eliminate this requirement, with the rationale being that too many courses can be used to meet the diversity requirement; yet this is exactly what the faculty senate wanted. In the winter of the 1991–92 academic year, the Academic Requirements Committee drafted a proposal outlining the criteria to be used in evaluating what constitutes a diversity course. The faculty senate would not approve the ARC's proposal, stating that the criteria were too narrow. The ARC was instructed to revise the criteria making it more inclusive, the result being that about 110 courses can be used to meet the diversity requirement. . . .

The proposal has substantial gaps when it comes to transfer students. According to the proposal, a transfer student who comes in as a sophomore (i.e., has 45 credits) does not have to take the freshman inquiry courses. A transfer student who comes in with 43 or 44 credits would be required to take 15 hours of Freshman Inquiry. This will cause much ill-will and animosity among these transfer students, not to mention the possible finan-cial implication for the students. Secondly, what happens to someone who takes the first Freshman Inquiry course and then does not attend school winter term? Will this person have to wait until next winter to continue the sequence? What if the core faculty have changed and the student has completed only two of the three required freshman courses? Does he have to start all over again? . . .

Prof. Reece: I'd like to point out that the proposal does indeed address diversity on pages 6 and 7. On the whole, the committee feels that there would be a good deal more, not less, teaching of diversity in the new program. Let me read the specific parts to you.

First, faculty teaching in the general education program will be re-quired to complete faculty development, which focuses upon how to include diversity issues within the courses they are developing or adapting for the program. The second element of our approach will be to insure that persons with expertise in developing and delivering courses related to diversity, particularly those faculty who teach in the Women's Studies and Black Studies Programs, are members of the General Education committee.

Dean Toulon (ex-officio): Look, this new curriculum is like architecture. When you start building, you do not start with the furniture. You start at the foundation. The question we should look at is on the quality of the concept. Many problematical issues of implementation will be resolved later. This document is as good as any we could develop. We could be here until next Monday if we want to list and examine all the details. The committee could have addressed all the details if it had developed a 300 or 400 page report. This is not feasible, and as it is, the proposal is quite lengthy. . . .

Dean Ahlbrandt (ex-officio): I agree with Dean Toulon. There would be problems with any new proposal, but this one addresses what attributes employers tell us they need from workers. Our new curriculum helps companies in our region and our students grapple with these issues. I would be proud to be associated with this new curriculum. We should move ahead now without a pilot because this is fundamentally good here. It is not right to make students wait while we work out all the nuts and bolts.

Provost Reardon: How we would assess a pilot given that there are no goals for the current program? And, if students were allowed to select an option, there would not be random selection.

Prof. Moor: I reserve the right to answer these questions at a later point.

Prof. DeCarrico: I don't think that a pilot would lead to full commitment of the faculty, so the results would be different if we substituted a pilot.

Dean Davidson (ex-officio): I have been involved with a similar program elsewhere, and the benefits for the faculty were strong with little cost. The faculty became engaged with people they had never worked with, enlivening themselves and revitalizing their careers.

Prof. Wineberg: But there are no comments about evaluation or implementation in the proposal. Who would be doing the implementation?

Prof. Bunch (nonvoting): I am impressed with the proposal, and the president did say that this may very well be the most important action taken on this campus in ten years. The deans are very positive about this. However, like the U.S. Senate is willing to deal with the details of NAFTA, perhaps we should do so as well. We might be moving too fast. The devil is in the details.

At some point, the whole faculty should be brought in on the decision-making if we want their commitment.

Dean Everhart (ex-officio): There are several problems with a pilot. By 1996, all high school students will be graduating from a curriculum that matches this one.

Prof. Wollner: I support what Deans Everhart and Ahlbrandt are saying. There are many external pressures and variables favoring a full-scale move into the program.

Presiding Officer: Without objection, shall we move back into regular session? Seeing none, it is so moved.

Prof. Moor: Let me at least answer the question as to how to assess a pilot. Now, it would be difficult to assess success of a pilot in the absolute. We could simply use outcome measures before and after for both programs. It is like finding a cure for cancer. If I pray and you use medicine, we can see the results and then make comparisons. I admit that there are many good concepts here, including the opportunity to engage in interdisciplinary work. But I really think we should do a pilot first.

Who called the question is not recorded in the minutes. The outcome is. Via a rare secret ballot, the motion to pilot the program failed, 32 to 15. The senate continued discussing the working group proposal, with White responding to another question about the full-year timeframe for FRINQ courses:

Prof. White: There has been much discussion about the issues: e.g., if a student takes off winter, could the student return in the spring? They could, and pick up what they missed in the summer. I prefer to keep students together for pedagogical reasons. Now, this is not required, but students would be advised to do so, and will have some flexibility to make their own decisions.

President Ramaley: Dean Toulon is right; the proposal is a lot like building construction. There are always changes after the blueprint has been approved. Here we want to define the structure from given goals, then work through the furniture, color of upholstery, etc. It is terribly important to trust our judgment and our faculty. We will be able to solve many of these problems later. We have escrowed the resources to do this, and so we don't have to argue about the dollars needed to make this work. The provost says the dollars are in the bank. This is the lowest-risk approach that we can take to solve this problem, and I commend all those who have spent their time and thoughtful attention on this.

Another secret ballot closed the meeting. The motion to approve the proposal passed, 37 for, 9 against. The presiding officer congratulated and thanked the group, adjourning the meeting at 4:45 with an invitation for everyone to enjoy a post-meeting glass of sherry.

PSU Case 1: Findings

As with the Olivet Case, the primary approach used to engage resistance at PSU was proactive. Early on, efforts were made to include a wide array of individuals in the planning process via membership in the working groups or forums designed to solicit feedback from faculty members. Despite these efforts, many faculty members either ignored or deliberately stayed away from participation in any planning activities as a means to resist. After the UNST proposal was finalized, the champions began in earnest to build a coalition of support going into the November 1993 faculty senate meeting. In particular, the deans of the various schools and programs were enlisted to convince others to vote for the proposal. Of course, voting against the proposal was an obvious form of resistance. Another was to suggest that the whole proposal be piloted as a way of preventing wholesale implementation. As was demonstrated in the ensuing senate meetings, the corresponding engagement practice by the champions was to make counterarguments and reason with individuals, as a way of building consensus before voting on the initiative. In this case, four approaches worked in combination to mitigate the number of contrarian votes. The campaign to run a pilot program failed, and the UNST initiative passed by large margins.

PSU Case 2: Attacking the Champion

No interviewees recalled overt instances of resistance during the second era, other than the faculty senate push in 1996 to evaluate University Studies (UNST). And that evaluation can be considered a genuine assessment, designed to pull the program into the regular governance process rather than to quash it. Resistance in this era mainly percolated beneath the surface, manifest, among other places, in the interactions between UNST director Chuck White and numerous campus constituents. White's case is an excellent example of how ordinary individuals willing to champion a cause must work through much resistance. It reveals a small portion of the complicated web of interpersonal interactions involving individually targeted resistance. I present this case not as one event or situation, but as a collection of vignettes that illustrate White's experience.

In 1992, Charles R. (Chuck) White was a typical PSU faculty member in the Political Science Department, teaching courses and conducting research. Little did he realize then that agreeing to chair a committee for the provost would embroil him—both personally and professionally—in defending a sweeping transformation of the general education curriculum. Indeed, White agreed to lead the General Education Working Group with a fair amount of naiveté, given that this was his first administrative post. Over time, White was strengthened by the belief that there simply had to be a better, more cohesive way to conduct GE at Portland State. He became energized, and his position as chair placed him naturally as one key champion for the cause. He could not have foreseen that chairing the group would place him at the front of a high-profile, winner-take-all campaign that would test his skill and fortitude during what was "a revolutionary and very exciting time, almost to the point of fanaticism" (Patton interview).

White's life was changed by his role in the transformation process. All interviewees place him at the center of the transformation, continually putting out "wildfires" where he personally "took a fair amount of whacks" (Flowers interview). By vigorously carrying out his role, White became more than a visible target; he became a lightning rod for resisters. According to one anonymous faculty member, White was like "Richard the Lionhearted off in the Holy Land fighting the Crusades, not realizing what the hell is going on in the homeland. But the sheriff of Nottingham [meaning CLAS Dean Kaiser] was up to some real naughty things himself, and that wasn't helping things."

White knew the task at hand was to deliver a plan that spoke to the faculty. This "meant that we needed to approach it in a scholarly way and be able to present evidence as to why this was what we were going to do" (White interview). Rich discussions among the working group members were commonplace, as many people had different ideas and solutions. A primary strategy for the team was to hold periodic open forums to get input and feedback on the plan as it developed. When a person offered critique or criticism, White would invite them to participate. For example, one professor in the Speech and Communications Department recognized that the proposal emphasized writing but no other forms of communication:

> I called Chuck White and I said, "My name is Devorah Lieberman, and you don't know me, but I am representing the Speech Department, and on behalf of the Speech Department, we think that if you are going to have communication as

a goal, you should have something in there about oral communication." And Chuck said to me, "If you feel strongly about this, why don't you join the committee." ... So, then I started going to the meetings. (Lieberman interview)

Even though he was able to entice a number of potential resisters to participate in the planning, White's lack of administrative experience may have resulted in some ill-advised moves. Ironically, some felt his approach was not politically astute. Undeniably, White said what he thought needed to be said, with little regard to how it would be received. This willingness to speak his mind made him the obvious champion to snipe at. Occasionally his seemingly minor statements, from another point of view, were perceived as antagonistic. For example, White's deriding of multiple choice examinations inflamed at least one faculty member during one forum:

> *I came out of there just absolutely angry because I knew what was going to happen.* ... He also took the time to make fun of multiple-choice questions. And pulling people out of upper division courses means that I am going to have to teach even more people. When I have got 170 students to a course, *I am not going to have any time to grade anything but multiple-choice.* (Crawshaw interview)

White believed an inherent lack of trust in the leadership by some faculty led to "an assumption by the resisters that either Michael or I was hiding something." And so, when asked to provide supporting documentation to the faculty senate, he "provided everything that I could think of, including budget documents and grant information" (White interview). Doing so turned resister perception to an assumption that they were now burying information. Some faculty claim White was too forceful in getting departments to support the program. He did make some enemies by pushing the proposal, saying, "If you don't get on board, you will be punished. Departments will be punished." Not only did such statements rile individuals and whole departments, but they were not quickly forgotten, creating a problematic residue of "memories of threats or promises that never happened" (Patton interview).

The UNST proposal specified only the academic plan—the GE curriculum transformation and its supporting rationale. There was no corresponding administrative, infrastructure, or budgetary plan. Who was to run it, where it was to be housed, and how it was to be operationalized were not clear. Anyone agreeing to spearhead implementation would inherit two specific challenges: (1) who and how to manage University Studies; and (2) how to get all the faculty involved.

As a condition of taking the job as dean of the College of Liberal Arts and Sciences (CLAS) at PSU in 1994, Marvin Kaiser had negotiated primary responsibility for University Studies and insisted that it be housed under the CLAS umbrella. He was not, however, given the corresponding budgetary authority, which remained under the provost's control. Dean Kaiser also inherited a new associate dean for University Studies. To the dean, it seemed logical to ask White to assume the post because he had the best understanding of the project. Against the advice of a colleague, White agreed to take the position and walked an "administrative tightrope," reporting administratively to Kaiser and answering fiscally to Provost Reardon. Kaiser later acknowledged that accepting responsibility for the program without the corresponding financial authority was a mistake:

> Obviously there were issues from the beginning as to where the real authority for this was to reside . . . that kind of divided notions of authority, more so than responsibility kind of dogged this thing from the beginning. . . . I should have either gotten to the place where I said, "either I have the authority along with the responsibility or I want neither." I should have come to that place. Now what would have happened, I don't know, but what happened in this kind of gulf between authority and responsibility was that, in fact, UNST became this entity unto itself. (Kaiser interview)

According to one long-term CLAS faculty member, the situation established a tension between White and Kaiser that is "famous in terms of its ongoing enmity and antagonism." Understandably, Kaiser's loyalties were split. Certainly, his first priority was the larger CLAS, and at times, CLAS priorities conflicted with UNST implementation. Before the UNST plan was implemented, every CLAS department had contributed faculty to teaching GE courses. Participation in UNST, on the other hand, was voluntary. One expected budget savings from the transformation would come from the elimination of large introductory-level GE courses. However, many of those courses had served a dual purpose, providing both GE credit and credit in the major field. With FRINQ courses filling the GE requirement, introductory-level courses would only serve as prerequisites in the major field. And faculty still had to teach these courses. Thus in practice, the 100-level courses could not be eliminated, negating any proposed savings. Moreover, with students selecting FRINQ courses instead, enrollments in the 100-level courses declined. The subsequent loss of Student Full-Time Equivalents effectively shrunk departmental budgets. Lower student enrollment also reduced the need for graduate student teaching assistants, affecting enrollment in graduate programs as well.

On occasion, the dean seemed to favor CLAS departments over University Studies. The dean also occasionally voiced the opinion that UNST was receiving too much money. The dean's office became a center where people could air their grievances. This was manifest during biweekly department chair meetings. With White in attendance, the dean did not stifle open critique of the program. Conversation ranged from legitimate concern to ridicule and snide remarks, and on at least two occasions broke into shouting matches between White and the strongest resisters. One chair present at those meetings admits that general criticism of UNST often deteriorated into open hostility toward White.

At a minimum, the dean's stance made it challenging to get anything related to UNST accomplished. Some go so far as to claim that the dean actively sabotaged the program. A number of interviewees reported that the dean used money earmarked for UNST programs for other purposes. In 1999, when Provost Reardon retired, Dean Kaiser was able to move the UNST budget to CLAS. In a surprise move, according to White, the dean " cut 100,000 dollars out of the base without ever talking to me. I walked into a department heads' meeting and there it was, just assuming that I could do it [make UNST happen with reduced funding]" (White interview). White recalled circumventing the dean to accomplish certain UNST goals.

> As it turned out, I understood the budget better than [he did], and I had to engage in some administrative stuff to keep the program whole. I would go talk to the budget office and he would be upset. From his perspective, to have a subordinate go independently to the budget office [was] an issue. But again, my responsibility was an all-university program, and my job was to make it work. And so I was entering into agreements with other deans and chairs. (White interview)

White was so busy advocating for the plan, disseminating information nationally, and meeting with funding agencies that he had to assign other faculty members to oversee elements of the UNST program. It appears as though the administrative structure and budgetary practices were invented on the fly. By default, a quasi–department structure emerged, comprising the people closest to and trusted by White. Outsiders saw it as a closed group, open only to those who had been part of the initial planning process. Moreover, while the planning process had been open and inclusive, implementation was not. The quick rollout schedule made it difficult for leadership to keep an ear open for criticism. Those who were critical of, or did not participate in, any portion of UNST were effectively cut out of the communication loop. White's primary objective was to support and protect faculty and departments who were already involved. To resisters, this move was seen as protectionism. The UNST "enclave" was thought to see itself as "beyond reproach." Outsiders were bitter, feeling the irony that such determined transformation advocates were not listening or not open to changing their practices or their plan:

> The lack of the degree to which we spoke to them [resisters] was either reconfigured as stonewalling or as [we] didn't hear or didn't say what [they] wanted to hear. Or, we simply were not responsive. It was that kind of challenge. Eventually it got so bad that maybe we pulled the covers up, circled the wagons a bit, and that got translated into stonewalling, as opposed to us getting tired of being hit over the head with brickbats. (Flowers interview)

Two strategies were used to recruit enough faculty members to teach FRINQ courses. The first was a "cash-for-bodies" exchange. That is, departments that committed a person to teach for at least two years in the program would be reimbursed from the UNST budget with a dollar amount that covered the position within the department. The allocation was typically used to cover the cost of either a tenure-track faculty member who could teach in the departmental major or someone who would be willing teach in FRINQ, thereby allowing existing faculty to continue doing what they'd been doing. A second strategy was to establish several postdoctoral "teaching fellowships" aimed at enticing new, energetic faculty to the PSU campus. They were required to teach FRINQ courses for two years and then were free to teach courses in the department that hired them. In the first year of the program, six newly minted Ph.D.s were hired.

White made these deals exclusively. As executed, the positions were not evenly distributed; nor were plans made to apply an across-the-board budgetary policy. Both strategies led resisters to claim that departments were treated inequitably. It did look as though the UNST administration was playing favorites, but at least one department was so against participating in UNST that it refused to deal.

Throughout the planning process, White was under tremendous pressure. His visible position placed his every action and word under extreme scrutiny. Even White admits he was not always successful. "Sometimes I would screw up. And so, my own administrative weaknesses became highlighted." There is no question that White was deeply invested in the process and the outcome.

Eventually, the lightning rod got hit one too many times, although exactly when is difficult to pinpoint. At some time during the rollout, it became too difficult for individuals to suppress the anger associated with their experience. The focus of resistance behavior shifted from the planning process, the plan, and its implementation to the people leading the effort. White was on the receiving end of resistance that got personal.

For White, the last straw may have come when attacks during department chair meetings ceased being professional. "They were not fun. They [resisters] were bashing and the dean wasn't stopping them" (White interview). White did not misjudge the action. Many observers verify that he was indeed attacked. "It got really ugly for Chuck . . . it was hard for him to deal with some of these people, as they would defame him and his skills as an administrator or manager" (Reece interview). It was apparent that it became personal between White and Kaiser, "just by the way they would talk with one another, and then later, [when] they wouldn't talk to one another" (Reardon interview).

> Did I handle all of the attacks well? Not necessarily. Some, sure . . . you see this is the problem I had. I became viewed as a person who was unwilling to change what had originally been created. Nothing can be further from the truth. Curriculum is a living, breathing kind of thing. As you learn, you don't teach the same way when you don't teach the same material. . . . They would ask things like, "Why are you not doing assessment?" And I would say, "We are, it is not just our initial strategy, and we are working it out." And they would say, "Don't be so defensive." *Bullshit, then don't ask that question! Don't say those things!* And so, people's conceptions and preconceived conceptions of me that evolved over time became important. (White interview)

The most dramatic manifestation of resistance affecting White personally occurred just eight years after the initial plan was developed and two years after the complete program was in place. The new provost (Tetreault) began the hiring process for the newly created position of vice provost. White applied. A committee of self-identified maverick faculty who had been resisting UNST all along effectively influenced the selection process against White. The group made sure that at least one of them was at each of White's interviews for the position. White recalls:

> I was certainly a target. And my experience as a leader for transformation was that I became a lightning rod for all the ills and a scapegoat for all the problems. . . .

One of these people would follow me around when I was going around for my interviews. If you can believe it, one of them would follow me around to raise questions and challenge whatever I was saying. They would come to the open forums and every meeting I had, one of them was there. It certainly affected my career and me because Mary Kay [Tetreault] made a decision to not give me the vice provost position. (White interview)

PSU Case 2: Findings

The primary manifestations of resistance demonstrated in this case are the numerous attacks aimed at one or more champions. Before Chuck White became the target, he had worked to include others in the planning. He had also tried to ensure that those who might be critics had an opportunity to be heard, listened to, and thereby incorporated into the planning process. He used discretionary funds, particularly those granted from foundations, to reward individuals and to make deals with departments to procure their cooperation. In the instances where these deals were made, they were highly successful in engaging and surmounting resistance. The English and History Departments are good examples of this. On the other hand, White also withheld such rewards from individuals and departments, or more aptly, threatened to do so, which was a way to try and coerce them to cooperate or punish them for not cooperating.

As the literature predicts, White's use of negative methods often further steeled the resisters against him or produced resistance among others, instead of reducing it. Also in this case, the intensity of the resistance was amplified in proportion to the power of the person doing the resisting. More specifically, the dean used his higher rank to coerce the faculty into supporting the plan. This gave the resisters further reason to attack champion White.

Another approach embedded in the making of deals was the hiring of new people who would willingly be integrated into the transformation. Resistance perpetrated by the dean was also interpreted by several champions as an active attempt to sabotage the program. When the resistance became more intense, another approach employed by those leading the transformation was to protect those on the front lines, effectively absorbing, deflecting, or ignoring attacks.

PSU Case 3: Student Surveys

A bell-shaped curve could represent participation and interest in University Studies over the years. Although there were almost 600 faculty members on the PSU campus, a relatively small number at one tail of the curve actively participated in the planning and implementation of UNST. The majority in the middle of the curve either approved of, were unaffected by, or held no opinion about the program. A small number of vocal opponents are represented at the other tail of the curve. In a mirror image, a parabolic curve could represent the amount of overt resistance behavior over time. The first fervent effort to resist UNST was made in 1993 by those who wanted to pilot the program. After that attempt died in the faculty senate, forms of resistance were comparatively passive (e.g., nonparticipation), more covert, or aimed at specific individuals. It was not until after the change in institutional leadership in 1998 and 1999 that resistance behavior again became intentional and overt. In this case, a portion of the faculty, represented almost exclusively by members of the science departments, began an initiative to evaluate the program. Compared to all other efforts, this was the strongest and broadest effort to stop University Studies. At the far end of both curves, the resistance hit its peak in the year 2000. According to one professor: "It got acrimonious and then it got emotional. You had to choose. There was no fence sitting after that. Those people [resisters] really lost credibility. I lost all respect for some colleagues in that process (Wetzel interview).

The small group of resisters included members of other departments as well, but the most aggressive were from the sciences. These people had a history of refusing to participate in any aspect of UNST (planning, implementation, or beyond). Larry Crawshaw, a tenured biology professor, emerged as one of the leaders [although Cranshaw would doubt that David Horowitz was easily as much of a leader] of the group. This case is extracted from his interview in order to give voice to the resisters and highlight the resistance area under the curve. While the following paragraphs are quoted material, I have removed superfluous words and sentences and made minor changes to facilitate the conversion from a natural human discourse to a written document.

> You know, faculty members are buffeted 90,000 ways with this or that initiative constantly washing over them. I might have had the opportunity to give input on University Studies, but there was no way to know at that time that it wouldn't be just another initiative that dies on the vine. So, I just ignored the whole thing. Not only that, but the decision to implement the new GE program was totally a done deal. We were looking at this several million-dollar bolus from the state to support it. There was no way a rational person would want to derail the process

because it was attached to that appropriation, which was earmarked for increasing retention. So I just figured "Oh, well, just forget it," and went back to work. So I was an observer, not an outspoken critic in 1992 and 1993. My part would come later.

Sure enough, the things that I predicted would make me angry when they happened did happen. First of all, UNST has done nothing to increase retention. Also for example, my upper-division Animal Behavior class went from 45 students to around 110. I now have to give a lot of people upper-division science credit because some of the courses are no longer available, as they are doing those requirements in UNST. I also must have talked to a hundred students who had entered under the old program and had a choice. Most of those students did not choose University Studies. I have never heard a student say, "I had a choice, and so I choose to take University Studies." Not once.

The propaganda the UNST people were putting out led us to believe that over 90 percent of the students were highly supportive of University Studies. Meanwhile, I am busy teaching in the lab, trying to get grants, and overwhelmed with everything, just ignoring the whole thing. And if you did bring something critical up, you were not met with a normal intellectual response. They would always say that you were opposed to change, that you were rigid and couldn't deal with new ideas. No one ever wanted to talk about different ideas. It was always a character assassination as opposed to an intellectual exchange. The usual argument was a personal attack. That is when I started getting heavily involved.

I was teaching Comparative Physiology in the winter [1999]. And I met a couple of kids I was teaching outside of class one day, and they just started going off on UNST. They just absolutely hated it. Now, the kinds of students that tend to hate it the most are older returning students 26 or maybe 30 years old. They have some life under their belts. It reminds me of my old professors that used to talk about the Korean War veterans. The veterans were just no-bullshit people. They wanted a degree and they wanted to get on with their lives.

These two students, this guy and his wife, were really good, bright students. And they could write. He was writing for the *Vanguard* [the student newspaper], and she was an elegant writer and one of the top students in my class. They could make computers dance around and do whatever you wanted. And they had to go through this University Studies program. The program put everybody randomly in classes. So they were in with people who had poor writing skills. They were basically past that whole thing. And here they were required to take 15 units in these classes and they hated it. There was no way out.

They couldn't test out. At PSU, the top quarter of the students could fit quite easily in just about any school. The bottom quarter, or fifth, will have a difficult time surviving academically. They are poorly qualified. What is the sense of putting those kids together? One group needs some fine-tuning of some very high-level writing skills and the other group barely knows what a subject and a verb are.

As I was talking to these two top students, it was obvious that they were totally angry. They kept saying that the PSU faculty members were gutless, that the faculty knew UNST was not a good program. They were basically asking me what was wrong with the faculty and why were we not fighting it. To me, it was one of a hundred fights. But, you know, because this was coming from these two very good students, I said, "This is serious. I wonder if there are other students who feel this way?" They said, "Oh, yeah, you guys are just not paying attention." So, I had to consider this possibility.

That quarter, I had two classes. In one I had about 40–45 kids, and I was pretty close to them. So, near the end of one lecture I gave them a blank piece of paper and told them to write down their feelings about UNST. Now, keep in mind that I was operating on the background assumption that there was an over 90 percent approval rating for the program. If you look at their answers, it is absolutely—well, you cannot avoid the issue. In the pile of responses you can see it in their writing. I almost fell out of my chair. Instead of 90 percent approval—well, there were some supportive answers, but there were more negative ones than positive ones. And some of the negative ones were absolutely hostile. I couldn't believe this, because as best I could tell I did not telegraph anything about my opinions.

So I did this again in the bigger course, which was Anatomy and Physiology. There are about 180 people in this course. I got back a lot more responses. Now, the responses were not quite as negative, but still it was more negative than positive. With a program that was supposed to have a 90 percent approval rating, I wondered, "What is going on? It doesn't make any sense." That same term, Gwen Shusterman had a big chemistry course and asked students in her class how they felt about UNST. There were almost 20 students there that were so angry that she sent some of them down to me to defuse the situation. They came to me asking what they could do. They were saying that they hated the program, "We just hate it."

Now, science students tend to be more focused than most. When they take the 15 UNST units that means that they cannot take some courses that they need in their freshman and sophomore year to keep their major sequence going. So, the UNST program just didn't reconcile with their needs. There was something really, really wrong here. I felt I just had to represent the students. I couldn't face myself in the mirror after speaking with those two students and getting the responses from the class. At that point, along with Gwen Shusterman and David Horowitz, a group of us decided to raise these issues with the administration.

I was truly surprised during that meeting. I have known some really good administrators that always want to know about the students. They would have thanked me for this kind of information. The response we got was exactly the opposite. I begged them to talk to the students and get serious about evaluating the program. They essentially said, "No, you guys are just way off base." We just kept getting told that, "Well, maybe there are some negative opinions of students in your program, but 90 percent like it." We had three or four meetings like that. They were even rude to us, saying that we had no right to talk about GE because we didn't participate. Even if they did listen to what we were saying, I am not so sure they really heard us.

I do remember one meeting where we were suggesting that there be alternatives to UNST or a way for students to test out of FRINQ courses. Their response was to say that they could let everybody out that scored particularly high on their SAT. I knew that not very many of our entering students were at that level. Even though they said that a lot would get out of UNST based on those criteria, I went and got the statistics to see if that was accurate. It turned out that about 25 students out of the whole entering class could be waived out based on that strict criterion. And I'll bet that half of those were in the Honors Program, and they were not required to take UNST anyway. So we are talking about somewhere around 13 people who could opt out of the program. What's the point? We have to be talking about something that impacts a reasonable number of students. We were just getting sandbagged right and left.

And so we got more and more vocal. A group of us got more people involved. And I think the administration started getting very nervous. Nobody would believe what we were saying. So we said, "Well hell, we know it is true because we see it in our classes." Gwen gets this cataclysmic anger response from her Chemistry students, and I get some of my very best students telling me I'm a chicken because I don't oppose UNST. We were particularly upset that they were telling us we had no idea about GE—and some of us had been involved in setting up the current system and were very fine teachers who received awards for quality teaching. So we resolved that if they didn't want to hear it directly, then we would go out and gather some data.

I contacted Barry Anderson, who is a cognitive psychologist specializing in decision-making, to help with the design of a survey that would let the administration know objectively and empirically what the students were thinking. In March of 2000 we went to the provost and a few others, including Dr. White, with a draft of the survey to get their support to conduct the study. Basically, we were dismissed and told that the questionnaire was totally biased and completely unacceptable. So a few others and I used our own money to distribute the survey to the students by buying advertisement space in the *Vanguard*. Responses were collected until May 12th. The following year, we did a similar survey of the faculty. The point of these surveys was to get the collected information analyzed and out into the open because, frankly, there really had never been any objective assessment of UNST. Once we got the surveys back, we compiled a results report. The packet was then distributed to the provost and the new vice provost. We also distributed the packet to the local newspapers—the *Willamette Weekly* and the *Oregonian*. We also contacted the *Chronicle of Higher Education* and they printed a story in the July 28, 2000, issue. Some students and faculty also wrote a number of *Vanguard* articles. So, basically, we made our point, and the message went out. (Crawshaw interview)

There were ten issues with UNST:

1. All entering freshmen not in the Honors College are required to enroll in the 15 credits of Freshman Inquiry. Their skills and backgrounds differ dramatically. This is true in writing, in mathematics, in life experiences, and in many other aspects of scholarly acumen. Some of these entering freshmen should be placed in basic skill building classes, while others should probably be allowed to move ahead to more advanced classes.

2. Students completing Freshman Inquiry do not necessarily become proficient in the basic skills.

3. Because so many credits are used up for the inquiry courses, key distribution courses are not required. Thus, neither the BA nor the BS has specific course requirements in History of Philosophy. The BA has no Mathematics requirement whatsoever, and the BS has no requirement in Fine Arts.

4. Most faculty are highly skilled in their areas of expertise, but are typically less adept in other academic areas.

5. The University Studies courses transfer poorly to many other schools.

6. Many faculty and students object to the moral imperatives that are embed-ded in some of the forced "volunteer" projects, and in certain of the class discussions.

7. On a more practical level, it is clear that the capstone and "volunteer" re-quirements were mandated before any clear evaluation or the ability of the university to produce such experiences was made.

8. The University Studies "system" has been applied in a rigid and coercive way and has not been successful at attracting voluntary faculty involve-ment. Departments that fail to meet University Studies "involvement quotas" are intimidated in various ways, such as by threats to withhold replacement appointments. Forced involvement with University Studies is written into many of the contracts of new faculty. When faculty object to any aspect of the "system," it is invariably assumed that they are "problem" faculty rather than acknowledging that the program itself might also have flaws.

9. Faculty and monetary resources are diverted away from upper division and graduate programs.

10. University Studies is an extremely expensive program, and many important sources of support have been overtly and covertly diverted to cover this en-deavor. The support for the peer mentors, for example, comes from scholar-ships that were previously utilized for undergraduate fellowships.[1]

According to materials provided in the survey results packet, there were a total of 248 returned questionnaires. Of those, 157 contained some positive comments and 214 contained some negative comments. There were 100 usable responses from students who had actually taken "one or more years of Univer-sity Studies in the proper sequence."[2] Sample sizes shrink further if they are broken down by the number of years students had participated in University Studies. Specifically, 57 respondents were reported to have taken only one year, 18 had taken two or three years, and only 16 respondents had participated in four complete years of the University Studies program. Nevertheless, the re-port's authors reached the following conclusions:

It is clear that University Studies is not for every student. Although a minority of students appear to find the program rewarding, there is strong indication of profound alienation among a substantial number of PSU students concerning general education reform. Certainly there is sufficient evidence of disaffection to begin a dialogue over continuing University Studies as an optional program and/or reducing its imprint on the undergraduate curriculum.[3]

The value of University Studies, since its inception, has been questioned by many university faculty members . . . the results cast considerable doubt on the claim that University Studies is a highly successful and widely popular program, justifying the great amount of university resources that have apparently been diverted to it (an analysis of cost is beyond the scope of this study). The results of this study place a heavy burden on the Portland State administration to submit University Studies to an independent, objective evaluation, without the flaws of either the present study or the "self-evaluations." The results also suggest that the administration and the faculty senate give serious consideration to allowing students the option of substituting the classic distribution requirement for University Studies.[4]

The same group of resisters conducted a similar survey of the faculty, which was distributed to all faculty members' mailboxes in the winter term of 2001. Again, there were a comparatively small number of respondents. With the fine arts and the professional schools heavily underrepresented, 99 surveys were analyzed. No information about whether the responding faculty member taught a University Studies course was collected. Again, the authors made recommendations:

1. Assign faculty members to teach only in areas in which they are trained.

2. Add a distribution requirement option to University Studies.

3. Implement placement tests for writing, mathematics, and computer skills.

4. Evaluate the cost-effectiveness of University Studies in comparison with the distribution model.

5. Look more deeply into differences of opinion regarding the Science and Quantitative Skills components of University Studies.

6. Look more deeply into differences of opinion regarding the University Studies teaching of Oral Communication.

7. Look more deeply into differences of opinion regarding ease of advising within the constraints imposed by University Studies.[5]

From the perspective of those leading the transformation, these surveys were more than a set of people looking for bad news: "It was a witch hunt, and it was a silly way of going about it" (Becker interview). One high-level administrator said that the survey was so flawed in both question construction and methodology that its results were suspect. He also noted that even if it had been well constructed he had never seen a questionnaire about general education that elicited primarily favorable comments from students (Terry Rhodes, personal communication, April 2003). Other champions also ignored the surveys, feeling that, to a large extent, the modest number of respondents was skewed toward students and faculty who had some kind of gripe with the program.

The whole scenario was very public. The student surveys were distributed via the campus student newspaper, and the survey sponsors distributed the results around the campus. Certainly they tried to publicly demonstrate that there were serious problems with UNST. The administration's position was that the whole study was flawed: there had been no consultation with the Human Subjects Office; the questions often had two or more action objects (asking two or three things in the same question); the sample was too small to be relevant; and using a student newspaper to distribute the survey and then relying on voluntary return was questionable research practice.

The administration's response to the whole series of events was pointed. Indeed, as indicated by Crawshaw, the new provost's first instinct upon hearing the concerns from the faculty was to meet with the group:

> After the six or eight faculty presented their grievances, I kind of had this gut reaction that I needed to know more about them and find out how they thought of themselves as teachers in particular. So, I asked them. Happily, I was very impressed by their commitment to teaching. After looking at the proposed questionnaire, I decided that I could not support it. It did not strike me as balanced and fair enough. I also felt that I had a responsibility to the whole university, and it really was just a thinly veiled effort to get rid of UNST. So I either told them that I wasn't going to do it [support the distribution of the survey], or I just kind of stalled. But of course, they went ahead and did it through the *Vanguard* anyway. (Tetreault interview)

After receiving a copy of the results packet, Provost Tetreault referred the documents to the director of Institutional Research and Planning (IRP) before making a public statement. She also had her new vice provost, Terrel Rhodes, meet with the group to rethink the survey. Rhodes appears to have gained favor with some of the survey's sponsors and continues to this day to be the point person for working with UNST critics. The IRP director strengthened the argument for ignoring the whole survey by criticizing it as flawed research. Plainly put by the UNST program director appointed to succeed White:

> If you look at the surveys, they are so poorly written that it is a travesty of scholarship. This group of faculty did it because they really do care about students, but what they did was so poorly conceived that it is scary in a way. It is weird what people do when they decide to resist something. (Patton interview)

A number of faculty members felt strongly enough that they entered the fray by writing opinion pieces published in the *Vanguard* criticizing the report and supporting UNST. Others said directly to the resisters, "You are not credible" (Latiolais interview) and then refused to listen to them. Indeed, for the most part the report was ignored. To give the resisters the last word in the case, we return to Larry Crawshaw's passionate point of view:

> We still have not gotten what we would consider an honest, rational kind of a dialogue between the critics and either the people running UNST or the administration of the University. It is the usual, "just suppress or ignore us, and hope we will go away." Well, we have not gone away. We have sort of gone quiescent. We all have work to do. My science was not getting done and nothing was happening, so I just said, "Screw it." If somebody else is not willing to pick up the ball on this, then I am not going to ruin my career over it. I just don't have time for it anymore. We got the *Chronicle* article out. We made our point.
>
> Yeah, they have the power. It is like we are in jail. We are not going to yell and scream and bang our heads on the bar and demand a revolt. We made the information known. The sad thing is that all around the country UNST is seen a model system that should be emulated. But in fact, it should be evaluated. Certain parts of it are good, but I don't think they have prevailed. In the long term, you have to have people's hearts. And I don't think they have people's hearts at this point. They are kind of like an occupying force. Just like Russia— they had East Germany, they had Yugoslavia, they had Poland, but they did not prevail.
>
> We have made our point. Sooner or later, I think it is going to collapse. It is expensive and many students and faculty don't like it. If you look at the original design, it was to be taught by regular tenure-track faculty. I am willing to put down 50 bucks right now that you cannot find more than three people who are normal tenure-track faculty in that program. They have to essentially bring in special faculty. They are good, hard-working people, and they are doing a really

difficult job, and I don't want to criticize any of them. But they are extremely expensive. This is a huge defeat. UNST faculty members are almost all two-year fixed-term adjunct faculty, and there are a few that they brought in for that program and to whom they gave tenure. But just normal faculty, people like me—there are zero, or perhaps one or two max, who are in the program.

The UNST people are going to eventually have to transform the program into something that is okay. Right now, it is not okay. The good students that come here don't want 15 units of that stuff. Some do, but a lot don't. So, why are we forcing them to do it then? I really believe that if they make it optional, the consumers will vote with their feet and UNST will wither and die.. . . . I do think we did more than make a statement. I think we have nailed it. It is kind of like a bull that has been stabbed. Like the matador, we have our back to the bull now and the bull is walking around trying to gore things, but it is basically going to go down. It has been fatally wounded. (Crawshaw interview)

PSU Case 3: Findings

Again in this case we see that, even though champions were trying to include everyone, the first inclination of the people against UNST was to decline to participate in the planning process. The primary form of resistance in this case, however, was the use of student surveys to build a case against UNST. In the end, students were leveraged in two primary ways to achieve that end. First, the case that a survey was needed was buttressed by reports of student frustration and negative feedback about UNST. Second, the survey instrument was privately funded by these faculty members and then administered and reported via the student newspaper. To generate more concern about the program, the results were also shared with the local and national print media as well. No new approaches were used by the administration in this case to engage and surmount resistance. Briefly, to review, first, the champions voluntarily met with the resisters and listened to their complaints; next, after choosing not to sponsor the survey, they criticized its methodology and ignored the results.

Forms of Engaging Resistance Not Illustrated in the PSU Cases

As mentioned earlier, the findings in this chapter are based on all cases of resistance, not just the three discussed. While all forms of resistance supported by the data were illustrated in the cases, not all approaches to engagement were. Unlike at Olivet College, at PSU no one was encouraged to leave the institution because of their resistance to the UNST plan. Only one person reported being removed from a post. Thus the data do not support the inclusion of firing or removal as an approach to surmounting resistance in this section.

Only two additional approaches not apparent in the three above cases need be reported in this section. One, early on, Provost Reardon was able to leverage grant monies to provide professional development opportunities as a way of gaining favor with the faculty. Two, the whole transformation at PSU was built on fostering and maintaining relationships among and between champions and the rank-and-file faculty.

Notes

1. Letter from Larry Crawshaw titled "An Explanation of my involvement with the University Studies Issue," no date.

2. Barry F. Anderson and Lee Haggerty (June 2000), "An Evaluation of Portland State University's University Studies Program," Appendix F of the survey results packet, p. 2.

3. Letter from David Horowitz, May 26, 2000, citing Horowitz's own "evaluation of the open-ended questions on the student questionnaire," May 22, 2000.

4. Appendix F of the survey results packet authored by Barry Anderson and Lee Haggerty, June 2000, p. 6.

5. Appendix in the packet titled "Seven Recommendations for the Faculty Survey on University Studies," by Barry Anderson, Larry Crawshaw, Stanley Hillman, and Ansel Johnson, pp. 1–4.

6 Engaging Resistance

Against the backdrop of the cases depicted in Chapter 5, the background stories offered in Chapters 1 and 3, and the prior conversation about the nature of resistance in Chapter 4, this chapter moves to a discussion of the findings and the formulation of a theoretical foundation for understanding the symbiotic relationship between resisters and champions. From the transformation experiences at Olivet College and Portland State University, it is possible to identify patterns of interactivity between champion and resister behaviors. These insights form the basis of a new theoretical framework for explaining how ordinary people can make transformation happen.

This new grounded theoretical model for engaging resistance has implications for both practitioners and scholars. More specifically, scholars should find the model useful for developing studies that further explain engagement and resistance behaviors, particularly in the quantitative realm. Practitioners may find the engagement model a useful lens through which to view reality as it unfolds, and also as a planning device for ensuring a more inclusive and positive change process.

The Comparative Analysis

Despite the obvious differences between Olivet College and Portland State University (e.g., size, location, types of students enrolled, etc.), the institutional sagas are remarkably similar, a fact that makes the comparative analysis more intriguing. Two institutional commonalties establish a context for the transformations and cases of resistance. Both schools were embroiled in crises that eventually led to dire fiscal concerns on the part of the respective boards and predicated the push for a change in leadership at the executive level. Both of the newly appointed presidents believed that the very existence of their institutions was threatened.

To be sure, the transformation narratives support the notion that transformation is facilitated when institutional actors are faced with a crisis, such as the fiscal ones at these institutions, although it is difficult to conclude that a crisis is a prerequisite for transformation. Organizational crisis does, however, amplify the readiness and sense of urgency to transform. At Olivet, at the very least, the racial incident and the departure of students, combined with the dire fiscal situation fueled by declining enrollment, fanned the flames of urgency. The crisis at Portland State was triggered in part by the passage of a state proposition that incrementally reduced the state tax base for funding public higher education. Enrollment had already dropped, and once again, state actors were working to divide and dole out various portions of PSU to other state schools.

Although today the Olivet and PSU programs are different from each other, before the transformations both institutions offered a traditional general education curriculum. Champions at both institutions targeted the components of the undergraduate curriculum for transformation and expected that an academic solution could be leveraged to fix cultural, behavioral, and economic issues as well as troubling curricular problems. Why the leaders at both institutions elected to pursue an academic solution to this set of circumstances remains a question. Perhaps it had to do with what is within the control of the faculty and staff. It could be that the champions were capitalizing on the existing conditions in order to make changes they had long been hoping for.

The planning phases at both Olivet and Portland State took just under two years to complete—from idea germination to majority approval by both faculties. It is notable that no one mentioned the speed with which the planning phases took place as a reason to resist transformation. Even so, the planning phase is where both schools' leaders began to employ successful engagement approaches. Because both planning processes were conducted outside of the usual faculty governance rubrics established by their faculty senates, the development of proposals and initiatives could proceed relatively smoothly and quickly. This is not to say that the leadership at both institutions intentionally avoided the faculty, as the planning teams were made up exclusively of faculty members, both volunteers and invitees. As planning progressed, these teams held open meetings to solicit feedback and gather input to build stronger proposals. Finally, by effectively using political and diplomatic approaches (e.g., coalition building, coercion, counterarguments, reasoning with resisters, relationship building, and consensus building) champions were able to mitigate resistance, bolster support, and gain the approval of the faculty senates for their respective transformation plans.

Although the transformation initiatives were well developed academically over time, it is striking that both sets of champions made no plans for a supportive and necessary administrative infrastructure. At the point when Olivet and Portland State faculty were asked to support the respective plans, the administrative details did not yet exist, and faculty were asked to trust the designers to complete those details once the plans had been approved. The faculties did so, but the ensuing dynamics may have led to more resistance in the long run. As a direct source of resistance caused by legitimate concern and uncertainty about the initiatives, the intentional omission of administrative infrastructure is most obvious in PSU Case 2: Attacking the Champion—particularly in the resulting dynamics among and between the dean of the College of Liberal Arts and Sciences, the provost, and the director of University Studies. However, it is difficult to stipulate from the data gathered which forms of resistance the lack of administrative plans may have caused.

Resistance

The comparative analysis of the six individual case studies empirically justifies the identification of only ten primary forms of resistance perpetrated by individuals or groups of stakeholders (see Exhibit 7) (though the case studies themselves revealed several others). They ranged from latent to extremely intense.

Like physical inertia, resistance to organizational transformation is dormant until some transformative action is set in motion. Extending the analogy, there is nothing to resist until the change (the virus or bacterium) is introduced to the organizational corpus. The resisters lie in wait for the invasive change. Latent resistance is passive, beginning with nonparticipation in planning or execution (R6) or voicing disagreement to allies (R9) rather than directly to the transformation leadership. Resistance is apparent and becomes more active as transformation plans are concretized and come closer to approval, and as champions move into the initiation phase. Certainly, as plans become more visible and imminent, resisters have something to point at and target. For example, at both institutions, it was excruciatingly difficult to know how much general education would cost to deliver. When the plans were presented, the costs became obvious. As such, when there was finally a plan to resist, resisters at Olivet and PSU tried to build a case against them (R2), offer alternatives (R7), disagree vocally (R9), and vote in opposition (R10) to the plans and initiatives. At the more extreme end of the intensity spectrum, individual champions were attacked (R1); media outlets were sought out (R3) to make issues public and "air dirty laundry." At times, students were used as pawns (R4) because resisters believed students were able to make powerful arguments to champions that they could not.

Eventually, the intensity of the resistance behavior for some becomes personal and it is impossible to divorce the emotive elements from the situation. Problematically, at the extreme level of intensity, emotionally charged perception often clouds the truth or is substituted as fact. At this point, resisters may sabotage elements of an initiative (R8), and eventually may leave a post or the institution completely (R5).

The intensity of resistance behavior typically matches the force of the initiatives and the strength of champion behavior, but this is not always the case. Sometimes resisters escalate the intensity of resistance beyond the level of action taken by change champions. The reverse can be true as well: champion behavior can exceed the force necessary to surmount the resistance. For example, some interviewees reported that the use of coercive approaches by champions caused them to resist more strongly.

From the comparative analysis and the discussion in Chapter 4, we know that there are nine primary reasons why people resisted transformation at Olivet and PSU. At a micro-behavioral level, there are probably as many other reasons to resist as there are people working in an organization. Any one source or cause could motivate a person to resist, but more typically, it was a combination of the following that pushed people to act. To review:

1. *The institutional culture inherited from prior administrations* had established patterns of behavior among campus stakeholders that led to a propensity for resistance. A good example of this is the "devil's bargain" struck with the Olivet faculty by the president before the transformation, in which faculty agreed to stay out of college governance in exchange for autonomy in their own departments. As a result, many faculty members grew to mistrust most administrators.

2. Reluctance to take on *new or additional work.* A transformation usually requires rank-and-file members of an organization to do new things or conduct business differently. Particularly on a college campus, highly trained faculty members may feel that transformation threatens their

expertise. They may balk at taking on additional work or learning new ways of working that transformation implies, particularly if the structures that reward old ways remain intact after the change.

3. *Protect the status quo.* The way that one is trained to work becomes the preferred practice. Practice leads to a sense of expertise that establishes a comfort zone within which organizational actors can easily navigate through the day. The sense that one has of being good or excelling at one's job also keeps people working with a method or pedagogy. Given the comfort organizational members have with current practice, resistance often stems from a desire to protect the status quo.

4. *Implication that the current system is broken.* When champions suggest that there is a need to transform, the people who worked hard to establish that system may resent the implication that it needs fixing. They may also fear that they will be perceived as disruptive or unnecessary components of a "new" status quo.

5. *Culture clash.* Transformation, by definition, cuts the very fabric of the institution, snipping the cultural fibers of tradition. Because these transformations threatened the academic freedom of some faculty, and asked faculty to teach outside their areas of expertise, resistance resulted from a clash of academic cultures. This was particularly true for people working in disciplines, such as the hard sciences, that did not mesh well with the new practice models.

6. *Fear.* Because transformation threatens the status quo at many different levels, fear about the initiatives also generates resistance. Reasons for fear range from not understanding the plans to uncertainty about new leaders. Surprisingly, threat of job loss in these cases was less a source of fear than the literature would have us believe. This may be because most of the faculty on these campuses held tenure, which does not exist in other industries.

7. *Legitimate concerns.* Many faculty members were justifiably worried about the fiscal impact of the proposed new programs, given the budget situations facing both organizations.

8. *Hypocritical or unfair champion behavior.* Resisters also stipulated that they simply had to act against the plans because they believed the behavior of the change champions was hypocritical, unfair, or bordering

on illegal. Regardless of intent, champion behavior can be perceived as negative. Resisters occasionally misperceive the well-intentioned actions of champions as unfair or underhanded. Budgeting and personnel decisions are frequent sources of this type of misperception. The burden lies with the champion to walk on the right side of a thin ethical line.

9. *Damaged relationships and personality clashes.* Because organizations are made up of people, personal beliefs and personalities come into play in all transformations. When relationships are damaged and personalities clash, resistance is a natural result. Organizational transformation always involves power dynamics, such as the interplay between the CLAS dean at PSU, the provost, and the UNST director. People may resist transformation simply because they do not like the champion. When power dynamics revolve around the redistribution of resources and funds, there are winners and losers. Feelings get hurt. Allies and enemies are created. Occasionally, battle lines are drawn.

It is important to note that the vast majority of the people on both campuses either supported or went along with the proposed initiatives. Only a small minority showed high levels of resistance. At both institutions, faculty members in the hard sciences perpetrated the more intense forms of resistance.

Much of the resistance that targeted the change processes at Olivet and Portland State took the form of complaints (R9) that the process was not inclusive. And most of the complaints began after the planning phases were concluded and after the programs were approved. But they used their earlier nonparticipation (R6) to justify their further nonparticipation in the new programs ("If I didn't help plan it, then I am not going to help execute it"). Resistance that targeted the products of the initiative at times stemmed from fear or legitimate concerns. However, much of the resistance was directed at protecting the status quo and balking at new and more work. Resistance aimed at the initiatives' champions was almost always more intense. As the champions were attacked (R1), they often felt the need to lash back, escalating the intensity. In all, there was only one instance in which resistance proved successful in stopping a small portion of the initiatives. This happened during the final stages of the planning process at Olivet College, when opposition to the Engaged Curriculum (the block plan) was so strong and convincingly argued that the administration dropped that portion of the initiative.

Engagement

Thirteen approaches used by change champions to successfully engage and surmount resistance are summarized in Exhibit 8. (Although champions used other approaches as well, these 13 are the ones that could be empirically validated.)

The complex mix of stakeholders (champions, supporters, resisters, and bystanders), initiatives, and intricate organizational contexts and cultures sets a complicated stage on which to make transformation happen. Perhaps swift planning helps to mitigate resistance, but interviewees did not mention this as an approach or strategy for doing so, only that the forces driving their transformations

Engagement Behavior	Description
A1. Coalition building	Using diplomatic skills to build a broad base of support among a diverse group of stakeholders so that they might convince others to also support the initiatives.
A2. Coercion	Using threats or pressuring people to support initiatives or to gain cooperation.
A3. Presenting counterarguments	Swaying the opinion of others by presenting or defending the transformation initiatives when challenged during meetings.
A4. Deal making	Offering something in exchange for support or cooperation.
A5. Ignoring resistance	Ignoring resisters or not responding to resistance behavior.
A6. Encouraging resisters to leave	Negotiating the departure of resisters from the institution or from their capacity or affiliation with the initiative, or terminating their employment outright.
A7. Hiring supportive individuals	Filling vacancies or newly created positions with individuals who understand and are willing to perform in accordance with the transformation initiatives.
A8. Including others in the planning	Proactively opening participant and leadership roles to diverse stakeholders through invitation or appointment, or by encouraging them to volunteer.
A9. Listening to resisters	Meeting with resisters to hear complaints, grievances, or critical statements.
A10. Reasoning with resisters	Interacting with individuals or small groups of individuals to sway their opinions.
A11. Building relationships	Cultivating and using personal and professional relationships with individuals to build allegiance to the initiatives.
A12. Rewarding constructive actions	Rewarding individuals or departments for positive contributions.
A13. Working toward consensus	Striving for the largest consensus possible before voting, implementing, or installing a new element of the plan.

Exhibit 8. Approaches to engaging resistance.

necessitated quick and decisive action. Indeed, engaging resistance is considerably more difficult than simply anticipating the types of resistance one might experience and then matching it with an appropriate engagement approach.

The comparative analysis of the data provides more generally applicable lessons about transformation and how to engage and surmount resistance. Before examining how ordinary people work to mitigate resistance, some intermediate questions can be asked. Specifically, how do champions know when they are facing real resistance rather than some other type of behavior? Even more specifically, how do we know when faculty members voicing concern (R10) about a particular initiative have crossed the line from honest feedback to resisting? Given the daily interaction champions have with supporters, resisters, and bystanders, how do champions decide which resister behavior to address? In other words, after making sense of and identifying a behavior that is one among many responses to change, what is the rationale for identifying it as "resistance" and engaging it, or not?

Making Sense of Resistance Behavior

From the analysis, there appears to be nothing scientific about making sense of the behavior one experiences while initiating transformation. In the views of my respondents, subjective interpretation and perception of individual and group behavior and intuition-based decision-making make it "way more art than science and every time a gamble" (Rutledge interview). There is "[no] quantitative measure that you can get. It is a feeling that you have" about the organization (Rabineau interview). Reactions to resistance are more visceral than mindful, and "what it does to you in your gut is largely a product of the kinds of experiences you have had" (Bassis interview). Championing change may exacerbate a person's ability to make sense of responses to change efforts, since the changer is naturally biased toward his own initiatives. The change champions at Olivet and PSU may have felt their initiatives were "the right thing to do and if someone doesn't agree with it then, obviously," they were the ones who were wrong (Latiolais interview).

Interestingly, champions at both institutions stipulate that they did not anticipate or conduct any meetings to discuss strategies for dealing with potential resisters or resistance. Given the emphasis on such strategy planning in the literature, it is difficult to believe that such a session would not be beneficial, and therefore not a necessary part of a transformation process. However, the nature of the transformations at both institutions left little time for such conversation, relegating much of the engagement of resisters and resistance to an ad hoc strategy. The lack of planning for resistance may also have been an artifact of the leadership style of the champions at these institutions Michael Bassis hints at this:

> I am not sure I was really fully prepared for how heavy the load at Olivet would be. There was so much to do that I was going to just roll up my sleeves and do it. I didn't have time to think everything through, and for the most part in the first six to eight weeks I was operating pretty much on instinct. I wasn't very systematic in thinking about or planning for that [resistance]. I didn't have the luxury of being able to stop and make a plan. I just did it all on instinct. Which was the way that I did most everything that first year. I didn't have the luxury of making any kinds of mistakes. If I made any kind of decent sized mistake, the institution was going to disappear. And that is really scary stuff. And the mistakes I made, I think, were not serious enough to derail anything, but I could have very easily made a very big one. (Bassis interview)

Rationale for Engagement

Because making sense of the responses to change efforts and interpreting resistance behavior is largely intuitive, and not all resistance is bad, choosing an engagement approach can be challenging. Say, for example, an English professor voices disapproval (R9) about an initiative, having spotted a major flaw in the proposal. Another person, the campus curmudgeon, also expresses disapproval of the same initiative. Should both be handled the same way? Something like this happened at both Olivet and PSU. The first resister was attempting to provide constructive resistance. The second may have been as well, but because of his previous behavior his objection was not perceived as constructive and was dismissed when it actually might have been wiser to embrace the curmudgeon. Regardless of how one feels about a person or the delivery, resistance can alert champions to problems that, when fixed, help produce a better product. Prejudging the quality of the latter person's resistance, or ignoring it (A5) altogether, could lead to stronger or more caustic resistance. Even the campus or company curmudgeon may have a valid point now and again.

The data suggest that the decision to engage resistance rests on the champion's subjective assessment of the source, focus, and intensity of the behavior, and on his or her past experiences with the individual or group doing the resisting. Selecting an engagement approach requires an intuitive reading of the organization based on the champion's familiarity with the people working in it. "It has to do with the degree that you have a real sense of the institution. You need to sort of do a read of the place, and say, 'is this [behavior] something that could go unresponded to?' But I don't think that I could tell you a hard and fast way to figure that out" (Reardon interview). Another champion reveals, "I won't pretend that I had a rational set of criteria or anything else" (White interview). There is a large emotional component to these decisions often linked to whether a champion felt she or he had both the time and the energy to deal with a particular individual or set of resisters. One former senate president reports:

> I was constantly moving around campus, talking to different people. If I felt like someone was giving positive, supportive comments, then I didn't waste my time. I didn't spend a lot of time talking to people who were going to ride along with it [the transformation] unless they had some kind of political clout that I thought I could use[A1].... If I felt like they were sort of quiet, mid-range, not very vocal, not very involved people, all I cared about was that we had their support and we moved on. It sounds more calculating than it is, but I am sure this was how my mind was working at the time. I look for where I think there will be glitches in the system, and go and see if I can smooth those out in advance of the vote or whatever is coming [A10].

The data also suggest that there was less opportunity to engage resisters than there was to react to events as they unfolded. Reactions to resistance are more improvisational and less systematic or rational than literature-based theory would have us believe (see, e.g., Weick, 2009). That is, a champion acts. This action produces a reaction—a response to change—interpreted as resistance of some kind, which can be deciphered or understood as positive and supportive, neutral, or negative (read: damaging to the transformation efforts). This reaction affects the next move by the champion, and the cycle continues.

Not every resistance behavior warrants engagement. In fact, ignoring people can be a successful approach (A5). When extreme resisters say, "I think it is wrong and there is no way in hell I will do it, and there is no way you can change my mind," then engaging them is simply a waste of time (Noyes interview). One faculty member expressed the caveat that "we need to keep the door open so that when their risk aversion is overcome, they can still jump in. But we should also always be willing and be happy to help those who are not with us to find a new job"[A9] (Homer interview).

In the main, the bulk of engagement energy early on at both organizations was focused on changing the minds of those who were "on the fence" about the transformation. Rather than addressing every instance of resistance, or subjecting themselves to the harsh criticism of the most outspoken critics, the champions found it most productive to engage and convince those who were undecided (A10). One good example was the use by one champion of the campus phonebooks to track opinion and gauge where to act next.

> The phonebooks are nothing fancy. That was just my way to try to be a little scientific about the resistance and classify people based on where you think people are going to vote—yes, no, question mark, maybe. So, I would go through these phonebooks with all of the votes on the vision [in mind], all of the elements of the Olivet plan, the design criteria, the learning outcomes, the alcohol policy and . . . label people. And if you were going to vote no, I was going to be talking to you [A10]. And I would be straight up. I would say, Aaron, you know what we are doing here, and here is why I think we need your support. . . . Now, I am not going to tell you what to do, but I am going to actually tell you that I think you should support this. And if they would give me some positive feedback, maybe I would switch it from question mark to a yes, or from a no to a question mark or a yes. And I would do that constantly. (D. Tuski interview)

No matter how intuitive and subjective the decision-making process, the data suggest two hard-and-fast rules by which champions acted quickly to engage resistance. Rule one: If the resistance behavior is going to either hurt the organization or derail the process, it must be addressed: "If people who have the votes are resisting you, or if there is someone at the position of dean or provost that is powerful enough to stop or block you, then you have got to pay attention to them" (Farr interview). Rule two: If resisters involve students (or customers in a business setting) as pawns (R4), then the champions must engage them in response. At both institutions, "Students would say, 'I was talking to a particular professor about how bad it [some aspect of the plan] was.' Then we knew we had to really take control before it got out of hand. That is when we would go to the professor and say, 'you have to simply come to us and complain, you can't engage students in those kinds of conversations. It is just unfair.'" (Rabineau interview). The new provost at PSU felt so strongly about this that she tried to stop the behavior by publicly denouncing it.

Toward a New Model for Engaging Resistance

To this point, I have been discussing the characteristics of resistance and engagement behaviors separately. Before we move to map the resistance and engagement behaviors as they interact over time, it is appropriate to review what engaging resistance means. Then I will clarify the relationships between the different engagement approaches and forms of resistance as they were used to successfully engage and surmount resistance behavior. The final task is to identify any emerging patterns that suggest a new theory for engaging and surmounting resistance during organizational transformation.

A Working Definition of "Engaging Resistance"

Originally, the term "engaging resistance" was coined to be neutral about the valence (positive, neutral, or negative) of champion and resister behavior. While neutrality is a part of good research design, a complete definition of "engaging resistance" must involve the direction of the behavior. Bear in mind that any one behavior can be perceived as positive and negative simultaneously by different people within the same organization. Because this study focuses on people who initiate transformation, a refinement of the definition hinges on the champion's perspective. While both champion and resister behavior can be negative, neutral, or positive, adding the qualifier "successfully" to the phrase implies a bearing, mainly toward action by the champion, that reduces or mitigates negative resister behavior. Specifically, *successfully engaging resistance* means to increase the positive participation in, support for, or mitigation of the damaging effect of resisters on transformation initiatives.

Successfully Engaging and Surmounting Resistance

Change champions successfully surmount resistance within their organizations mainly in an ad hoc fashion, based on their intuitive sense of the resister behavior they experience. Indeed, it is the continual sensemaking of the possible and actual resistance sources and focuses, coupled with an interpretation of the intensity and direction of resister behavior, that moves champions to act. The mezzo- and macro-levels of analysis reveal specific patterns of interactivity between resistance and engagement that champions use to surmount impediments to organizational transformation. From these patterns, one may gather which engagement approaches are the most useful and when to use them.

Exhibit 9 shows which of the 13 approaches to engaging resistance succeeded in surmounting each of the ten forms of resistance. Not every approach was used to counter every form of resistance, but each approach successfully

Forms of Resistance

Engagement Approaches	R6. Not participating	R9. Voicing disagreement	R7. Offering contrary alternatives	R2. Building a case against	R10. Voting in opposition	R3. Criticizing in the media	R4. Using students as pawns	R1. Attacking champions	R8. Sabotaging	R5. Leaving a post or the institution
A8. Including others in the planning	**S**	S	S	S	S					
A9. Listening to resisters	S	**S**	S	S	S	S				
A1. Coalition building		S	S		**S**					
A3. Presenting counter-arguments		S		**S**	S	S		S		
A4. Deal making	**S**									
A10. Reasoning with resisters	S	S	**S**	S	S		S	S		
A11. Building relationships	S	S	S	S	**S**					
A12. Rewarding constructive actions	**S**	S								
A13. Working toward consensus		**S**	S	S						
A7. Hiring supportive individuals	**S**	**S**								S
A5. Ignoring resistance	S	S	S	S		**S**		S		
A2. Coercion							**S**		S	
A6. Encouraging resisters to leave							S	S	**S**	

Notes: S = indicates that an approach was successful in engaging and surmounting resistance. **S** indicates that an approach was the most strategically successful in surmounting resistance.

Exhibit 9. Successful approaches to engaging resistance.

mitigated one or more forms of resistance to differing degrees. This is not to say that these approaches eliminated resistance altogether. And in fact, elimination of all resistance should not be the ultimate goal when it comes to instigating organizational change or transformation. What we know is that a variety of engagement strategies work in combination to ameliorate resister behaviors such that champions were able to successfully implement the transformations.

Although the change champions did not explicitly devise a strategy to engage possible resistance, in hindsight two approaches they considered to be good planning practices also turned out to be effective proactive engagement strategies. The most effective was including a wide array of stakeholders in the planning (A8). The data indicate that involving a diverse set of individuals in transformation planning results in a stronger proposal, as well as increased participation in and acceptance of it. The second proactive approach was allowing for numerous opportunities to provide feedback during planning and listening to criticism (A9), whether it resulted in alterations to the plans or not. Giving people a forum to speak their minds and provide feedback, when combined with an inclusive planning process, diminishes the tendency for a resister to voice disagreement with the process (R9).

Although a small number of faculty members at Portland State and Olivet stipulated that a noninclusive process was one reason for their resistance, the processes were sufficiently open that the champions had little trouble refuting that argument (A3) and could justify ignoring certain resisters (A5) if they persisted. Faculty were provided with numerous opportunities to be a part of the planning process and offer feedback and input; if they did not volunteer, speak up, or contribute in any way, then they effectively abdicated their right to resist.

A number of the approaches applied during the planning and pre-approval phases could be characterized as diplomatic or politically astute strategies for engagement. Building consensus (A13), relationships (A11), and coalitions (A1), reasoning with individuals (A10), making deals (A4), and presenting counterarguments (A3) are all strategies that facilitated the approval of initiatives at Olivet and Portland State. It is difficult to conclude from the data whether these were proactive or reactive measures because they were often executed in the daily endeavor to build viable solutions acceptable to a majority of campus stakeholders. Even so, the comparative analysis suggests the following. Coalition building (A1) was primarily effective in shrinking the number of opposition votes (R10) on both campuses. On many occasions, champions were able to sway opinions by presenting counterarguments (A3) as resisters were building cases against particular initiatives (R2). Deal making (A4) and rewarding people and departments for constructive actions (A12) were primarily effective at increasing participation (R6) in initiative development and plan rollout. Working toward consensus (A13) gave those who voiced disagreement (R9) an opportunity to share their opinions and also convinced some to support the initiatives.

Resistance was not completely arrested once a majority of the faculty had approved the plans. Further engagement was required to work through continuing and other forms of resistance perpetrated by a smaller number of individuals. After the plans had been approved, only those most opposed to them continued to resist. After approval, the strongest resisters attacked the champions (R1), criticized the plans in the media (R3), recruited students to the cause (R4), and sabotaged the transformations (R8); and a small number of resisters left their posts or the institution altogether (R5).

As the intensity of resister behavior increases, champion engagement approaches change as well. The primary approaches used after plans had been approved were reactionary rather than proactive, save one—hiring supportive individuals (A7). Bringing people on board who are already in line with the transformation is the most neutral approach to surmounting resistance. Nevertheless, hiring new individuals, such as the young faculty at PSU, boosted participation in the new initiatives. Less neutral engagement responses involved coercive tactics (A2) such as pressuring faculty to teach particular material and encouraging faculty to leave their positions or the institution (A6). If all of those approaches failed and resisters still remained, champions often just ignored them (A5). This strategy was used most successfully in dealing with people who used the media to criticize the initiatives. Coercion (A2), although difficult to make work, seemed to be best applied to stop people who were using students as pawns (R4). And only a small number of individuals were encouraged to leave the organization or asked to step down from a post (A6) (those who sabotaged the transformations at Olivet College).

A New Model for Engaging Resistance

The forms of resistance and engagement approaches displayed in Exhibit 9 show patterns that suggest the beginnings of a new model for understanding one segment of the transformation process. Exhibit 9 identifies the most successful approaches to mitigating particular forms of resistance.

In general, each engagement approach was most successfully deployed during a specific period of the transformation planning and initiation phases.

This does not mean that individual approaches could not also work at other times. However, each engagement approach seemed to work best in response to certain categories of resistance at specific times (identified in Exhibit 10 as phases 1, 2, and 3). The curve reflects the fluctuating level of resistance intensity over time, from latent to extreme. Bear in mind that because the foundation for this model is a qualitative study, there is no calculus that pertains to the slope of the curve. It is meant as a visual representation. As champions successfully engage and surmount resistance, the number of resisters decreases over the duration of a transformation from the planning phase (Phase 1), to the push for approval (Phase 2), through implementation rollout and beyond (Phase 3).

Phase 1: Planning

During Phase 1 the most successful approaches to engaging resistance can be called "good planning practice." They are a fundamental, proactive part of achieving a transformation. The planning phase continues until plans have been written down but are not yet approved. The number of resisters during

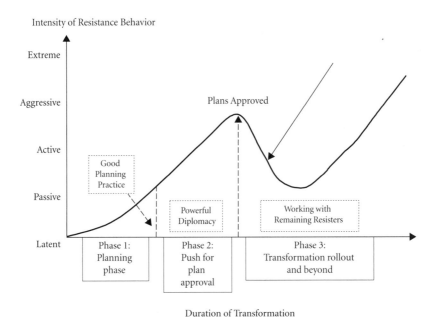

Exhibit 10. A model for engaging resistance through three phases. The dashed vertical lines represent the point when each phase is complete and the plans are put in writing.

this time period is the greatest. Resistance behavior moves from latency to its least intense passive and active forms, occurring mainly as nonparticipation (R6), voicing disagreement (R9) and people offering contrary alternatives (R7). Including others in the planning (A8) and listening to resisters (A9) are the primary strategies used to surmount resistance during this phase.

Because it is difficult for champions to differentiate the people who are honestly critiquing their efforts from those who are resisting for other reasons, a more inclusive approach to planning may be more time-consuming but can save work later by appeasing a substantial number of resisters (Axelrod, 2002). Because transformation plans evolve, confusion and ambivalence among those not directly involved in the planning are common sources of resistance. The ambiguity of unsettled plans threatens the status quo and may strike fear among some resisters; the low levels of resistance intensity are a cause for concern, but do not stir great levels of angst among champions. Wise and practiced champions know that recognizing and embracing positive resistance is a means of improving their overall effort.

Phase 2: Push for Plan Approval

During Phase 2, "powerful diplomacy" is the most successful approach to convincing others in an organization that transformation is desirable and surmounting resistance. Push for plan approval begins after concrete plans have been drafted (represented by the first dashed line under the curve) and ends after official permission to initiate the plans is granted (represented by the second dashed line under the curve). Because some resisters were involved in the design process or felt that they were listened to during Phase 1, the number of resisters shrinks and is smaller in Phase 2. But resistance behaviors in Phase 2 become more active and intense, and they peak whenever any kind of vote is taken. Resistance during this period is aimed primarily at the process and the plans and takes the form of nonparticipation (R6), voicing disagreement (R9), offering contrary alternatives (R7), building a case against (R2), and voting against the initiatives (R10). The diplomatic efforts used to build support among resisters include the coalition building (A1) influencing opinion and votes, making counterarguments (A3), deal making (A4), reasoning (A10), relationship building (A11) with individual resisters, rewarding people for positive actions (A12), and working diligently toward the largest consensus (A13).

During this portion of a transformation process, plans become more tangible and are a more conspicuous target for resistance than the ideas or suggestions for plans in Phase 1. Because plans have not received the green light, resisters believe there is still a chance to stop the whole process. The stakes are high for both those leading and those resisting the transformation. Because the whole organization has yet to commit to the plans, the intensity of the tussle is amplified. Resisters act according to their strength, the bandwidth for action, and their commitment to protecting the status quo. As it becomes apparent that earlier resistance efforts had no effect, small numbers of resisters escalate the intensity of the active forms of resistance. They also pursue more aggressive behaviors such as critiquing plans in the media (R3), using students (customers) as pawns (R4) and attacking champions outright (R1). Champions address these more aggressive forms of resistance during Phase 2, primarily by using diplomatic approaches to win over those on the fence, thus increasing the critical mass of support for the initiatives.

Some are won over, but inevitably the intensity of resistance and level of aggressiveness escalates among a small number of others.

Phase 3: Rollout and Beyond

During Phase 3 the number of resisters declines precipitously, and the primary engagement approach is "working with remaining resisters." The period begins just after the plans receive official approval and encompasses the rollout and the implementation of the plan. Although number of individuals still resisting in this period is small, they require a substantial amount of attention and emotional energy because their tactics tend to be more caustic and negative, including: criticizing in the media (R3), using students (customers) as pawns (R4), attacking champions (R1), leaving a post or the institution (R5), and sabotaging the efforts of the champions (R8). The more successful approaches in dealing with these forms of resistance during Phase 3, besides hiring supportive individuals (A7), are also caustic and can be perceived by resisters as negative. Champions can match or surpasses the aggressiveness of and intensity of the resistance by ignoring (A5), coercing (A2), or encouraging resisters to leave a position or to leave the organization altogether (A6).

As champions move from transformation planning to implementation, resisters in this phase realize that the plan has received approval from a majority of the voting members. Outside of the academy, by this time the efforts of the champions may be perceived as a fait acompli, particularly if the transformation has been ratified by a company's board and endorsed by its executive officers. The vast majority of resisters up to this point have capitulated for four primary reasons. They may believe: (1) in following the lead of a democratic voting process or the direction of corporate leadership; (2) that the initiatives will eventually fail but that it is now out of their hands; (3) that they have done all they could and have no energy to continue the fight; or (4) after having been engaged via powerful diplomacy in Phase 2, they may actually have changed their views to support the plans. Occasionally, some of the strongest resisters become active participants in the new programs. Thus, from plan approval forward, only a small number people who care deeply about their position continue to actively resist.

This small group of active resisters, well aware of their status as a minority, may band together. Seeing that all previous attempts to resist the transformation have been thwarted, they resort to more intense, aggressive, and extreme forms of resistance. The vitriolic minority are no longer able to speak for a silent majority, no longer able to act as the organizational conscience, and must completely own their opinions. At this point, the act of resisting becomes personal. Having lost the battle to stop the transformation before implementation, resistance becomes less about criticizing the process and the plans, and more about picking holes in the program by publicly identifying weaknesses as it is rolled out and discrediting the leadership. Weaknesses in the program, such as the lack of infrastructure planning, as well as mistakes or hypocritical acts by champions, are particularly vulnerable targets for resisters. Some individuals work in subversive ways to undercut new programs. A few realize that that they no longer fit within the new system, and of their own volition abandon the organization altogether.

Bolstered by a supportive majority, champions who roll out the initiatives as planned during Phase 3 effectively minimize the effect resisters have on the transformation by ignoring them altogether or dismissing the resistance. Over time, champions who are unable to completely ignore continued resistance, or who have not steeled themselves against personal attacks, find it difficult to divorce their subjective emotional reactions from the resistance in order to make rational decisions about what to do next. Resistance that is sharply pointed and laced with negativity causes angst among the champions, and can reciprocally spur negative engagement. Although championing the transformation all along may have been a deeply personal endeavor for the change champion, at this point the engagement process becomes personal as well. The champion may choose to engage the more extreme resisters by silencing them or by dismissing them from the organization. At the most extreme intensity levels, anger, hate, and vengeance can drive actions on both sides. Discussions between champions and resisters are heated, if they occur at all.

There is one additional aspect of the engagement process that is difficult to illustrate graphically. Over the duration of a transformation, as the action and intensity of resister behavior fluctuates, there is also an ebb and flow to engaging resistance.

The Ebb and Flow of Engaging Resistance

Rather than anticipate and formally plan to engage resistance as an antecedent to transformation, the findings suggest that champions decide what action to take based on the sense they make of different forms of resistance as they occur and their perceptions about the individual resisters. Emotions and intuition permeate the engagement process. People improvise. Champions' subjective assessment of the source, focus, and intensity of the resistance behavior, as well as their history with a resister, figure prominently in the choice to execute a particular engagement approach. Simultaneously, champions' interpretation of these variables shapes their perception of the valence (how positive, negative, or neutral is it?) of resistance behavior, which serves as a basis for selecting a specific engagement act or acts.

In practice, the intuitive sense a champion has about the valence of resistance behavior is usually, but not always, matched with a particular engagement approach. When champions recognize the valence of the resistance behavior as positive, they may engage resisters with an equally positive and embracing approach. One example from PSU was the Speech Department's objection to the omission of oral communication from the University Studies plan; their complaint led the champions to invite the department's messenger to join the planning process.

One resistance behavior can be ascribed different valences if executed in more than one period or with different intent. For example, although many people at Olivet and PSU resisted the transformations by not participating during the planning period, they were largely ignored because they were not threatening the process. When forms of resistance are seen as neutral or having a null effect (or valence), they are met with neutral approaches. Nonparticipation is engaged quite differently when it is viewed as detrimental. At PSU, for example, the champions used rewards to gain participation by the English Department in University Studies. Because writing was to be a large component of the Freshman Inquiry program, the threat of nonparticipation by the English Department was too great to ignore.

Negative forms of resistance can also be engaged with positive tactics. For example, during the planning phase, when resisters use aggressive approaches such as voting against small components of a transformation, positive and proactive strategies of listening to and including others are often effective. But when forms of resistance are considered negative or detrimental to the transformation process, champions usually choose similarly aggressive and negative engagement approaches. The aggressive resistance tactic of using students as pawns can be stopped with a coercive engagement approach, such as hauling faculty members into closed-door meetings to discuss the ramifications. Extremely negative forms of resistance are engaged with similarly extreme approaches. A good example of this occurred at Olivet College, when resisters who had attempted to sabotage the college's accreditation review were encouraged by the school's leaders to leave the college. Of course, this was not a cleanly executed operation but involved a bitter battle and the threat of a lawsuit in the end.

Although I didn't set out to discover the following, the data suggest that two additional interesting phenomena further explain the ebb and flow of engaging resistance throughout a transformation.

Positive Pull and Negative Bounce

The interactions between champions and resisters depend on the each individual's sense of the other's behavior. Just as the valence of resistance behavior factors into a champion's approaches to engagement, the valence of champion behavior affects the resister's future action. There are nine possible combinations of interactions between champions and resisters. These are identified in Exhibit 11. The following discussion is limited to positive and negative engagement and resistance, for two reasons. First, neutral resistance—that which neither helps nor

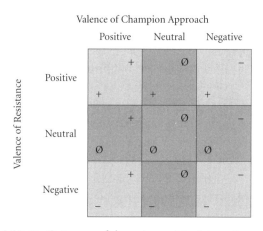

Exhibit 11. Outcomes of champion-resister interactions.

hinders a transformation—tends to be ignored. Second, neutral engagement approaches, by definition, have no real tangible effect on resister behavior.

Those who wish to embark on a transformation within their own organizations may want to consider the pattern of champion and resister interactions demonstrated by the actors at Olivet and PSU. First, the champions' use of positive engagement approaches tended to yield positive results, along with a corresponding deflation of intensity and mitigation of future resistance. I call this phenomenon "**positive pull**." The use of negative engagement approaches tended to yield an escalation in intensity or spur other, more aggressive forms of resistance. I call this phenomenon "**negative bounce**." Despite the complexity of human behavior within organizations, particularly those involved in sweeping transformation, the concepts of "positive pull" and "negative bounce" are quite simple.

Positive Pull

When champions face resistance, their choice of a positive engagement approach is likely to have a positive effect on resisters. The power of the positive engagement approach pulls resisters toward initiatives rather than reinforcing or strengthening their resistance. In effect, the resister becomes convinced that the transformation plans are necessary and right, or the champions are able to adapt or alter their plans in a way that is acceptable to the resisters. At worst, resisters so positively engaged become neutral. More than likely, they become supporters of the transformation. As positive interactions continue, resisters become more favorably disposed toward the cause, and the number of resisters decreases. When deployed appropriately, approaches like including others in the planning (A8), listening to resisters (A9), coalition building (A1), deal making (A4), relationship building (A11), rewarding constructive actions (A12), working toward consensus (A13), and hiring supportive individuals (A7) can exert a strong "positive pull" on resisters and prove effective in surmounting resistance.

Such engagement approaches do not work to mitigate all forms of resistance, however. Certainly, it is difficult to work though impediments to organizational transformation one at a time. During the different periods of a transformation, champions are busy deploying several different approaches simultaneously to engage many forms of resistance. If one approach appears not to work, champions should change their engagement strategy. Champions may experience the negative bounce phenomenon when they engage a particularly negative form of resistance (e.g., personal attack or sabotage) with a similarly negative approach.

Negative Bounce

Champions who engage resisters with a negative approach are not likely to improve their chances of succeeding. When engagement approaches are perceived as damaging or insulting, they tend to sustain the resistance behavior or to escalate its intensity rather than mitigate resistance. In short, the deployment of negative engagement approaches produces an effect that is opposite from the desired result; instead of helping, they produce **negative bounce**: sustaining existing or producing more aggressive and intense forms of resistance. Some approaches champions believe to be positive can be interpreted as negative by the resisters (e.g., presenting counterarguments (A3)). At the very least, negative approaches to surmounting resistance temporarily sustain the existing resistance. Without exception, the findings suggest that approaches such as coercion (A2) initially escalate rather than mitigate resistance. The most extreme strategies, such as encouraging people to leave the organization (A6), end the resistance for one person but can boost the intensity of the remaining resistance by creating martyrs.

Using a combination of approaches, champions are eventually able to mitigate resistance once a transformation becomes embedded within the organization. That is why I call this phenomenon a "bounce": resistance is not eliminated completely, but is surmounted to the degree that the remaining resisters have a null effect on the transformation.

Positive Pull and Negative Bounce in Practice

At the outset of the planning phases at both Olivet College and Portland State University, the institutions' leaders were preoccupied with developing solutions to potentially debilitating organizational crises. Even these leaders did not fully appreciate the scale and scope of the changes that the resulting initiatives would entail. As many others came to realize, they were compelled to act primarily because *not* changing threatened the very existence of the organization.

Champions began the planning (Phase 1) as they would any other initiative, while also realizing that the gravity of the situation required a more inclusive than dictatorial approach. The default strategies for engaging resisters at this point were positive planning practices rather than explicit strategies for working through resistance. As people resisted by not participating, voicing disagreement, and offering alternatives, the champions quite naturally invited them to participate in the process. At that time, resistance was mainly seen as constructive criticism and treated accordingly. Early on in the planning phase, the champions circulated iterations of the plans around campus and sought contrarian opinions, with the objective of listening to resisters and altering the plans based on the feedback. Many people, including some resisters, became supportive of the transformation initiatives because they participated in the planning phases, either as task force members or by providing feedback.

It was not until the transformation plans were concretized that resistance became increasingly active and more intense. For champions, the objective shifted from plan development to pushing for broad organizational approval of the initiatives (Phase 2). Because the time for inclusive plan development had passed, the primary strategies for engaging resisters moved toward convincing, powerful, diplomatic approaches. On many occasions, what the champions considered negative forms of resistance, such as building a case against the plan or voting against an initiative, were turned by the power of positive approaches such as reasoning, rewarding constructive acts, consensus building, or coalition building.

Although positive diplomatic approaches worked on many resisters, they did not work on everyone. Nor were the resisters always met with a positive engagement strategy. When one approach didn't work, champions tried others.

Before discussing the use of negative engagement approaches to surmounting negative resistance, however, it is important to address what happens when positive resistance is addressed with a negative engagement approach because it is at this point in the negative bounce phenomenon that resistance can become personal for the resister. The key here is to consider how a resister perceives and interprets the engagement action. Just as the valence of resistance is an important consideration for champions, the valence of the approach matters deeply to the resister.

Because champions tend to operate from positions of power within an organization, the burden of responsibility weighs more heavily on their shoulders to act appropriately when working to surmount resistance. Even so, the ebb and flow of engagement behavior is largely dependent on the quality of a champion's perception and sensemaking skill. Because transformation is messy, people are not perfect, and in some instances transformation leaders may not consider or care how their actions are perceived (e.g., by acting unethically), champions are not immune from committing the error of meeting a positive form of resistance with a negative engagement approach. Regardless of intent, doing so usually inflates or sustains the existing resistance until it is mitigated in some other way.

One example of this negative bounce happened at Olivet College. When one resister loudly expressed legitimate concern about the cost of the plan at several meetings, the champions dismissed his arguments with counterarguments that he interpreted as personal attacks. In response, he escalated his resistance by drafting his own alternatives to the Olivet Plan. In that instance, the champions misperceived the resistance, attached the wrong valence to it, and responded inappropriately.

Such errors are honest mistakes when a champion misperceives the resistance and attaches the wrong valence to it (e.g., such as when the curmudgeon unexpectedly offers good advice). The behavior is disingenuous, though, when champions knowingly use a negative approach to mitigate positive resistance; in that event their behavior is hypocritical and serves as fodder for more intense forms of resistance—even the severance of a champion's own employment. There are two salient examples from the cases: (1) Charles White's admitted mistakes, his failure to be promoted, and his subsequent resignation as chair of the University Studies program; and (2) James Halseth's alleged use of a blacklist and his subsequent departure from the college. Although the men engaged positive resistance with a negative approach, it is difficult to conclude that this was the reason they lost their leadership positions. At most, the data indicate that their use of negative engagement approaches to surmount positive forms of resistance resulted in a negative bounce that intensified the existing and more aggressive forms of resistance.

The data suggest that there is a natural tendency to match or exceed the valence and intensity of a resistance action when executing an engagement approach. Positive resistance is usually met with a positive approach. Early on in a transformation (during Phases 1 and 2), champions tend to engage many forms of resistance with positive approaches. Resisters are swayed by the positive pull of inclusive planning and powerful diplomacy. Even so, when a champion is confronted with negative forms of resistance (see the bottom row of Exhibit 11), it is difficult to counter the strong desire and, as one interviewee put it, "hit back with a bigger brick."

As the champion continually defends the initiatives and successfully navigates through and surmounts resistance, the number of resisters shrinks to a strongly committed few. The level of resistance intensifies, becoming aggressive to extreme, and the valence is definitively negative. Over time, it becomes very difficult to respond to negative forms of resistance without a similarly defensive approach: a counterargument; a protective mechanism such as circling the wagons; or encouraging people to leave the institution. The litmus test for more aggressive engagement action is the point at which a champion comes to believe that a particular form of resistance is powerful enough to damage, derail, or stop the transformation altogether. At that tipping point, like rams locking horns, negative forms of resistance are met with equally or more negative engagement approaches, which escalates the resistance (the negative bounce).

Oddly, these types of confrontations—negative resistance met by negative engagement—occurred mainly after both programs were well into the rollout phase of the transformations (Phase 3). The organizations were long past the point of no return, having committed considerable resources to the transformation endeavors. When negative resistance behaviors are met with more intense and extreme negative approaches, the interactions, or lack thereof, go beyond professional and become deeply personal for a small number of people on both sides. It then becomes difficult for people, also on both sides, to separate their ill feelings from the actions; relationships deteriorate, and interactions become too abrasive to continue. Ultimately, one party or the other leaves a post or the institution, or beats a hasty retreat to the old ways of behavior, and the antagonists ignore one another.

Curiously, there are people still working on both campuses who refuse to participate in the new programs but are allowed to remain. More than likely, this is because they no longer threaten the transformations. Such an outcome is more significant for a small campus like Olivet, with a small faculty, than it is at the larger Portland State, where participation in University Studies is still voluntary.

7 Lessons from the Field

*There are some enterprises in which a careful
disorderliness is the true method.*
—Melville, *Moby-Dick*

The central purpose of this book is to explain how change leaders handle the
resistance they encounter as they undertake the transformation of their organizations. I do not want to suggest that all change begets resistance. It does
not. Even so, to gain a solid understanding of how ordinary people rise to the
challenges of moving change efforts forward, it is necessary to examine transformations that entail acknowledged forms of resistance. In doing so, one can
then draw empirically valid conclusions about resistance, both to further the
scholarship in this area and to inform change champions.

This examination of the turbulent transformations at Olivet College and
Portland State University provides insight into why people resist change, what
shape their resistance takes, and the strategies that can be successfully deployed
to surmount resistance. The new model presented here for successfully navigat-
ing the messy change process has two intended outcomes: to advance the literature and future research, and to equip ordinary people to engage and surmount
the resistance they encounter in their own organizations.

Review of the Findings

I selected Portland State University and Olivet College as sites for this study
because both institutions were transforming their undergraduate curriculums
over essentially the same ten-year period of time. Both transformations were
fueled by financial problems and instigated by the two colleges' new presidents.
In addition to fixing troubling curricular issues, the leaders hoped that their
strictly academic transformation plans would also remedy the cultural, behavioral, and economic problems plaguing the campuses. Planning committees

were staffed with volunteer and invited faculty members. These committees conducted their work outside the standard curriculum change procedure, which is usually the purview of a faculty senate. Both the Olivet Plan and PSU's University Studies proposal were submitted for approval to their respective faculty senates minus any concrete plans for an administrative infrastructure (who would run it, how it would be financed, etc.). Both proposals were approved by a majority of the voting faculty, with only a small number of dissenting votes. Upon approval, both sets of initiatives were offered to entering freshmen and then rolled out as the students progressed through to their senior year.

I encourage the curious reader to visit the web sites for both organizations and examine their current programs. Because web sites evolve to reflect current organizational culture, individuals will need to assess for themselves whether these transformations succeeded. At this writing, the two institutions continue to operate with their transformed general studies programs. The Olivet Plan and the University Studies operations are thoroughly woven into the curriculums of both institutions. Their web sites provide robust discussions of the schools' philosophies and approaches, and offer guidance to students about how to take advantage of general education delivered in this manner.

Resistance

This study revealed ten forms of resistance experienced by change champions as they worked through organizational transformation and nine sources or causes of resistance to change. Resistance behavior during organizational transformation is aimed primarily at the transformation process (planning and implementation), the goals or outcomes of the transformation (the products), and the individuals leading the efforts (the change champions). Early during a transformation's planning phase, resistance is mainly latent and not intense. As plans become more concrete, thereby visible and imminent, resisters have something to target; the intensity of their resistance escalates and becomes more overt. As the level of intensity increases, resisters become more personally invested in stopping the transformation, and it becomes difficult for people on both sides to divorce their emotions from their actions. At its most extreme, resistance may become intensely personal and people may resort to extreme actions such as leaving a post or an institution, or even sabotage.

People operating within an organization have no reason to resist until they become aware that a transformation has been initiated. The primary first resistance action, in fact a nonaction, is nonparticipation (R6) in the change planning or effort. This type of resistance, as well as some others (e.g., voicing disagreement (R9) and voting in opposition (R10)) also occurred during the planning and initiation phases.

Although I expected the change champions to have anticipated and planned how to engage resistance, the findings suggest otherwise. Champions at both institutions reported that they did not anticipate resistance, but responded to resistance in a mainly intuitive, ad hoc manner. The one exception was the proactive approach of involving potential resisters in the planning process (A8). Even though listening (A9) was one engagement approach, because allowing feedback and flexibility is a normal element of a good planning process, it is difficult to identify listening as an intentional approach to engaging resistance. What we do know is that champions intuitively assessed the intensity of resistance and attended to resisters and resister behavior on the basis of their sense of the potential for that action to derail the initiatives. In fact, sensemaking was the main tool that champions used to gain an intuition-driven perception about resister behavior.

Engagement

Champions at Olivet College and Portland State University successfully used 13 approaches to engaging and surmounting resistance. Most of the approaches they took became apparent only in retrospect. Rather than anticipate and plan, champions tended to engage resistance in an intuitive and improvisational fashion, deciding to use an approach or tactic on the basis of an intuitive read of the organization, a sense of the resistance behavior (source, focus, and intensity), and prior experience with the resister.

Arguably the two most powerful and favored approaches were proactive: (a) including others in the planning (A8); and (b) listening to critics (A9) through soliciting feedback and input into the planning process. While not every form of resistance was engaged, and in fact, ignoring some resistance (A5) can be an effective approach, two strict rules of engagement are obvious from the data. Rule 1: If the behavior is going to either hurt the organization or derail the process, it must be addressed. Rule 2: If resisters involve students/customers as pawns, then they must be engaged.

In order to succeed, the champions of organizational transformation must interact with, or intentionally *not* interact with, resisters as a way of increasing their positive participation in and support for change and mitigating their damaging effect on the initiatives. The most useful approach to mitigating resistance are listed in Exhibit 8. Exhibit 10 illustrates the intensity of resistance behavior (latent through extreme) as an organization passes through three phases of engagement (1. Planning; 2. Push for plan approval; and 3. Transformation rollout and beyond).

The phenomena of "positive pull" and "negative bounce" reflect the organic ebb and flow of engaging resistance. An engagement approach that resisters view as positive is likely to increase their neutrality about a transformation or even turn them into supporters; this is positive pull. When champions deploy an engagement approach that resisters consider to be destructive or insulting, they are likely to sustain or escalate the intensity of their resistance, at least temporarily; this is negative bounce.

Toward a New Theory of Engaging Resistance

On the one hand, strategic change processes can be difficult to understand, given their intangible nature. On the other, a retrospective analysis allows us to see what was difficult to grasp while it was happening. Exhibit 12 establishes the broader contextual picture from which the engagement model emerged. It shows the flow of resistance and engagement interaction, the symbiotic dance that one should expect during any transformation. Before and during the planning phase, external and internal forces coalesce to create a crisis or circumstances that make the need for change obvious. The champions recognize the need to transform and make the decision to act. At both Olivet and PSU, the champions stipulate that their only option was to transform the institution or face extinction.

The third element of the model is where reality diverges from the literature. My expectation was that people championing transformation would anticipate and strategize ways to mitigate some forms of resistance before it materialized. Instead, other than including others in the planning process (A8) and listening to resisters (A9), champions at both institutions did not anticipate resistance, but mainly addressed it as it occurred. Thus the arrow from the third box to the resistance triangle shows the direct link to the planning process. People do resist transformation during the plan development, mainly by not participating (R6), but also by offering alternatives (R7) and voicing disagreement (R9).

The transformations at Olivet and Portland State were neither benevolently offered to nor malevolently thrust upon the organizational actors. The fourth element of the model, approval by the faculty, indicates that, particularly in academic organizations dealing with curricular transformation, approval by the faculty must come before implementation begins. In the for-profit sector, such approval may come from the CEO, the board, or other executives.

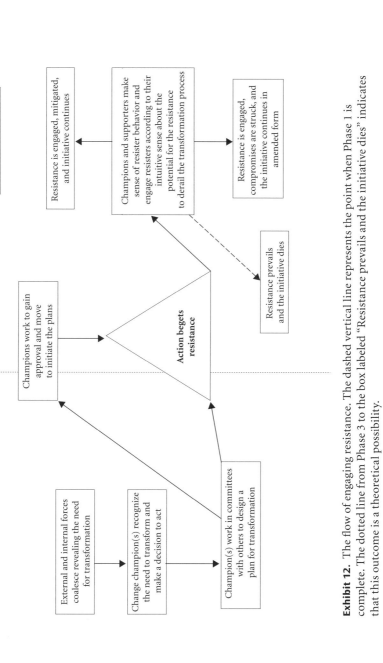

Phase 1:
Planning Phase

Phase 2:
Plan Approval

Phase 3:
Transformation Rollout and Beyond

External and internal forces coalesce revealing the need for transformation

Change champion(s) recognize the need to transform and make a decision to act

Champion(s) work in committees with others to design a plan for transformation

Champions work to gain approval and move to initiate the plans

Action begets resistance

Resistance prevails and the initiative dies

Resistance is engaged, mitigated, and initiative continues

Champions and supporters make sense of resister behavior and engage resisters according to their intuitive sense about the potential for the resistance to derail the transformation process

Resistance is engaged, compromises are struck, and the initiative continues in amended form

Exhibit 12. The flow of engaging resistance. The dashed vertical line represents the point when Phase 1 is complete. The dotted line from Phase 3 to the box labeled "Resistance prevails and the initiative dies" indicates that this outcome is a theoretical possibility.

Most resistance during the approval process took the form of voting in opposition (R10), voicing disagreement (R9), offering alternatives (R7), and building a case against the initiatives (R2). Approaches that were used to surmount resistance during the approval process were working toward consensus (A13), coalition building (A1), offering counterarguments in meetings (A3), reasoning with individuals (A10), and building relationships (A11).

During the transition between planning and implementation, successful engagement approaches include a mixture of old-fashioned diplomacy and ad hoc political responses. Upon approval, the initiation phase is activated in earnest. After experiencing and reacting to resistance behaviors, there are three possible outcomes for change initiatives: (1) resistance prevails and the initiative dies; (2) resistance is engaged, compromises are struck, and the transformation continues in amended form; or (3) resistance is engaged or mitigated, and the initiative continues. One literature-based and logical assumption is that one outcome of a failed engagement action by the champion is the demise of an initiative. Thus that element remains a theoretical piece of the model. This study leads me to conclude, however, that failure is unlikely after a plan has been approved by more than half of the organization's members.

The framing process model (Exhibit 12) and the new theoretical model (Exhibit 10) offer an empirical explanation for how champions work to successfully engage and surmount resistance. There are three periods that help us bound and identify the more successful approaches for engaging and surmounting resistance.

During the Planning Phase, champions face low-intensity levels of passive or active resistance, which is best surmounted by including others in the planning and listening to the resisters. During the Push for Plan Approval, the intensity of resistance is greater, peaking as plans are put forward for an up-or-out vote by an authorizing body. The hallmarks for successfully mitigating resistance during this period include application of diplomatic and political tactics such as counterarguments, deal making, reasoning with and building relationships with individual resisters, rewarding positive shifts in behavior, and consensus building. After a voting majority approves the initiatives, resistance declines precipitously and is perpetrated by only a dedicated and vocal few. During this phase—Plan Rollout and Beyond—champions mainly face small numbers of resisters who use aggressive and extremely intense forms of resistance. Champions mitigate resistance during this period by hiring supportive individuals, ignoring resistance, coercing individual resisters, and encouraging resisters to leave their positions or the organization altogether.

Just as there is an ebb and flow to the intensity of resistance, there is an ebb and flow to engagement behaviors. The valence of the resister behavior (positive, negative, or neutral) is usually, but not always, matched with a similarly charged engagement approach. Positive resistance is surmounted mainly with positive approaches. Neutral resistance is generally ignored because it usually has no bearing on the transformation initiatives. Negative engagement approaches are sometimes used to surmount negative resistance. Champions may mistakenly diagnose the valence of resistance and apply an inappropriate approach. Just as the valence of resister behavior is an important consideration in a champion's choice of an engagement approach, the valence of the engagement behavior affects the resisters' future behavior. Because there is a tendency for positive engagement approaches to change resisters' minds (the positive pull phenomenon), mistakenly diagnosing a negative (a false positive) form of resistance is not a critical error. Also, intentionally applying a positive approach to negative resistance can be quite effective in surmounting resistance.

On the other hand, because champions tend to match the valence and exceed the intensity of resistance behavior, misdiagnosing a positive form of resistance as negative could prove to be a large mistake. At the very least, negative approaches to engaging and surmounting resistance tend to sustain or temporarily intensify current resistance and can give rise to more aggressive and extreme forms of resistance (the negative bounce phenomenon). At this point the interactions between champion and resister can escalate to very intense levels. The thrust and parry can become bitter, and at its most extreme, someone may decide to exit the situation (e.g., by resigning a position or leaving the organization).

The Wisdom of Practice

As stand-alone elements of the transformation process, these findings about resistance and engagement approaches are among the first empirically justified additions to the literature. The case narratives provide a context for each form and illustrate the symbiosis between change and resistance.

Indeed, because each set of champions was successful in moving their transformations forward, it is safe to state that these approaches worked for them. Which approaches will work best in another situation will necessarily depend on the initiatives themselves, the inputs, the players, and the context. Even so, the theoretical advancements described in Chapter 6 suggest that certain approaches are more effective for surmounting particular forms of resistance during specific periods of a transformation. The "positive pull" and "negative bounce" phenomena also offer guidance for those interested in transforming their organizations. Specifically, positive approaches to surmounting resistance work better than negative engagement strategies, which appear to, at least temporarily, exacerbate resistance.

It is dangerous to apply any model strictly and expect it to work in every situation. But if you treat a model as a framework for understanding what *might* happen rather than a recipe for what *will* happen, you will likely become a much more skilled and effective change agent.

The tools and strategies described here worked for the change agents in these cases. The nature of your own experience may differ from those reported in this book. At some point, you may have to abandon these tools or tactics and adapt to unexpected or different circumstances (Weick, 2009). The following nine lessons correlate with the data and may further inform practitioners about how to navigate through resistance while championing organizational transformation. They are derived from the case studies of Olivet College and Portland State University and are supported by the words of those who lived through the transformations at those institutions.

Lesson 1: Expect Resistance

The very reasons we organize are antithetical to the nature of change. Cementing the values of an organization, creating consistency, establishing a routine, and becoming expert in one's field are some of the main purposes of organizing. Organized individuals have a natural tendency to resist change, particularly when it involves large-scale initiatives. Thus champions of change should expect resistance from established, organized, or comfortable members of their organization.

As one interviewee said, "You are probably doing something wrong if you don't get opposition" (Rhodes interview). And according to PSU's chair of the General Education Working Group, "When [a plan] becomes visible and affects the entire institution, a lot of grievances and history get rolled into that [resistance] and focused on the new target" (White interview). It would be a mistake to view all resistance as bad (Piderit, 2000; Burke, 2008). Resistance is a natural and necessary part of the transformation process and can be, according to one high-level administrator, "your best force of inspiration, because through it you can find out where the weaknesses are in your argument," and it allows you to pinpoint the underdeveloped parts of the transformation.

Lesson 2: The Inertia of the Status Quo Is Strong

At the outset of any transformation, the inertia of the status quo is difficult to overcome (Lewin, 1947). Said one who witnessed the transformation at Olivet: an "organization does not want to be transformed. It pays lip service to it. It spends millions of dollars on the idea of it. It trains, it talks, and it does everything. But the powers that be, in their little fiefdoms, do not want to be changed." Moreover, there is always a double standard at work. "If you advocate the status quo, you don't have to justify it. But if you are advocating change, you are held to a very high standard of proof, which someone advocating the status quo would never accept by definition" (Hayhow interview). Perhaps what was unique about the situations at both Olivet and Portland State was that because of the pending sense of crisis, the people within each organization were primed for change. Although one interviewee said, "If you really want to make transformation happen, you really need to face a crisis" (Dole interview), it is difficult to stipulate the corollary, that "It takes a crisis to precipitate transformation."

Lesson 3: Transformation Is a Long, Arduous,
and Sometimes Dangerous Journey

It is important to "be mission-driven and clear about your mission. Then you can set your vision and the goals that follow." However, it is not safe "to assume that because one is possessed of this idealistic vision that everyone is therefore going to immediately be persuaded by the glory of it. Transformation is going to take very, very lengthy and patiently skilled work with your colleagues, near Machiavellian cunning, and a constant willingness to dedicate yourself to this onerous task that will see very few results outside of the classroom for many, many years" (Kaiser interview). One characteristic champions share that allowed them to be successful was that they were unbending,

> stubborn, and determined. You have to stay the course, and you have to do it for a long time. You can't just do it for a couple of years. Now that we are eight years downstream of the first course that we ever taught in University Studies, we are now probably feeling comfortable with the idea that we now know how to do this. But, I am not sure that we still have it right. So, you have to be dedicated for the long haul. (Pratt interview)

Transformation is difficult to prepare for and when embarked upon requires painstaking attention to detail. Once the planning period is over and approval is given, the "sexy part of transformation is over. It becomes ugly, gritty, dirty, nasty, work—boring, infrastructure crap. But it was necessary to keep the ideal going forward" (Rutledge interview). "Cézanne used to put a line on a painting and then the whole thing would have to be changed. It was never done. Getting these alignments in a big sense and a small sense is the hardest part of the whole [transformation] process" (Rowe interview).

> Arthur Chickering used to say [in consulting with the champions at Olivet], "you have won the air war, and now the going gets tough because now you are into the ground war. Just because you won the air war, does not mean that you are going to win the ground war." When the planning stopped and the implementation began, that is when it got tough. That was when you discovered how much work it was going to take, how many resources it was going to take, and you discover that some of the things that had to be changed were not going to be comfortable necessarily. Reality sets in. In any kind of transformation or major change, this is bound to happen. But when you are in the euphoria [of planning], you don't tend to think of it. You think, "Oh, it will be all right." (Hayhow interview)

A champion also has to "have the will for it [transformation]. . . . And you have to be prepared for people to say nasty things about you" (Reardon interview). It is like that old folk saying: "If you want to be a pioneer you have to be willing to take some arrows in the back. And you want those people who are going to take some arrows to feel supported" (Nelson interview). In many ways, championing transformation is, according to a PSU administrator, "like Russian roulette. Every day you wake up, and you spin the chamber and you hope the bullet isn't in it. But you know if you are trying to change the institution, you are always going to piss off a certain group of people. At some point, you probably have pissed off enough people that there is a groundswell, and you are not in favor anymore."

> Don't be discouraged or disheartened because transformation gets messy. You are going to have to adjust things on the fly and there is going to be a lot of ambiguity. And sometimes it is going to be two steps forward and three steps back because the next day you will take four and one. You better have a lot of energy and persistence because this is a long-distance race and not a sprint. And you better find a way to get refueled emotionally because it can get really draining trying to play a leadership role in a transformation, which is especially true for a president whose job is really lonely anyway. (Bassis interview)

Lesson 4: Transformation Must Be Comprehensive and Indiscriminate

Often, "what is frequently called institutional transformation isn't that. It is really just tinkering. Once you start something like this it has got to consume the campus. The scale and scope [of the Olivet transformation] is something that I would commend to others" (L. Tuski interview). Any hint that some sacred cows are to be left standing leaves a champion open to criticism and resistance. Transformation must be comprehensive, "and closely related to that, it cannot be done on the periphery. It has to be done at the core and deal with the core business of the institution" (Halseth interview). One characteristic of the efforts at both institutions was that transformation of the organizational infrastructure was not designed alongside the curricular plans. This left a large portion of the transformation to be conducted ad hoc and opened up the champions to several forms of resistance. "You can't implement curricular change unless you implement at the same time organizational change. It won't happen. You cannot get a grassroots change in your curriculum unless you are also willing to redesign structures" (Toth interview).

Lesson 5: Take Time to Know Your Organization, Its Culture, and Its People

As a means of making sense of the sources of resistance, it pays to "understand the culture of your institution. To understand what motivates the faculty, you need to know what kind of institution it is, what drives it, and what the problems are that the faculty face" (Tetreault interview). Knowing the culture extends beyond simply accepting the rule of thumb espoused by PSU president Judith Ramaley: "A third of the faculty are going to be interested and come along, and a third are going to wait and see what is going to happen, and a third you are never going to get to" (Reardon interview). You need to do your homework because champions are likely to be challenged on many different fronts: "I knew enrollment patterns and hiring patterns. I knew which departments had lost and which hadn't. I knew budget distributions. I took the time to learn all those things because I knew I needed to know them" (White interview).

Although the speed with which the transformation planning took place at both institutions was swift, it behooves the champions to also take the time to know all the people in the organization. You do not want to give up on any particular person or "kick them out too fast because some of your most ardent resisters can become your biggest supporters" (Kohl interview).

> The relationship that you have with faculty and staff and students is important. You can never have enough of the right kind of communication—listening to students, being accessible to faculty and staff. I go to events and I talk to students. And that is how you stay in connection with some of the resistance. People tell me [about] resistance, and people tell me some things about my performance or my decisions that hurts some times, but I thank them profusely. You can't pay for that kind of feedback and advice. It's good old-fashioned politics. Nothing beats good, on-the-ground, interpersonal recognizance, and feedback. Nothing beats that. You talk to enough people and you establish sincere relationships. (D. Tuski interview)

Lesson 6: Good Process Tends to Lead to Good Outcome

The perception or reality of poor process can spark resistance. One of the key elements of planning at Olivet and PSU included giving faculty "ownership of the process. Once we [the faculty] had it, we were not letting go of it" (Knapp interview). Because these plans were academic in nature, "clearly, we were going to need a document that spoke to the faculty; which meant that we needed to approach it in a scholarly way and be able to present evidence as to why this was what we were going to do" (White interview). This was one element of the process at PSU that worked very well. "We studied. We read. We brought the literature. We talked to other experts" (Kaiser interview). External validation, whatever the form (for example, a grant from the Kellogg Foundation or an award from the Pew Charitable Trusts), is also important because it lends legitimacy to the program and "our institutions tend to want to know how [the transformation] is being viewed on the outside, and you need to be able to respond to that" (White interview). Focus on building consensus. "Negotiate, dicker, and compromise, so that you get pretty general wholehearted support. Don't rely on the strength of a bare majority of the faculty or whoever needs to approve because it is too weak a base" (Moor interview). Finally, one process element neglected in both transformations, and lamented by resisters, was an assessment and reevaluation process:

> If you think you are done with it, you are in trouble. And you have to build into the system a continual reexamination. There has been a significant transforma-

tion that has occurred, and to a degree the college has been transformed, but unless you leave open the opportunity for continual reevaluation, you set up the stage where people become comfortable once again, and people can get too comfortable. (Blackman interview)

Lesson 7: Include Stakeholders from All Levels

This lesson received the most support and corroboration from the interviewees. The proactive approach of including others in the planning was the most-favored strategy for surmounting resistance on these two campuses. Axelrod (2002) calls this expanding the "circle of involvement." Although inclusion can lengthen the process, champions must be sure that the process is as "open and inclusive as possible in the leadership. By inclusive, I mean being open to all points of view, and being humble about how we approach that" (Kaiser interview). Importantly, if someone declines an invitation to join the process, don't force him or her to join. "What we always did was make sure that we never closed the door. You could always join in again" (Rutledge interview). One Olivet College trustee echoes this view:

> You have got to bring them into tent. I have seen so many [other] cases in which leadership does not include in the process those in the organization who are perceived or could be considered resisters. It won't work. You can't get everybody but the resisters to some point and then try to include the resisters. There will always be resisters, and they will be hardened and they won't come up. You have got to get everybody from the most vocal resister to the strongest supporter involved in the process. Now, you may not be able to change that resister's mind. The worst thing you can do is leave the resister out and they turn into guerrillas at the fringe of the system. Bring everybody to the table. Hassle it out. Come to the best consensus as you can. Compromise and reason and communicate. It won't work otherwise. (Hayhow interview)

Lesson 8: Listen and Amend the Plan Accordingly

Simply listening to resisters can prevent many of the hard feelings that are based on the familiar complaint that no one listened. "If you listen to them initially, most people will ultimately realize that if they are free to express their opinion and the majority does not agree with it, then that is fine. At least they had their say" (Schroth interview). More strongly, inclusion as an approach to surmounting resistance is a barren strategy if not coupled with honest listening and amending of plans when necessary. The hypocrisy of inclusion and listening to critics but then failing to adapt and adjust plans accordingly was seen as a cause of further resistance. Every reason for resistance contains an element of truth, and champions can "improve the quality of the product" by listening to the resisters (Bassis interview). In fact, comments by resisters can provide "invaluable information. You can't pay for some consultant from the University of Michigan to come in and tell me that kind of stuff" (D. Tuski interview). There is one caveat to this lesson:

> The key ingredients are the same for any advice you ever get about how to maintain a good working relationship or a good friendship. Be honest about what you are doing. Listen extremely carefully to what they are saying and realize that what they are saying may only be the surface of what they are feeling, especially in an environment where emotions are generally not revealed directly, but generally indirectly because of the emphasis on cognition rather than emotional complexity. (D. Tuski interview)

Lesson 9: Coercion Is Very Tricky to Make Work

Both campuses achieved transformation. However, only one set of champions found it necessary to remove people who had remained steadfast and stubborn in their resistance. It may be necessary, and even appropriate, to encourage some resisters to consider leaving the organization. However, "beating up people, just trying to intellectually pistol whip people, doesn't work. If you have got to use the brick, use it sparingly" (D. Tuski interview). Approaches such as creating a blacklist, or even just the impression that there is one, can damage the process and the champion's reputation. Even deal making, if done unevenly or seen as unjust, can cause more resistance rather than mitigate it. Above all, "if you are going to act, then do it ethically, do it morally, and do it with concern for people's dignity" (Schroth interview).

Reaching a Conclusion

Hindsight reveals a number of elements of the Olivet College and Portland State University transformations that could be related to engaging and surmounting resistance, but this particular study was not designed to analyze them. Certainly this project's limitations, as with all research and theory building, are no more a cause for consternation than they are an opportunity for improvement and advancement of the field. Indeed, the limitations of the data precipitate several questions that might lead scholars in new research directions.

Possible Limitations

As noted earlier, there has been a shift in the literature since the start of the new millennium, and since I began this research more than ten years ago. If I had had at my fingertips the excellent scholarship that exists today (e.g., Burke, 2008; Piderit, 2000; et al.), would I have designed this study any differently? In all honesty, probably not. Clearly, there is today a greater understanding of resistance and organizational change in general than there was when I started my research. But using more nuanced variables would not necessarily have led me to different results or findings. More important, I had already made the mental shift away from viewing resistance as a strictly negative phenomenon. Even though scholars encourage us to think of resistance along a continuum of responses to change efforts, there are very few empirical works that advance our understanding of the symbiosis between resisters and champions. As such, this volume plows new ground and supports this new direction in organizational change theory.

Although grounded-theory analyses are strong tools for theory development, qualitative methods do not usually lend themselves readily to generalizable results. This issue is mitigated somewhat by the fact that the transformations studied here were remarkably similar in many respects and draw on a large volume of data from six different cases of resistance. Even so, one should wonder whether, if the study were replicated, it would yield the same or similar results. More specifically, to better understand resistance, it would be profitable to ask the same protocol questions at other organizations that have undertaken different types of transformation.

Further, was the research method deployed adequate to grasp the phenomenon it was intended to examine? This study rests heavily on interviews, which by their very nature rely completely on people's recollections. Fortunately, working through resistance is a memorable experience, but memory can be faulty and selective. The use of archived primary documents in triangulating with the interview data during the analysis moderates this issue. In the future, perhaps scholars acting as (a) consultants to organizations initiating transformation, (b) agents in some transformation effort, or (c) champions for organizational transformation at their own institutions could use those experiences to develop studies using experimental and control groups, participant analysis, or other action research methods.

Future researchers may also want to investigate some of the financial elements that are germane to the subject. Indeed, the fiscal aspects of transformation and resistance were briefly mentioned by only a few interviewees and
seen in some of the document data. I did find that the uneven distribution of
soft money via deal making and the like was a cause for some resistance. And
questions surrounding who was to control what portions of any newly created
or redirected resource pools affected the dynamics between individuals at both
institutions. But the data are less clear about most other financial aspects of
these transformations.

Clearly, the present study could have been designed to more thoroughly
examine the economic effects of transformation on resistance behavior. For
example, resistance at Portland State was aimed primarily at Freshman Inquiry
and not at the senior year portion (Senior Capstone) of the University Studies program. Perhaps that had something to do with the fact that faculty were
given four thousand dollars to conduct Capstone programs.

The fact that both sets of change champions left the fiscal and infrastructure
design elements out of their curricular transformation plans is notable. Their
omission from the transformation planning process may or may not have had
a larger effect on resistance. Subsequently, as one vice president for finance said,
it could be wise in a future study to "follow the money." Indeed, it would be
interesting to explore how the distribution and redirection of resources affect
transformation and resistance because, as March and Simon (1958) suggested
long ago, you get what you reward.

Finally, although this was an exploration of the interplay among and between various organizational actors, one might wonder how the power dynamics inherent in an organization affected the outcomes. I was not familiar
enough with the transformation narratives to build an examination of this
into the research design. But it is possible that authority, responsibility, and
the use of power in making change happen either exacerbated or ameliorated
resistance in these organizations. For example, a total of six presidents (including an interim president) led Olivet College over the course of 12 years
(1990–2002) after the negotiated departure of the longtime president. At PSU,
the transition of leadership, particularly at the president and provost levels (in
1996 and 1999), may have led to renewed efforts to resist the transformation
even after University Studies had been well established. Leadership issues and
the related power dynamics particularly warrant specific attention by researchers in future studies.

Some Questions for Future Research

Because this study focused on successful approaches to engaging and sur-mounting resistance from the champion perspective, it was difficult to get people to discuss their mistakes and failures. Olivet College Case 1 (The Block Plan) offers a small window into the circumstances and conditions under which resisters may prevail. However, the champions spun this as a particularly suc-cessful strategy ("lose one battle to win the war"). Of course that interpretation is debatable, and because it was not replicated at PSU it was not presented in the findings. Inasmuch as we can learn from success, some explanatory power may be gained by studying instances where champions failed to surmount re-sistance: where "resistance prevails and the initiative dies" (see Exhibit 12). I set that possibility aside in favor of exploring the other two threads.

When exploring the symbiosis between resisters and champions, there are likely many lessons to be discovered by extracting them from the cases where resisters prevail over champions. The twist here is that resistance may be ex-tremely valuable to the organization by stopping potentially harmful change. Resistance that conquers detrimental change may be considered very positive and resisters a heroic, vital part of the operation.

It was surprising that the champions in these cases did no advance planning to develop strategies or approaches to surmount anticipated resistance. Given the emphasis in the planning literature on considering all obstacles before ini-tiating change, it would be interesting to explore why these institutions did not do so. There is a large intuitive and emotional element to both resistance and decisions about how and when to engage it. Could it be that having an intangible plan is advantageous and helps to mitigate resistance, or is human behavior within organizations so unpredictable that it is impossible to make such plans? Alternatively, is the dependence on one's ability to improvise by acting intuitively a necessary characteristic of change champions? It may well be that intuition and improvisation are keys to an effective transformation in which an agile process is able to engage and surmount resistance because the targets are in flux.

While conducting the interviews I became increasingly aware of a turning point in the intensity of resistance, when what had been strictly professional became deeply personal for both resister and champion. Although I was able to build a theoretical explanation for this in the closing sections of Chapter 6 (where champions attempt to mitigate negative resistance with equally or ex-cessively negative engagement approaches), I was unable to pinpoint when this happens. Intuitively, and from some of the evidence, it appears that when the actions on one side trump those on the other, this spurs a more aggressive response. For example, after the Olivet leaders were suspected of using a blacklist, resistance behavior became more intense (the negative bounce phenomenon). Still, it is challenging to discern from this data anything beyond the theoretical suggestion that particular champion behavior precipitated more or less resistance. In some of the later interviews, I asked the precise question, "When does resistance or surmounting resistance become personal?" The answers were somewhat vague. A better question might have been: "Why did you stop resisting, and if you did not, why not?"

An answer may rest somewhere in the exploration of positive pull and negative bounce. At the very least, because my research only identified and did not set out to explore these phenomena, a test for positive pull or negative bounce should be devised lest they become relegated to the folk wisdom dustbin along with "you can catch more flies with honey than with vinegar."

To leverage this completed work, the research can be advanced by testing the provocative elements of the different grounded-theory-based models and findings presented herein by utilizing proven quantitative research methods to advance the theoretical constructs. The results of this study should be tested in different industries and in other nonprofit settings. One of the last questions in my protocol was designed to extract some wisdom from the practitioners. Specifically, I asked if each person to offer some lessons drawn from their experience (they are reported above). Future studies geared toward validating or invalidating those lessons would serve us well.

The largest opportunity for those who would advance the research in this area is to consider placing future studies of resistance in a new theoretical position as a necessary and healthy component of any change operation. There are myriad opportunities to reshape the literature in this vein, which identifies resistance along a continuum of responses to and a more organic and natural part of any change process. Perhaps, as Piderit (2000) suggests, the old paradigm of thinking about resistance using a physics-driven metaphor has taken us as far as it can go.

Conclusion

Other scholars have been asked to comment about their own lives in organizations. Weick offered the sage advice that our "referent is yesterday's organization and [our] experience of it. However, that organization no longer exists.

Yesterday's organizing, viewed in hindsight, is all the tangible social reality we have to live with and theorize about. There is good reason to be humble" (Weick, 2009, 274).

Perhaps how leaders wrestle with resistance and engage those who perpetrate it will become a way to gauge an organization's health overall health. Whereas effective organizations can be assessed by how constructively their members deal with conflict, insightful employees know that the absence of conflict is a sure sign of illness or dysfunction. Likewise, the absence of resistance while organizational change or transformation is in the air should be cause for concern. The hallmark of a healthy and functional operation may be one where resistance is encouraged and resisters are embraced as necessary and natural.

It should be evident that all of the resisters and champions portrayed in this book cared deeply about their respective organizations. As an indication of their personal investment and stakeholder-ship, perhaps we should view those who resist the most fiercely not in a negative light, but as those who care the most. A champion who deploys the proper combination of engagement approaches may find that her or his most ardent resister becomes the transformation's strongest supporter.

Appendix A
Olivet College

Olivet College Timeline

April 2, 1992: Racial incident on campus sparks media frenzy and causes African American students to walk off campus.

May 1, 1992: President of past 15 years announces his resignation.

June 30, 1992: Gretchen Kreuter is hired as interim president.

July 15, 1993: Michael Bassis assumes the presidency; immediately appoints the advisory Presidential Staff Group.

September 4, 1993: First campus-wide faculty forum held, ending with the selection of members of the Vision Commission.

December 6, 1993: Faculty forum debates and ratifies the new vision statement, with 88 percent voting in favor.

December 18, 1993: Select faculty delegation presents the *Education for Individual and Social Responsibility* vision statement to the board of trustees and receives a standing ovation.

January 22, 1994: Bassis convenes a third faculty forum and issues a charge to implement the new vision.

January 26, 1994: Board of trustees votes unanimously to adopt the new vision statement.

February 21, 1994: Bassis convenes another faculty forum to discuss and debate the learning outcomes developed by the committee. After being modified slightly, the outcomes and objectives were approved by 84 percent of the faculty.

March 1994: Bassis convenes another faculty forum and issues a new charge to the faculty.

April 1994: W. K. Kellogg Foundation awards a $15,000 planning grant to support the working groups' progress.

June 1994: President Bassis hires James Halseth as vice president.

September 2–3, 1994: Two-day faculty working retreat to discuss proposals.

October 1994: Board of trustees approves the basic concepts of the Olivet Plan.

April 10–12, 1995: North Central Association accreditation review.

Fall 1995: First class enters under the Olivet Plan.

Spring 1996: Graphical representation of Olivet Plan developed.

April 2, 1997: President Bassis convenes an all-day, all-campus meeting to develop a set of community standards or principles later dubbed the Olivet College Compact.

May 1997: Faculty, staff, and student senates all ratify the Compact.

June 1997: Board of trustees endorses the Compact.

August 1998: Michael Bassis steps down as president and Dean Halseth is appointed as interim acting president.

June 1999: Acting President Halseth resigns.

July 1999: Federico J. Talley assumes the president's post.

Summer 2000: Talley is given the option to retire as president; Donald Tuski is appointed acting president.

Spring 2001: Donald Tuski is officially made the 25th president of Olivet College.

Olivet College Vision Statement
Education for Individual and Social Responsibility

Our Vision

Olivet College is dedicated today, as it was in 1844, to the principle that the future of humanity rests in the hands, hearts, and minds of those who will accept responsibility for themselves and others in an increasingly diverse society. This principle of individual and social responsibility is realized in the context of a distinctive liberal arts experience which nurtures in our students the emergence and development of skills, perspectives, and ethics necessary to better themselves and society. We seek to involve our students in an active academic community which cherishes diversity of thought and expression. In so doing, we will help our students discover ways they can most effectively contribute to the common good.

Our Aspirations
We aspire to provide a campus-wide academic culture such that our students will come to understand the need to serve others as well as themselves, to celebrate both the wealth of human diversity and the bond of human similarity, to care for the earth and all its resources, and to strike a balance among their intellectual, physical, emotional, and spiritual capacities. It is our hope that each graduate will embrace our essential principle in his or her life's work.

Our Commitment
Driven by our academic vision, Olivet College maintains a learning environment that encourages scholastic excellence among students, faculty, and the wider campus community. Students at Olivet College are committed first to their learning. Faculty at Olivet College are committed first to their teaching. And, the institution is committed first to providing the necessary resources and support to achieve these goals both within and beyond the classroom.

Our Heritage
The foundation of our guiding principle was established one hundred and fifty years ago by the founders of Olivet College when they wrote,

> We wish simply to do good to our students, by placing in their hands the means of intellectual, moral and spiritual improvement, and to teach them the divine art and science of doing good to others.
>
> Adopted by the Olivet College faculty December 6, 1993;
> adopted by the Olivet College board of trustees January 29, 1994

The Olivet Plan

The Olivet Plan is a powerful and comprehensive vehicle with which to deliver the College's Vision. Faculty designed the Olivet plan which encourages students (1) to integrate what they learned from the full range of their experience; (2) to engage in active learning both inside and outside the classroom; and (3) to take genuine responsibility for their own learning. The Olivet Plan consists of the following: First Year Experience, Portfolio Assessment, General Education, Learning Communities, Service Learning, and the Senior Experience. In addition, the Olivet Plan has required in each element a strong commitment to cultural diversity. The plan also includes some important changes to our academic calendar. Wednesdays have been reserved for activities that cannot be accommodated easily within regularly scheduled classes. These include a late spring three and one half (3.5) week Intensive Learning Term (ILT) during which students may enroll in only one course. The Intensive Learning Term allows students and faculty to pursue special projects on and off campus free of conflicts with other course obligations.

The First Year Experience (FYE)

Our goal is to provide Olivet undergraduates with a rigorous and systematic orientation to Education for Individual and Social Responsibility during the first semester of study. The FYE course will prepare students for the challenges of college learning in general and of the particular learning which is valued by Olivet College.

Olivet requires entering students to take a three (3) semester hour First Year Experience course during the first semester. Specific course objectives are: (1) to introduce students to Olivet College learning outcomes in which students must demonstrate competency to graduate; (2) to demonstrate the multiple ways such learning can take place (with particular attention to experiential learning beyond the classroom); (3) to help students to assess, upon entrance, where they stand relative to these learning goals (self-reflection, testing, etc.); and (4) to ensure that students define goals for learning and explore how to pursue those goals fully. Through the FYE course students participate in a series of intercultural dialogues designed to help them better understand and appreciate cultural differences. The course is taught in sections of twenty (20) students by full time faculty, assisted by academic support and student services personnel. The course is designed to engage students through multiple pedagogies, especially those that promote active learning.

Portfolio Program

The goal of the portfolio program is to assist students in taking on responsibility for their education through a process of: (1) self-assessment, (2) educational planning and goal-setting, and (3) development of individual portfolios demonstrating each student's learning, competency and academic achievement. This program helps students develop a commitment to learning beyond individual courses and course grades; it helps them develop the ability to integrate learning from the full range of learning experiences, including involvement in co-curricular activities. The long-term involvement with a mentor and a cohort group allows students to establish the relationships that will help them succeed at Olivet College and in the future.

Beginning in the first year, and continuing until the student's graduation portfolio is completed, every student will enroll in a required one (1) credit Portfolio Seminar conducted by a faculty mentor. Unlike other courses, a failing grade in any Portfolio Seminar cannot be replaced by a passing grade in any subsequent semester. In these seminars, students compile a portfolio of their best work to date that addresses each of the five broad areas of learning outcomes. The portfolio also serves to demonstrate that every student is progressing toward his or her educational goals and plans. Each semester portfolios are evaluated by the faculty mentors. Additionally, formal validation of student competency occurs as a student moves from lower-division to upper-division course work and as a student presents himself or herself for graduation.

General Education

General Education requirements infuse the concept of individual and social responsibility throughout the curriculum to maximize student achievement of the learning outcomes. General Education consists of a sequence of required courses providing common learning and shared experiences for all undergraduates.

The General Education plan consists of eleven (11) core courses which link skills, orientations, learning outcomes, and competencies with Olivet's Academic Vision of Education for Individual and Social Responsibility. Thematically linked courses are delivered through a variety of formats and teaching/learning styles including integrated, cross-disciplinary teams, and collaborative teaching. Active and integrative learning are key features. The subjects of these courses will include: Self and Community I and II; Writing and Rhetoric I and II; Arts Exploration; Creative Experience; Nature, Technology and Humanity; Science Experience; Civilization Studies I and II; and Exploration of the Liberal Arts: Living in a Diverse World. These courses explore the relationship between Individual and Social Responsibility in the context of one's personal and social identities and the bonds of human similarity as well as the wealth of human diversity.

Service Learning

Olivet's goal is to provide a course-based Service Learning Project that will address community needs while at the same time instilling in our students the ethic of Education for Individual and Social Responsibility. The new college-wide

Service Learning requirement combines first-hand community service experience with careful and extensive reflection on that experience.

At least once during their undergraduate experience, students at Olivet are required to complete a three (3) credit service learning course offered by an academic department. Each Service Learning course requires students to spend a minimum of forty (40) hours serving the needs of the community. Such service is accompanied by reflection on that experience under the direction of faculty. A faculty member serving as the Director of Service Learning will assist the President in convening on-going dialogues among community leaders to identify opportunities to serve needs meaningful to the community. In addition, the Director will assist faculty in the placement and supervision of students enrolled in Service Learning courses.

Senior Experience

The Senior Experience is designed to help students integrate what they have learned about Individual and Social Responsibility and apply that learning to the transition from student life into family, career, advanced degree pursuits, and civic life.

A three (3) semester hour Senior Experience will be offered to students preparing to graduate from Olivet. The course is designed to provide practical experience in the world with reflection on that experience facilitated by faculty and off-campus mentors. A director of the Senior Experience will assist faculty in identifying and coordinating placement opportunities and mentors. Ten (10) departmentally-based Senior Experience courses will be offered each year, beginning in 1998-1999.

Learning Communities

The goals of this element of The Olivet Plan are to encourage students to assume responsibility for their own learning and to engage in active learning beyond the confines of the classroom. Learning communities are designed to allow students to explore important themes and issues through interactions with each other and with experts from beyond the campus.

Course-based learning communities consist of cohorts of students who enroll concurrently in three (3) different but thematically linked courses. For example, students may enroll in courses in biology, economics, and art, all linked thematically to the issue of the natural environment. Work in all three courses is supplemented by enrichment activities that extend beyond the boundaries of the classroom into the broader community. These enrichment activities are organized through the active participation of the students themselves with the team of faculty serving as facilitators. Participation in learning communities is optional, but once fully implemented, the College plans to offer five (5) different course-based learning community opportunities each semester.

Lecture & Symposium Series

In addition to these course-based learning communities, Olivet provides an ongoing thematically based lecture and symposium series to link the entire College as a learning community. This ongoing series is held on Wednesdays during the academic year to explore the many dimensions of Individual and Social Responsibility. The series culminates in May during the Intensive Learning Term (ILT) with a major event marking the formal conclusion of the academic year.

Excerpts from especially noteworthy lectures and proceedings are published periodically and distributed to individuals and organizations within higher education and in the broader community.

The Olivet College Compact

Olivet College is founded on and devoted to student learning, growth and development. The College values diversity within a community built on trust, participation and a sense of pride. As a member of this community, I affirm the following commitments:

I am responsible for my own learning and personal development. We recognize the critical importance of taking ownership for our learning. We seek to learn from the full range of our experience, to be open to new experiences and new ideas and to continuously pursue excellence and fulfillment in our intellectual, social and spiritual pursuits.

I am responsible for contributing to the learning of others. Every learner benefits when each shares ideas, insights and experiences with others. We value differences of opinion and perspective as well as open, respectful dialogue about these differences as central to the ongoing learning process.

I am responsible for service to Olivet College and the larger community. People working together for the common good is a key to growth for both the individual and the community. We commit ourselves to participating in community service and volunteer activities, both on and off campus.

I am responsible for contributing to the quality of the physical environment. Enhancing environmental quality is critical to the College, the community and ultimately to the survival of our planet. We will act to maintain and improve our facilities and grounds, to enhance the safety, the security and the appearance of our surroundings and to protect the ecology of our larger community.

I am responsible for treating all people with respect. We aim to create a positive and inclusive campus culture celebrating both the individual and cultural differences which make each of us unique and the similarities which bond us together. We recognize the need to seek to understand others as the first step to developing mutual understanding, caring and respect.

I am responsible for behaving and communicating with honesty and integrity. We build trust when we communicate openly, when we seek justice and fairness for all people, regardless of role or position, and when we honor our values and commitments in our private as well as our public behavior.

I am responsible for the development and growth of Olivet College. We reach outward and seek to inform, involve and recruit new students, employees and friends who share the vision and principles of Olivet College.

In joining this community, I commit myself to these principles and accept the obligation entrusted to me to foster a culture of responsibility at Olivet College.

Appendix B
Portland State University

Portland State University Timeline

Summer 1946: Stephen Epler opens the Vanport Extension Center (VEC) with the mission of serving veterans returning from World War II.

Memorial Day 1948: Floodwaters destroy the VEC campus and community of Vanport, Oregon.

Fall 1948: Vanport moves and welcomes the first student to a converted abandoned shipyard affectionately dubbed Oregon Ship.

April 15, 1949: The governor of Oregon signs House Bill 213 allocating the funds to purchase a building (the old Lincoln High School) for the permanent home of the Vanport Extension Center in downtown Portland.

Winter 1952: Epler successfully works with the faculty to change the name of the institution to Portland State Extension Center and is more commonly referred to as Portland State College.

Fall 1952: Oregon Ship moves into the old Extension offices in downtown Portland.

December 1952: Consultant to the State Board of Higher Education recommends extending four-year degree-granting ability to Portland State.

Fall 1953: A second building—a converted Safeway grocery story—is acquired to house the Engineering Department.

1949–55: The organization fights with the governor's office, and with opponents from the University of Oregon and Oregon State University, to become a legitimate and separate four-year institution of higher education specializing in teaching teachers within the city limits of Portland.

February 10, 1955: The governor of Oregon signs a bill granting official four-year status to Portland State. Its name is changed officially to Portland State College.

1969: Portland State receives authorization to grant doctoral degrees and changes its name from College to University.

1970–1986: President Joseph Blumel presides over the institution as it grows from college to comprehensive urban institution. In the process, the president sets up an adversarial relationship with the faculty through a series of management blunders.

1978: The faculty votes to unionize as a chapter of the American Association of University Professors (AAUP).

August 3, 1979: The first collective bargaining contract is signed at 3:02 a.m.

September 16, 1981: President Blumel declares a fiscal crisis.

October 3, 1983: In another bout with fiscal crisis, President Blumel asks the faculty for advice on how to avoid declaring another financial emergency.

Mid-1980s: An attempt to redefine the distribution system fails miserably in the faculty senate.

1986–1988: Natale A. Sicuro becomes president of the institution; ongoing problems lead the faculty to threaten a no-confidence vote.

1990: Oregon voters pass Proposition 5, restricting the use of taxpayer dollars to primary and secondary education.

1990: Judith Ramaley selected as the first female president of PSU.

1992: President Ramaley and Provost Reardon decide to reform the general education distribution requirements.

1992: Two all-campus faculty forums were conducted to discuss the possible transformation of the distribution system and to solicit volunteers for working groups.

Fall 1992: Two committees are formed: the Interdisciplinary Committee and the General Education Committee.

1992: Charles R. White installed as chair of the GE Committee;

—Retreat at the Oregon Coast to set the agenda for the two committees;

—Provost sends the groups to the American Association of Colleges (AAC) meeting in Seattle;

—Interdisciplinary Committee disbands and the GE Committee picks up steam.

1993: Forums are held to present the working proposals of the GE Committee to the faculty, staff, and students and to get input for modification and improvement of the plan.

Fall 1993: The plan is finalized in a brief document, distributed, and then submitted to the faculty for a vote in the senate.

November 1993: The faculty senate votes to approve the working group plan after a proposal to make it a pilot program failed.

1994: With its work done, the GE Working Group is disbanded and a new task force headed by White starts work on building the first-year Freshman Inquiry (FRINQ) program.

Summer 1994: Faculty meet over the summer to build the curriculum from scratch.

1994–95: The name University Studies is given to the new GE program.

—The first year of Freshman Inquiry begins with five sections and about 200 students participating.

—The Center for Academic Excellence (CAE) is formed to support the professional development of faculty needing new skills in order to teach in the collaborative, interdisciplinary style. Devorah Lieberman takes the helm as the CAE's director (she was also one of the first FRINQ instructors).

—Marvin Kaiser is hired as the dean of CLAS and negotiates to retain the direction of the University Studies program. Provost Reardon agrees but retains control of the University Studies budget.

—PSU receives a grant from the W. K. Kellogg Foundation to participate in the Network for Institutional Transformation (NIT).

1995–96: First year of Sophomore Inquiry; tinkering with the Junior Cluster to accommodate a possible cohort consisting only of only transfer students.

—First five Senior Capstone courses piloted by the CAE with a grant from the Corporation for National Service.

October 10, 1996: PSU receives the Leadership Award for the Renewal of Undergraduate Education from the Pew Charitable Trusts—one of the first three institutions to be so recognized.

1996–97: First year of Junior Cluster.

1997–98: Full-blown Senior Capstone program offered for the first time.

1997: Judith Ramaley resigns as president of PSU. Daniel Bernstein becomes the next president.

1998: First students graduate under the new GE requirements.

—President Bernstein commissions a group of faculty to conduct an assessment of the institution.

February 1998: The faculty senate appoints its own committee to conduct an assessment of the University Studies Program. Results are submitted to the full senate on June 2, 1998.

1999: Michael Reardon steps down as provost and is replaced by Mary Kay Tetreault.

—Provost Tetreault moves the University Studies program out of CLAS and makes it its own department with oversight by the provost's office.

—Provost Tetreault hires Terry Rhodes as the new vice provost for undergraduate studies and curriculum.

May 2000: A group of faculty, mainly from the sciences, survey the students for their opinions of University Studies.

July 2000: The Chronicle of Higher Education publishes an article critical of University Studies.

Winter Term 2001: The same group of faculty who surveyed the students conduct a faculty survey about University Studies.

General Education Working Group Report and Recommendations [September 1993]

Purpose

The purpose of the general education program at Portland State University is to facilitate the acquisition of the knowledge, abilities, and attitudes which will form a foundation for life-long learning among its students. This foundation includes the capacity and the propensity to engage in inquiry and critical thinking, to use various forms of communication for learning and expression, to gain an awareness of the broader human experience and its environment, and appreciate the responsibilities of persons to themselves, to each other, and to community.

Goals

Goal 1. Inquiry and Critical Thinking

To provide an integrated education experience that will be supportive of and complement programs and majors and which will contribute to ongoing, life-long inquiry and learning after completing undergraduate education at Portland State University.

Strategies

1. Assist development of critical reasoning and the ability to engage in inquiry.
2. Assist development of the capability to evaluate differing theories, modes of inquiry, systems of knowledge, and knowledge claims.
3. Achieve an intelligent acquaintance with a range of modes and styles of inquiry and social construction.
4. Assist development of the ability to understand and critically evaluate information presented in the form of graphics and other visual media.
5. Assist development of the ability to use writing as a way of thinking, of discovering ideas, and [of] making meaning as well as expressing it.
6. Assist development of the ability to critically evaluate numerical information.
7. Enhance student familiarity with science and scientific inquiry.
8. Enhance student familiarity with and capabilities to employ current technologies to facilitate learning and inquiry.
9. Enhance awareness of and appreciation for the interconnections among the specialized areas of knowledge encompassed by disciplines and programs
10. Provide awareness of choices among academic disciplines and programs.
11. Provide students with an opportunity to explore applications of their chosen fields of study.

Goal 2. Communication

To provide an integrated educational experience that will have as a primary focus enhancement of the ability to communicate what has been learned.

Strategies

1. Enhance student ability to express what is intended in several forms of written and oral communication.
2. Assist students to develop the ability to create and use graphics and other forms of visual communication.
3. Enhance student ability to communicate quantitative concepts.
4. Develop student ability to employ current technologies to assist communication.

Goal 3. Human Experience

To provide an integrated education that will increase understanding of human experience. This includes emphasis upon scientific, social, multicultural, environmental, and artistic components of that experience and the full realization of human potential as individuals and communities.

Strategies

1. Enhance awareness and appreciation of societal diversity in the local, national, and global communities.
2. Explore the evolution of human civilization from differing disciplinary and cultural perspectives.
3. Explore the course and implications of scientific and technological change.
4. Develop an appreciation of the aesthetic and intellectual components of the human experience in literature and the arts.
5. Explore the relationship between physical, intellectual, emotional, and social well-being, including the means by which self-actualization is developed and maintained throughout life.
6. Explore and appreciate the aesthetics of artistic expression and the contributions of the fine and performing arts and of human movement/sport/play to the quality of life.
7. Develop the capacity to adapt to life challenges and to foster human development (including intellectual, physical, social, and emotional dimensions) amongst self and others throughout the life span.

Goal 4. Ethical Issues and Social Responsibility
Provide an integrated educational experience that develops an appreciation for and understanding of the relationships among personal, societal, and global well-being and the personal implications of such issues as the bases of ethical judgment, societal diversity, and the expectations of social responsibility.

Strategies

1. Appreciate the impact of life choices on personal, social, and environmental health.

2. Gain an understanding of ethical dilemmas confronted by individuals, groups, and communities and the foundations upon which resolution might be possible.

3. Practice and test one's capacities to engage the ethical, interactive, and organizational challenges of the present era.

4. Explore the personal implications and responsibilities in creating an ethical and safe familial environment, neighborhood, work environment, society, and global community.

5. Explore and appreciate the role of diversity in achieving environmental, social, and personal health.

6. Gain familiarity with the values, foundations, and responsibilities of democratic society.

Recommended Requirements

1. Freshman Core—Three Core Courses [later named Freshman Inquiry]—15 Credits

2. Sophomore Year—Three 4-credit courses selected from different interdisciplinary programs or general education tracks—12 Credits.

3. Junior and Senior Years—Complete one interdisciplinary program or general education track (four, 3-credit courses)—12 Credits

4. Senior "Capstone" Experience—6 Credits

   Further information about current Senior Capstone courses can be found at www.ous.pdx.edu.

2002—Mission and Goals

The purpose of the general education program at Portland State University is to facilitate the acquisition of the knowledge, abilities, and attitudes that will form a foundation for lifelong learning among its students. This foundation includes the capacity to engage in inquiry and critical thinking, to use various forms of communication for learning and expression, to gain an awareness of the broader human experience and its environment, and appreciate the responsibilities of persons to themselves, to each other, and to community.

Appendix C
Engaging Resistance: Interview Protocol

Introduction: First, let me thank you in advance for agreeing to speak with me about your involvement in the transformation here at Portland State [Olivet College]. Please review and sign the consent form. To begin, let me explain my purpose here [explain purpose]. Do you have any questions before we begin? I will be recording this interview for later analysis. Can I have your permission to do so? Please state your name and position for the record.

1. What are the milestones of the transformation at Portland State University [Olivet College]?

   Prompts to be used if necessary:

   ☐ Characterize the state of the readiness for this transformation.

   ☐ What were the forces that caused you to move forward on the transformation initiative?

   ☐ What were the organizational issues that these initiatives were designed to solve?

   ☐ Describe the main objective of the transformation initiative.

   ☐ Describe your vision for this transformation.

   ☐ Was this the same vision you held during your recruitment/selection process?

   ☐ Describe your strategy for this transformation?

2. What was your experience in relation to these milestones?

    Prompts to be used if necessary:

☐ Describe how you used your position to work through the transformation initiative.

☐ Characterize your role in relationship to the transformation initiative.

☐ Why did you feel that this transformation was necessary?

3. Describe the forms of resistance that you experienced during the planning and initiation phases of the transformation.

    Prompts to be used if necessary:

☐ How did the actions of the transformation effort lead to resistance?

☐ What forms of resistance did you encounter?

☐ Please give me three examples of resistance that illustrate concrete behavior exhibited by resisters.

☐ What behaviors were exhibited that you could identify that were clues you were facing resistance?

☐ Describe the various forms of resistance you encountered as you planned for implementation.

☐ Describe the various forms of resistance you encountered during implementation.

☐ Where there different levels of intensity of the resistance behaviors? How would you describe them?

☐ Describe the critical decision points revolving around the resistance.

☐ How did you make the decision to respond to some resisters and not others?

☐ Why do you suppose these individuals would be resisting this particular initiative?

☐ Do you feel that it was necessary to address all forms of resistance?

☐ Were you over- or under-prepared to meet the resistance? Why?

☐ Where were the pockets of resistance emanating from: within your planning team; in the greater campus community; or outside the campus altogether?

☐ What were the targets of the resistance? Or, were resisters objecting to the targets of the transformation, the plan itself, the process, or the individuals involved in moving the plan?

4. At any time during the process of the planning or initiation of the transformation, did you feel that you needed/wanted to resist? If so, why, and what did you do?

5. What approaches did you use to deal with the resistance and resister behavior you experienced?

Prompts to be used if necessary:

☐ Articulate your strategy for mitigating resistance.

☐ In the cases that you did, why and how did you engage the resisters?

☐ Outline the steps, approaches, or tactics that you took to surmount the resistance.

☐ Why did these steps work?

☐ Were they modified as you progressed?

☐ Was this a part of your anticipated plan?

☐ What was the reaction of the resisters as you carried out your approaches?

☐ What is your sense of the amount of time it took you to deal with resistance?

☐ Did resistance prevail, cause you to augment the transformation, or disappear? Why?

☐ Three outcomes are possible when working through resistance. First, you convince the resisters that your way is correct and they join you. Second, you listen to the resisters and augment the plan and they join you. Third, the resistance is successful and the transformation process is stopped. Are you aware of any cases in which this third option happened?

☐ How did you know that you had surmounted the resistance? Or, how did you know that you were successful in mitigating the resistance?

☐ How did you know when to move to another approach?

- ☐ How do you know that the resistance didn't go underground?
- ☐ What were the tactics that didn't work to successfully engage the resisters?

6. Given your experience at Portland State, what lessons would you offer to those who are embarking on a transformation of their own?

7. Given that I don't know what I don't know, is there some question that I didn't ask that I should have? What is it, and what would your answer to that question be?

8. Is there anything else that you would like to share given our conversation (for example, someone else I should talk to)?

Thank you for participating. [I then explained that results would be posted and available online once I had a successfully defended product.]

References

Interviews

Readers interested in knowing more about the interviews conducted by the author at Portland State University and Olivet College should contact him directly.

Works Cited

Alfred, R. L. and Carter, P. (1993). Rethinking the business of management. In Alfred, R. L. and Carter, P. (eds.), *Changing Managerial Imperatives: New Directions for Community Colleges*, 7–19. San Francisco: Jossey-Bass.

Anderson, A. D. (2000). *Explaining Transformation in Higher Education: A Grounded Theory of Transforming a Small Liberal Arts College*. Unpublished white paper, University of Michigan, Center for the Study of Higher and Postsecondary Education, Ann Arbor.

Argyris, C. (1985). *Strategy, Change and Defensive Routines*. Boston: Pitman.

Ashkenas, R., Ulrich, D., Jick, T., and Kerr, S. (1995). *The Boundaryless Organization: Breaking the Chains of Organizational Structure*. San Francisco: Jossey-Bass.

Astin, A. W., Astin, H. S., et al. (2000). *Leadership Reconsidered: Engaging Higher Education in Social Change*. Battle Creek, Mich.: William K. Kellogg Foundation.

Atwater, L. E. and Atwater, D. C. (1994). Organizational transformation: Strategies for change and improvement. In Bass, B. M. and Avolio, B. J. (eds.), *Improving Organizational Effectiveness through Transformational Leadership*, 146–172. Thousand Oaks, Calif.: Sage.

Azároff, L. V. (1996). *Physics over Easy: Breakfasts with Beth and Physics*. River Edge, N.J.: World Scientific.

Axelrod, R. (2002). *Terms of Engagement: Changing the Way We Change Organizations*. San Francisco: Berrett-Koehler.

Backer, T. E. and Porterfield, J. (1998). Change at work: Why it hurts and what employers can do about it. In Klarreich, S. (ed.), *Handbook of Organizational Health Psychology*, 203–217. Madison, Conn.: Psychosocial Press.

Bain, A. (1998). Social defenses against organizational learning. *Human Relations* 51 (3): 413–429.

Bainbridge, C. (1996). *Designing for Change: A Practical Guide to Business Transformation.* Toronto: John Wiley and Sons.

Baldridge, J. V. (1975). Organizational innovation: Individual, structural and environmental impacts. In Baldridge, J. V. and Deal, T. E. (eds.), *Managing Change in Educational Organizations: Sociological Perspectives, Strategies, and Case Studies*, 151–175. Berkeley, Calif.: McCutchan.

Barnett, R. (2000). Reconfiguring the university. In Scott, P. (ed.), *Higher Education Re-formed*, 114–129. New York: Falmer Press.

Bechler, C. T. (1993). A study of crisis communication from a modular perspective: The framing and shaping of meaning in Olivet College's response to a racial clash. Unpublished Doctoral Dissertation, Bowling Green State University, Ohio.

Beckhard, R. and Pritchard, W. (1992). *Changing the Essence: The Art of Creating and Leading Fundamental Change in Organizations.* San Francisco: Jossey-Bass.

Bennis, W. and Nanus, B. (1985). *Leaders: The Strategies for Taking Charge.* New York: Harper and Row.

Bensimon, E. M., Neumann, A., and Birnbaum, R. (1989). *Making Sense of Administrative Leadership: The 'L' word in Higher Education.* ASHE-ERIC Higher Education Report No. 1. Washington, D.C.: School of Education and Human Development, The George Washington University.

Bergquist, W. H. (1992). *The Four Cultures of the Academy: Insights and Strategies for Improving Leadership in Collegiate Organizations.* San Francisco: Jossey-Bass.

Bergquist, W. (1993). *The Postmodern Organization: Mastering the Art of Irreversible Change.* San Francisco: Jossey-Bass.

Birnbaum, R. (1988). *How Colleges Work: The Cybernetics of Academic Organization and Leadership.* San Francisco: Jossey-Bass.

Bovey, W. H. and Hede, A. (2001) Resistance to organizational change: The role of defense mechanisms. *Journal of Managerial Psychology* 16(7/8): 534–549.

Boyer Commission on Educating Undergraduates in the Research University (1998). *Reinventing Undergraduate Education: A Blueprint for America's Research Universities. http://naples.cc.stonybrook.edu/Pres/boyer.nsf,* SUNY Stony Brook.

Brill, P. L. and Worth, R. (1997). *The Four Levers of Corporate Change.* New York: AMACOM.

Brinkman, P. T. and Morgan, A. W. (1997). Changing fiscal strategies for planning. In Peterson, M. W., Dill, D., and Mets, L. (eds.), *Planning and Management for a Chang-*

ing Environment: A Handbook on Redesigning Postsecondary Institutions, 288–306. San Francisco: Jossey-Bass.

Brown, A. D. and Starkey, K. (2000). Organizational identity and learning: A psychodynamic perspective. *Academy of Management Review* 25 (1): 102–120.

Bryan, M. (2006). Talking about change: Understanding employee responses through qualitative research. *Management Decision* 44 (2): 246–259.

Bryson, J. M. (1995). *Strategic Planning for Public and Nonprofit Organizations: A Guide to Strengthening and Sustaining Organizational Achievement*. San Francisco: Jossey-Bass.

Burke, W. W. (2008). *Organization Change: Theory and Practice*. Thousand Oaks, Calif.: Sage.

Burke, W. W., Lake, D. G., and Paine, J. W. (eds.) (2009). *Organization Change: A Comprehensive Reader*. San Francisco: Jossey-Bass.

Calabrese, R. L. (2003). The ethical imperative to lead change: Overcoming the resistance to change. *International Journal of Education Management* 17 (1): 7–13.

Cameron, K. S. and Ettington, D. R. (1988). The conceptual foundations of organizational culture. In Smart, J. C. (ed.), *Higher Education: Handbook of Theory and Research*, 356–396. New York: Agathon Press.

Cameron, K. S. and Quinn, R. E. (2006). *Diagnosing and Changing Organizational Culture*. San Francisco: Jossey-Baas.

Cameron, K. S. and Tschirhart, M. (1992). Postindustrial environments and organizational effectiveness in colleges and universities. *Journal of Higher Education* 63 (1): 87–108.

Cameron, K. S. and Ulrich, D. O. (1986). Transformational leadership in colleges and universities. In Smart, J. C. (ed.), *Higher Education: Handbook of Theory and Research*, vol. 2, 1–42. New York: Agathon Press.

Cameron, K. S., Kim, M. U., and Whetten, D. A. (1987). Organizational effects of decline and turbulence. *Administrative Science Quarterly* 32: 222–240.

Carchidi, D. M. and Peterson, M. W. (2000). Emerging organizational structures. *Planning for Higher Education* 28: 1–15.

Cawsey, T. and Deszca, G. (2007). *Toolkit for Organizational Change*. Thousand Oaks, Calif.: Sage.

Chaffee, E. E. (1985). The concepts of strategy: From business to higher education. In Smart, J. C. (ed.), *Higher Education: Handbook of Theory and Research*, 133–172. New York: Agathon Press.

Chaffee, E. E. and Jacobson, S. W. (1997). Creating and changing institutional cultures. In Peterson, M. W., Dill, D., and Mets, L. (eds.), *Planning and Management for a Changing Environment: A Handbook on Redesigning Postsecondary Institutions*, 230–245. San Francisco: Jossey-Bass.

Champy, J. and Nohria, N. (1996). Into the storm: The cycle of change quickens. In Champy, J. and Nohria, N. (eds.), *Fast Forward: The Best Ideas on Managing Business Change*. Boston: Harvard Business Review.

Cheldelin, S. I. (2000). Handling resistance to change. In Lucas, A. F. (ed.), *Leading Academic Change: Essential Roles for Department Chairs*, 55–73. San Francisco: Jossey-Bass.

Christenson, D. D. (1982). Changes in higher education: Forces and impacts. In Hipps, G. M. (ed.), *Effective Planned Change Strategies: New Directions for Institutional Research* 9 (1): 5–17.

Clark, B. R. (1991). The organizational saga in higher education. In Peterson, M. W. (ed.), *Organization and Governance in Higher Education*, 46–52. Neeedham Heights, Mass.: Simon and Schuster.

———. (1997). Foreword. In Peterson, M. W., Dill, D., and Mets, L. (eds.), *Planning and Management for a Changing Environment: A Handbook on Redesigning Postsecondary Institutions*, xiii–xviii. San Francisco: Jossey-Bass,

———. (1998). *Creating Entrepreneurial Universities: Organizational Pathways of Transformation*. New York: Pergamon.

———. (Jan./Feb. 2000). Collegial entrepreneurialism in proactive universities: Lessons from Europe. *Change* 32 (1): 10–19.

Collins, L. K. and Hill, F. M. (1998). Leveraging organizational transformation through incremental change and radical approaches to change: Three case studies. *Total Quality Management* 9 (4 & 5): s30–s34.

Corbin, J. and Strauss, A. (2008). *Basics of Qualitative Research: Techniques and Procedures for Developing Grounded Theory*. Thousand Oaks, Calif.: Sage.

Crane, T. R. (1963). *The Colleges and the Public, 1787–1862*. New York: Teachers College, Columbia University.

Creswell, J. W. (2009). *Research Design: Qualitative, Quantitative, and Mixed Methods Approaches*. Thousand Oaks, Calif.: Sage.

Cutcher, L. (2009). Resisting change from within and without the organization. *Journal of Organizational Change Management* 22 (3): 275–289.

Day, M. T. (1998). Transformational discourse: Ideologies of organizational change in the academic library and information science literature. *Library Trends* 46 (4): 635–667.

de Caluwé, L. and Vermaak, H. (2003). *Learning to Change: A Guide for Organizational Change Agents*. Thousand Oaks, Calif.: Sage.

de Jager, P. (2001). Resistance to change: A new view of an old problem. *The Futurist* 35 (3): 24–28.

Demers, C. (2007). *Organizational Change Theories: A Synthesis*. Thousand Oaks, Calif.: Sage.

Dill, D. D. (1999). Academic accountability and university adaptation: The architecture of an academic learning organization. *Higher Education* 38, 127–154.

Dodds, G. B. (1996). *The College That Would Not Die: The First Fifty Years of Portland State University, 1946–1996*. Portland: Oregon Historical Society Press.

Drucker, P. F. (1994). The age of social transformation. *Atlantic Monthly* 274: 53–80.

Duderstadt, J. J. (2000). *A University for the 21ˢᵗ Century*. Ann Arbor: University of Michigan Press.

Dunphy, D. and Griffiths, A. (1994). Theories of organizational change as models for intervention. Working paper. Center for Corporate Change, University of New South Wales, Australia.

Eckel, P. D. (2000). The role of shared governance in institutional hard decisions: Enabler or antagonist? *Review of Higher Education*, 24 (1): 15–39.

Eckel, P., Hill, B., and Green, M. (1998). *On Change: En Route to Transformation*. Washington, D.C.: American Council on Education.

Fairweather, J. S. (2000). Diversification or homogenization: How markets and governments combine to shape American higher education. *Higher Education Policy* 13: 79–98.

Farmer, D. W. (Fall 1990). Strategies for change. In Steeples, D. W. (ed.), *Managing Change in Higher Education. New Directions for Higher Education* no. 71: 7–18. San Francisco: Jossey-Bass.

Fitz-enz, J. (2000). *The ROI of Human Capital: Measuring the Economic Value of Employee Performance*. New York: AMACOM.

Fletcher, B. R. (1990). *Organizational Transformation Theorists and Practitioners: Profiles and Themes*. Westport, Conn.: Praeger.

Ford, J. D. and Ford, L. W. (2009). Decoding Resistance to Change. *Harvard Business Review* 87 (4): 99–103.

Ford, J. D., Ford, L. W., and D'Amelio, A. (2008). Resistance to change: The rest of the story. *Academy of Management Review* 33 (2): 362–377.

Ford, J. D., Ford, L. W., and McNamara, R. T. (2002). Resistance and the background conversations of change. *Journal of Organizational Change Management* 15 (2): 105–122.

Furst, S. A. and Cable, D. M. (2008). Employee resistance to organizational change: Managerial influence tactics and leader-member exchange. *Journal of Applied Psychology* 93 (2): 453–462.

Galpin, T. J. (1996). *The Human Side of Change: A Practical Guide to Organization Redesign*. San Francisco: Jossey-Bass.

Geller, E. S. (2002). Leadership to overcome resistance to change: It takes more than consequence control. *Journal of Organizational Behavior Management* 22 (3): 29–49.

Gilgeous, V. and Chambers, S. (1999). Initiatives for managing resistance to change. *Journal of General Management* 25(2): 44.

Gioia, D. A. and Thomas, J. B. (1996). Identity, image and issue interpretation: Sense-making during strategic change in academia. *Administrative Sciences Quarterly* 41: 370–403.

Glaser, B. G. and Strauss, A. L. (1999). *The discovery of grounded theory: Strategies for qualitative research.* Hawthorne, N.Y.: Aldine de Gruyter.

Godkin, L. and Allcorn, S. (2008). Overcoming organizational inertia: A tripartite model for achieving Strategic organizational change. *Journal of Applied Business and Economics* 8 (1): 83–95.

Goltz, S. M. and Hietapelto, A. (2002). Using the operant and strategic contingencies models of power to understand resistance to change. *Journal of Organizational Behavior Management* 22 (3): 3–22.

Goodchild, L. F. and Wechsler, H. S. (1989). *The History of Higher Education.* Needham Heights, Mass.: Simon and Schuster.

Green, M. F. (1997). Institutional leadership in the change process. In Green, M. F. (ed.), *Transforming Higher Education: Views from Leaders around the World,* 27–52. Phoenix: Oryx Press.

Green, M. F. and Hayward, F. M. (1997). Forces for change. In Green, M. F. (ed.), *Transforming Higher Education: Views from Leaders around the World,* 3–26. Phoenix: Oryx Press.

Greiner, L. E. and Schein, V. E. (1988). *Power and Organization Development: Mobilizing Power to Implement Change.* New York: Addison-Wesley.

Gross, N., Giacquinta, J. B., and Bernstein, M. (1971). *Implementing Organizational Innovations: A Sociological Analysis of Planned Educational Change.* New York: Basic Books.

Gumport, P. J. (2000). Academic Restructuring: Organizational Change and Institutional Imperatives. *Higher Education* 39: 67–91.

Gumport, P. J. and Pusser, B. (1997). Restructuring the academic environment. In Peterson, M. W., Dill, D., and Mets, L. (eds.), *Planning and Management for a Changing Environment: A Handbook on Redesigning Postsecondary Institutions,* 453–478. San Francisco: Jossey-Bass

Guskin, A. E. and Bassis, M. A. (March 1985). Leadership styles and institutional renewal. In Davis, R. M. (ed.), *Leadership and Institutional Renewal. New Directions for Higher Education* no. 49: 13–22.

Hamel, G. (2000). *Leading the Revolution.* Boston: Harvard Business School Press.

Hamel, G. and Prahalad, C. K. (1994). *Competing for the Future.* Boston: Harvard Business School Press.

Hammer, M. and Champy, J. (1993). *Reengineering the Corporation: A Manifesto for Business Revolution.* New York: Harper Business.

Hearn, J. C. (1988). Strategy and resources: Economic issues in strategic planning and management in higher education. In Smart, J. C. (ed.), *Higher Education: Handbook of Theory and Research,* 212–281. New York: Agathon Press.

Hearn, J. C. (1996). Transforming U.S. Higher Education: An Organizational Perspective. *Innovative Higher Education* 21 (2): 141–157.

Hermon-Taylor, R. J. (1985). Finding new ways of overcoming resistance to change. In Pennings, J. M. (ed.), *Organizational Strategy and Change*, 383–411. San Francisco: Jossey-Bass.

Heydinger, R. B. (1997). Principles for redesigning institutions. In Peterson, M. W., Dill, D., and Mets, L. (eds.), *Planning and Management for a Changing Environment: A handbook on redesigning postsecondary institutions.* San Francisco: Jossey-Bass, 106–123.

Hipps, G. M. (1982). Summary and conclusions. In Hipps, G. M. (ed.), *Effective planned change strategies. New Directions for Institutional Research* 9 (1): 115–122.

Hultman, K. (1998). *Making change irresistible: Overcoming Resistance to Change in Your Organization.* Palo Alto, Calif.: Davies-Black.

Jansen, K. J. (2000). The emerging dynamics of change: Resistance, readiness, and momentum. *Human Resource Planning* 23 (2): 53–56.

Judson, A. S. (1966). *Changing Behavior in Organizations: Minimizing Resistance to Change.* Cambridge, Mass.: Blackwell Business.

Keller, G. (1997). Examining what works in strategic planning. In Peterson, M. W., Dill, D., and Mets, L. (eds.), *Planning and Management for a Changing Environment: A Handbook on Redesigning Postsecondary Institutions*, 158–170. San Francisco: Jossey-Bass.

Klein, A. and Klein, D. C. (1999). SimuReal. In Davane, T. and Holman, P. (eds.), *The Change Handbook: Group Methods for Shaping the Future.* San Francisco: Berrett-Koehler.

Klimecki, R. and Lassleben, H. (1998). Modes of organizational learning: Indications from an empirical study. *Management Learning* 29 (4): 405–430.

Knight, P. T. and Trowler, P. R. (2000). Department-level cultures and the improvement of learning and teaching. *Studies in Higher Education* 25 (1): 69–83.

Koteen, J. (1989). *Strategic management in public and nonprofit organizations.* New York: Praeger.

Kotter, J. P. (1996). *Leading Change.* Boston: Harvard Business School Press.

Kotter, J. P. (1999). Leading change: The eight steps to transformation. In Conger, J. A., Spreitzer, G. M., and Lawler E. E., III (eds.), *The Leader's Change Handbook: An Essential Guide to Setting Direction and Taking Action*, 87–99. San Francisco: Jossey-Bass.

Kraatz, M. S. and Moore, J. H. (2002). Executive migration and institutional change. *Academy of Management Journal* 45 (1): 120–143.

Kriegel, R. and Brandt, D. (1996). *Sacred Cows Make the Best Burgers: Developing Change-Ready People and Organizations.* New York: Warner Books.

Kuh, G. D. and Whitt, E. J. (1988). *The Invisible Tapestry: Culture in American Colleges and Universities. ASHE-ERIC Higher Education Report* No. 1. Washington, D.C.: Association for the Study of Higher Education.

Labianca, G., Gray, B., and Brass, D. J. (2000). A grounded model of organizational schema change during empowerment. *Organization Science* 11 (2): 235–257.

Laframboise, D., Nelson R. L. and Schmaltz, J. (2003). Managing resistance to change in workplace accommodation projects. *Journal of Facilities Management* 1 (4): 306–321.

Levin, J. S. (Summer 1998). Organizational change and the community college. In Levin, J. S. (ed.), *Organizational Change in the Community College: A Ripple or a Sea Of Change? New Directions for Community Colleges* no. 102: 1–4. San Francisco: Jossey-Bass.

———. (Summer 1998b). Making sense of organizational change. In Levin, J. S. (ed.), *Organizational Change in the Community College: A Ripple or a Sea of Change? New Directions for Community Colleges* no. 102, 43–54. San Francisco: Jossey-Bass.

Lewin, K. (1947). Frontiers in group dynamics. *Human Relations* 1: 5–41.

———. (1947b). Quasi-stationary social equilibria and the problem of permanent change. In Burke, W. W., Lake, D. G. and Paine, J. W. (eds.), *Organization Change: A Comprehensive Reader*, 73–77. San Francisco: Jossey-Bass, 2009.

Likert, R. (1961). *New Patterns of Management.* New York: McGraw-Hill.

Lucas, A. F. (2000). A teamwork approach to change in the academic department. In Lucas, A. F. (ed.), *Leading Academic Change: Essential Roles for Department Chairs*, 7–32. San Francisco: Jossey-Bass.

———. (2000b). A collaborative model for leading academic change. In Lucas, A. F. (ed.), *Leading Academic Change: Essential Roles for Department Chairs*, 33–54. San Francisco: Jossey-Bass.

Macri, D. M., Tagliaventi, M. R., and Bertolotti, F. (2002). A grounded theory for resistance to change in a small organization. *Journal of Organizational Change Management* 15 (3): 292–311.

MacTaggart, T. J. (1998). Why the time is ripe for restructuring. In MacTaggart, T. J. (ed.), *Seeking Excellence through Independence: Liberating Colleges and Universities from Excessive Regulation*, 3–20. San Francisco: Jossey-Bass.

March, J. G. and Simon, H. A. (1958). *Organizations.* New York: John Wiley and Sons.

Maxwell, J. A. (1996). *Qualitative research design: An interactive approach.* Thousand Oaks, Calif.: Sage.

McLendon, M. K. (1999). *Olivet College: Reinventing a Liberal Arts Institution X, Y, and Z.* Publication of Managing Institutional Change and Transformation in Higher Education at the Center for the Study of Higher and Postsecondary Education, University of Michigan, Ann Arbor.

Merriam, S. B. (1988). *Case Study Research in Education: A Qualitative Approach.* San Francisco: Jossey-Bass.

———. (2002). *Qualitative Research in Practice: Examples for Discussion and Analysis.* San Francisco: Jossey-Bass.

Miles, M. B. and Huberman, A. M. (1994). *An Expanded Source Book of Qualitative Data Analysis.* Thousand Oaks, Calif.: Sage.

Mintzberg, H. (1994). *The Rise And Fall of Strategic Planning: Reconceiving Roles for Planning, Plans, Planners*. New York: Free Press.

Mintzberg, H. and Quinn, J. B. (1996). *The Strategy Process: Concepts, Contexts, Cases*. Englewood Cliffs, N.J.: Prentice Hall.

Nadler, D. A. (1988). Organizational frame bending: Types of change in the complex organization. In Kilmann, R. H. and Covin, T. J (eds.), *Corporate Transformation: Revitalizing Organizations for a Competitive World*, 66–83. San Francisco: Jossey-Bass.

———. (1998). *Agents of Change: How CEOs and Their Companies Are Mastering the Skills of Radical Change*. San Francisco: Jossey-Bass.

Nevis, E. C., Lancort, J., and Vassallo, H. G. (1996). *Intentional Revolutions: A Seven-Point Strategy for Transforming Organizations*. San Francisco: Jossey-Bass.

Newman, K. L. and Nollen, S. D. (1998). *Managing Radical Organizational Change*. Thousand Oaks, Calif.: Sage.

NCA (North Central Association). (1995). Report of a Visit to Olivet College, April 10–12.

Nutt, P. C. and Backoff, R. W. (1996). Walking the vision and walking the talk: Transforming public organizations with strategic leadership. *Public Productivity and Management Review* 19 (4): 455–486.

———. (1997). Facilitating transformational change. *Journal of Applied Behavioral Science* 33 (4): 490–508.

Olivet College Narrative Summary. Report to the W. K. Kellogg Foundation, September 1998.

Oreg, S., et al. (2008). Dispositional resistance to change: Measurement equivalence and the link to personal values across 17 nations. *Journal of Applied Psychology* 93 (4): 935–944.

Overton, B. J. and Burkhardt, J. C. (1999). Drucker could be right, but . . . : New leadership models for institutional-community partnerships. *Applied Developmental Science* 3 (4): 217–227.

Owens, R. G. and Steinhoff, C. R. (1976). *Administering Change in Schools*. Englewood Cliffs, N.J.: Prentice-Hall.

Pardo del Val, M. and Fuentes, C. M. (2003). Resistance to change: A literature review and empirical study, *Management Decision*, 41 (1/2). 148–156.

Peterson, M. W. (1982). An outsider's view: Prelude, interlude, or postlude. In Hipps, G. M. (ed.), *Effective Planned Change Strategies. New Directions for Institutional Research* 9 (1): 123–130.

———. (1995). Images of university structure, governance, and leadership: Adaptive strategies for the new environment. In Dill, D. D. and Sporn, B. (eds.), *Emerging Patterns of Social Demand and University Reform: Through a Glass Darkly*, 140–158. Oxford: Pergamon Press.

———. (1997). Using contextual planning to transform institutions. In Peterson, M. W., Dill, D., and Mets, L. (eds.), *Planning and Management for a Changing Envi-*

ronment: A Handbook on Redesigning Postsecondary Institutions, 127–157. San Francisco: Jossey-Bass.

Peterson, M. W. and Dill, D. D. (1997). Understanding the competitive environment of the postsecondary knowledge industry. In Peterson, M. W., Dill, D., and Mets, L. (eds.), *Planning and Management for a Changing Environment: A Handbook on Redesigning Postsecondary Institutions,* 3–29. San Francisco: Jossey-Bass.

Peterson, M. W. and Spencer, M. G. (1990). Understanding academic culture and climate. *New Directions for Institutional Research* 17 (4): 3–18.

Pfeffer, J. (1994). Conditions for the use of power. In French, W. L., Bell, C. H., and Zawacki, R. A. (eds.), *Organization Development and Transformation: Managing Effective change,* 450–459. Burr Ridge, Ill.: Irwin.

Pfeffer, J. and Salancik, G. R. (2003). *The External Control of Organizations: A Resource Dependence Perspective.* Stanford, Calif.: Stanford University Press.

Piderit, S. K. (2000). Rethinking resistance and recognizing ambivalence: A multidimensional view of attitudes toward and organizational change. *Academy of Management Review* 25 (4): 783–794.

Portland State University (PSU). (September 1993). General Education Working Group Report and Recommendations.

Pratt, D. (June 1998). Reflecting backward, looking forward: Notes from a visiting scholar. Manuscript for a Special Invited Issue of the *Journal of General Education.*

Presley, J. B. and Leslie, D. W. (1999). Understanding strategy: An assessment of theory and practice. In Smart, J. C. (ed.), *Higher Education: Handbook of theory and research,* 201–239. New York: Agathon Press.

Quinn, R. E. (1996). *Deep Change: Discovering the Leader Within.* San Francisco: Jossey-Bass.

———. (2000). *Change the World: How Ordinary People Can Achieve Extraordinary Results.* San Francisco: Jossey-Bass.

Rennie-Hill, L. and Toth, M. A (1999). Introduction. *Journal of General Education* 48 (2): 63–64.

Rhodes, G. (2000). Who's doing it right? Strategic activity in public research universities. *Review of Higher Education* 24 (1): 41–66.

Romanelli, E. and Tushman, M. L. (1994). Organizational transformation as punctuated equilibrium: An empirical test. *Academy of Management Journal* 37 (5): 1141–1166.

Rowley, D. J., Lujan, H. D., and Dolence, M. G. (1997). *Strategic Change in Colleges and Universities: Planning to Survive and Prosper.* San Francisco: Jossey-Bass.

Rudolph, F. (1990). *The American College and University: A History.* Athens: University of Georgia Press.

Rush, S. C. (1995). Searching for solid ground. In Johnson, S. L. and Rush, S. C. (eds.), *Reinventing the University: Managing and Financing Institutions of Higher Education,* 3–17. Toronto: John Wiley and Sons.

Ryan, K. D. and Oestreich, D. K. (1991). *Driving Fear out of the Workplace: How to Overcome the Invisible Barriers to Quality, Productivity, and Innovation.* San Francisco: Jossey-Bass.

Sastry, M. A. (1997). Problems and paradoxes in a model of punctuated organizational change. *Administrative Science Quarterly* 42: 237–275.

Schein, E. H. (1992). *Organizational Culture and Leadership.* San Francisco: Jossey-Bass.

Scott, B. (2000). *Consulting on the Inside: An Internal Consultant's Guide to Living and Working inside Organizations.* Alexandria, Va.: American Society for Training and Development.

Scott, P. (2000). *Higher Education Re-formed.* New York: Falmer Press.

Senge, P. M. (2000). The academy as learning community: Contradiction in terms or realizable future? In Lucas, A. F. (Ed), *Leading Academic Change: Essential Roles for Department Chairs*, 275–300. San Francisco: Jossey-Bass,

Senge, P. M. and Sterman, J. D. (1992). Systems thinking and organizational learning: Acting locally and thinking globally in the organization of the future. In Kochan, T. A. and Useem, M. (eds.). *Transforming Organizations.* New York: Oxford University Press.

Slowey, M. (1995). *Implementing Change from within Universities and Colleges: Ten Personal Accounts.* London: Kogan Page.

Sporn, B. (1999). *Adaptive University Structures: An Analysis of Adaptation to Socioeconomic Environments of U.S. and European Universities.* Philadelphia: Jessica Kingsley.

Stanley, D. J., Meyer, J. P., and Topolnytsky, L. (2005). Employee cynicism and resistance to organizational change. *Journal of Business and Psychology* 19 (4): 429–461.

Stark, J. and Lattuca, B. (1997). *Shaping the College Curriculum: Academic Plans in Action.* Boston: Allyn and Bacon.

Syer, J. and Connolly, C. (1996). *How Teamwork Works: The Dynamics of Effective Team Development.* San Francisco: McGraw-Hill.

Thompson, G. (1997). Changing universities: From evolution to revolution. In Armstrong, S., Thompson, G. and Brown, S. (eds.), *Facing Up to Radical Changes in Universities and Colleges*, 1–8. London: Kogan Press,

Trice, H. M. and Beyer, J. M. (1993). *The Culture of Work Organizations.* Englewood Cliffs, N.J.: Prentice Hall.

van Vught, F. A. (1994). Policy models and policy instruments in higher education: The effects of governmental policy-making on the innovative behavior of higher education institutions. In Smart, J. C. (ed.), *Higher Education: Handbook of Theory and Research*, 88–125. New York: Agathon Press,

Vollmann, T. E. (1996). *Achieving Market Dominance through Radical Change.* Boston: Harvard Business School Press.

Waddell, D. and Sohal, A. S. (1998). Resistance: A constructive tool for change management. *Management Decision* 36 (8): 543–548.

Weick, K. E. (1976). Educational organizations as loosely coupled systems. *Administrative Science Quarterly* 21 (1): 1–19.

———. (1979). *The Social Psychology of Organizing.* San Francisco: McGraw-Hill.

———. (1987). Perspectives on action in organizations. In Lorsch, J. W. (ed.), *Handbook of Organizational Behavior,* 10–28. Englewood Cliffs, N.J.: Prentice-Hall.

———. (1995). *Sensemaking in Organizations.* Thousand Oaks, Calif.: Sage.

———. (2009). *Making Sense of the Organization: The Impermanent Organization.* San Francisco: John Wiley and Sons.

Weis, R. S. (1994). *Learning from Strangers.* New York: Free Press.

Wilson, A. (2000). Strategy and management for university development. In Scott, P. (ed.), *Higher Education Re-formed,* 29–44. New York: Falmer Press.

Winstead, P. C. (1982). Planned change in institutions of higher learning. In Hipps, G. M. (ed.), *Effective Planned Change Strategies: New Directions for Institutional Research* 9 (1): 19–31.

Yin, R. K. (1993). *Applications of Case Study Research.* Thousand Oaks, Calif.: Sage.

———. (1994). *Case Study Research: Designs and Methods.* Thousand Oaks: SAGE Publications.

Young, A. P. (2000). "I'm just me." A study of managerial resistance. *Journal of Organizational Change Management* 13 (4): 375.

Zoller, H. M. and Fairhurst, G. T. (2007). Resistance leadership: The overlooked potential in critical organization and leadership studies. *Human Relations* 60 (9): 1331–1361.

Index